Swami Dayanand Saraswati's

Satyarth Prakash

(A True Face of Hinduism)

&

(An Agenda for Reformation of World Religions)

Chapter 1-6

English Translation with Notes

By

Prof. Ravi Prakash Arya

Indian Foundation for Vedic Science

1051, Sector-1, Rohtak, Haryana, India

Contact No. 09313033917; 09650183260

vedicscience@rediffmail.com; vedicscience@gmail.com

https://vedic-sciences.com

First Edition

Kali era: 5115 (c. 2014)

Kalpa era : 1,97,29,49,115

Brahma era: 15,55,21,97,29,49,115

ISBN 81-87710-64-0

Contents

Swami Dayanand Saraswati: An Ideal Architect for the Modern World 7

Founder of Dharma 11

Dayanand's Vedic Altruistic Socialism 13

Staunch Exponent of Scientific Awareness 14

An advocate of co-existence 14

Awareness towards the preservation of Environment 15

An advocate of Education 15

An advocate of Equal Status to women 16

INTRODUCTION 17

PREFACE 20

CHAPTER 1 29

Exposition of different names of God 37

CHAPTER 2 66

CHAPTER 3 80

Middle Brahmacharya 101

(Raudra Brahmacarya) 101

Highest Brahmacharya 102

(Āditya Brahmacharya) 102

5.1 Pratyakṣa Pramāṇa (Perception) 120

Anumāna (Inference) 121

Upamāna (Analogy) 122

Śabda (Authority) 123

Aitihya (History) 124

Arthāpatti (Cause-Effect Syllogism)...124
Abhāva (Absence)...125
Teaching and Leaning Scheme...148
CHAPTER 4...170
Brahmacharya or Student life...170
Age for marriage...176
Types of Marriage...194
Best Time of Marriage...196
3. Pitṛyajña...208
4. Vaiśvadeva-yajña...212
5. Atithi Yajña...215
Characteristices of hypocrites...220
Qualifications of a student...229
CHAPTER 5...256
Retirement and Renunciation...256
Vānaprastha (Retirement)...256
CHAPTER 6...282
Introduction...283
Qualifications of Ministers, Officers, Subordinate Staff and Ambassadors to be appointed...298
Tax Collection...304
War Ethics...305
Liabilities of the Head of a State and his Assembly...309
King's Routine...318
Invasion...325
Rate of Taxes...333

Other Books published on Swami Dayanand Saraswati

1. Rishi Dayanand through the Eyes of West
2. Tributes to Renaissance Rishi
3. Signatures of Time (A Collection of 231 letters written by Swami Dayanand Saraswati in 19th Century India) English

Swami Dayanand Saraswati

An Ideal Architect for the Modern World

Here it would not be out of context to recollect some of the significant contributions made by Swami Dayanand Saraswati for the elevation of the human race in the strife-torn modern world. If his principles and ideas are followed without any prejudice or pre-conceived notions, we may be able to develop a heaven on the earth.

All of us know that today the burning issues before the modern world are growing poverty (hunger), exploitation of poor and deprived, environmental pollution, communalism, religious bigotry, terrorism, discrimination of human beings based on gender, colour, creed, race, region or religion. Rishi Dayanand was a great seer of the modem age. He was the Yuga draṣṭā (Renaissance Rishi) and Viśva Guru (World teacher). He could visualize all these problems of the modern world in the middle of the 19th century itself and gave an amicable solution to all such problems that the world was likely to face in the years to come. The solution was given by him in the form of ten principles of Arya Samaj, Satyartha Prakash and many other books written in conformity with Vedas. He discarded the various religious sects in the name of Mata and Matantaras and set into motion a new movement in the name of Arya Samaj (academic, social, and spiritual agenda of reforms) in 1875 with the Vedic motive of 'kṛṇvanto viśvam āryam', to make the whole world noble and civilised, to purge the modern world of its various ailments and notions for the coexistence of human beings on the globe, to remove poverty, exploitation, communalism, religious bigotry, discrimination of human beings and to create social and environmental awareness. Initially, he was not willing to give any name to his movement for the fear of its being branded as a religion (religious sect) like others in the world.

In addition to above, Rishi Dayanand was a revealer of the truth. His magnum opus 'Sathyarth Prakash' "Revealing the Truth" is a glaring example of this fact. His contribution may also be counted towards shaping the prosperous, enmity free modern world of friendship and fraternity. First time in the modern history of humankind, he put forward the principles of coexistence. He was a staunch advocate of Vedic Altruistic Socialism, Altruistic Nationalism or Internationalism.

Rishi Dayanand's life was an ideal example of a good citizen. The concept of good man has been distinguished from the concept of a good citizen. A good man is endowed with good personal qualities, but he has no role to play in the society and national development except that he is a good man. In other words, a good man is a passive person who neither acts nor reacts to what is happening in the society. Nevertheless, a good citizen is an active person who reacts with good or bad happening in the society. A good citizen has the guts to declare wrong as wrong and right as right without any regard to his selfish interests. Rishi Dayanand was a good citizen. He never hesitated to point out rights and wrongs of British rulers and the Indian society irrespective of gender, caste, creed, region and religion. He was a person who praised the Queen for her justice but when the British Viceroy asked him to praise the British rule in his public lectures, he plainly refused to do so and spoke candidly to British Viceroy that it is better to live in a self-ruled State howsoever bad it is than to live under a good State ruled by foreigners. Once when his attention was drawn to the unhappiness of British rulers for his comments, Dayanand says, I have no fear from any ruler or king as far as the exposition and propagation of truth are concerned. Thus, Rishi Dayanand's life teaches one to be a good citizen of one's own country. This notion lies in line with the Ṛgveda's slogan vayam rāṣṭre jāgriyām purohitāḥ 'Let us be awakened like a leader/ good citizen in the nation.

Rishi Dayanand was a staunch exponent of Altruistic Welfare in the Call for Globalisation. Today the entire World is talking about globalisation under the pressure of America. The American concept of globalisation is based upon the exploitation of weak and poor nations for selfish interest or say for further enriching its capital. This type of capitalist globalisation will prove fatal for humanity at large especially for poor and developing nations. Long back in the middle of 19th century, Dayanand also advocated globalisation, but his concept of globalisation was based upon two principles (1). The well-being of the entire world as advocated by him in the sixth principle of Arya Samaj (The welfare of the entire world should be our aim). He defines the term welfare or upakāra as the promotion of physical, spiritual and social well-being).

According to Swami Dayanand, an Individual person's welfare lies in the welfare of entire society. Similarly, a nation's welfare is considered in the welfare all nations. He advocates in the ninth principle of Arya Samaj (An Individual's welfare lies in the welfare of whole Society). These principles, if followed in a campaign of globalisation, will change the entire look of the world.

With the rise of socialism in the world the concept of

a welfare state came to a forefront in a democratic set up to curtail the capitalism. The American concept of a welfare state curtails capitalism within its internal setup since it is not based upon the exploitation of its own citizens. It gives rise to another type of capitalism, which is based upon the exploitation of poor, developing and under developed nations. Dayanand's welfare State in the light of the 6th and 9th principle of Arya Samaj becomes the real welfare state which not only considers the welfare of its own citizen but the welfare of the other poor nations in the world. The Veda says, kevalāgho bhavati kevalādi, i.e., a person/nation who eats alone eats sin. The Vedic prayer in Hindi also reads as follows- bhukhā pyāsā paḍā paḍausi tune roṭi khāi to kyā. 'There is no greatness in filling up one's own stomach if the neighbour is suffering from hunger and thrust. 'Today's capitalist countries would like to throw their surplus grain to oceans instead of transferring them to the needy and poor countries. The real welfare state in a democratic set up can be created only by following the principles of Rishi Dayanand.

Today's India can benefit a lot from Rishi Dayanand's vision for developed and prosperous India. He was the first practitioner of applied democracy in India. He was the first to introduce the element of election in Arya Samaj in 1875. Keeping in view the instability of Government in a democratic set in India, we may follow the great visionary saint Rishi Dayanand. He because of the statement of Vedas stressed the element of election. King, as he interprets, is to be the president of the assembly. According to him, the wisest and the most learned among the members of an Assembly are to be elected the king or the president. Thus, he provides a tangible solution to the present crisis of instability of the Government in India in the parliamentary form of

Government. According to him, the prime minister should be elected by the parliament and not by the party. If this norm is made prevalent, there will be no instability of the Government for five years. In parliament, the prime minister may be voted out and not the Government. Another prime minister will be elected irrespective of consideration of majority or minority and the stability of the Government will he ensured and there will be no need for re-elections or midterm polls.

Dayanand's nationalism discards the radical nationalism prevalent today and supports altruistic nationalism, which is based upon the internationalism. He is a nationalist in the world perspective. His concept of nationalism does not stand at the cost of other nations. He introduces the idea of 'live and helps others to live'. He does not like to overlook his national interest but at the same time, he does not want to interfere with others' interest. According to the 10th principle of Arya Samaj: An individual should be free to act so far as individual welfare is concerned but should not act freely so far as altruistic welfare (welfare of all individuals/ persons/ or nations) is concerned. He is not in favour of the kind of nationalism prevalent in America where one's own national interests are carried out at the costs of other nations. For our own progress, we cannot exploit others.

Founder of Dharma

Krishna in Gita tells Arjuna: dharma sansthāpanārthāya saṁbhavāmi yuge yuge. "The People like me take birth to found the lost Dharma, yuga after yuga. Thus after Krishna, it was Rishi Dayanand who founded the Lost Dharma. Today Dharma has been replaced by religion. According to Dayanand, Dharma is not a religion but eternal laws and human values based on the truth, which sustains universe, and biological and human life on the earth. He himself defines Dharma in the fifth principle of Arya Samaj as, 'We all should act according to Dharma. i.e. with the consideration of what is truth and what is untruth.' Thus, his Dharma or Vedic concept of Dharma propagated by him was not the concept of a religion created by human beings just like different religions of the present day. Dayanand never trusted man-made things since human beings create things for their selfish purposes. Man made rules, or things cannot address the universal problems. Since they have a limited range and limited things do not have universality in them. Dayanand's Dharma is the fountainhead of Science. He never accepted the things in the name of religion. According to him, Vedas were not the religious books like Bible or Koran rather they are the books of all true sciences and knowledge. He quotes Yāska: sakṣāt kṛt dharmāṇo ṛṣayo babhuvu, i.e. 'There were born Rishis to whom was revealed the entire knowledge'. Thus, his Dharma is not immune of science, whereas the religion, as we have seen presently and in the past, has been the antithesis of science. To top it all, he could visualise that all these religions are the business shops marketing human beings. The religions are dividing human beings from human beings by way of their vicious agendas, rituals, dress codes, a way of worship and propaganda. That is why; he discarded the idea of the existence of religious sects or Matas. In the I2th, 13th and 14th chapter of Satyartha Prakash he attempted to reform the religions to make them more pro-science or knowledge based. He raped all these bigoted religions prevalent in the world whose business is thriving upon innocent human beings. These religions are the root cause of various altercations and terrorism in the world. Today we have been talking about interfaith dialogues. However, following Rishi Dayanand's notion, I would emphasise that today the need is not for the interfaith dialogues but the faithless dialogues. If we want the true welfare of the humankind on the earth, we shall have to discard all these religions out-rightly. If the world wants to survive the destruction caused by quarrels of religions and terrorism propelled by religions, religions would have to be discouraged (as done by Rishi Dayanand) and replaced by spirituality and the Vedic concept of Dharma would have to be followed in true spirit.

Here it may not be odd to inform that Vedic concept of Dharma is based upon Spirituality. Spirituality informs us that entire humanity is one. What to say of humanity, all creatures are the creation of God. As such killing even of an animal is a crime. That is why Rishi Dayanand propagated vegetarianism. He was so confirmed about it that he even avoided sharing meals at the houses of non-vegetarians.

Dayanand's Vedic Altruistic Socialism

Dayanand's Vedic Altruistic socialism is similar to Marxian scientific socialism as far as Marx advocates that the right given to an individual in the socialistic set up are not for the benefit of the individual alone but for the benefit of the entire society. According to Rishi Dayanand (9th Principle of Arya Samaj), an individual /person or nation should not content with his/her own welfare but an individual person's/nation's welfare lies in the welfare of all individuals/nations. Marx's Scientific Socialism is based on the principles of cause and effect. He discards religion whereas Rishi Dayanand brings Dharma in its true form of spirituality and human values in his socialism.

Staunch Exponent of Scientific Awareness

Today we have ushered in the era of science. For the true advancement of science, scientific awareness is mandatory. Howsoever, the scientific advancement takes place in the world, but as far as the scientific awareness is lacking, a society cannot be said to be scientifically advanced in the real sense of terms. Rishi Dayanand lays the foundation of scientific awareness among human beings, by coining the fourth principle of Arya Samaj. He observes, 'One should always be ready to accept the truth and give up untruth'. The concept of truth is the underlying factor for scientific awareness. First time in the human history, we find such a principle that advocates adherence to truth without following any religious dogma. There are so many examples in the history where truth was suppressed in the name of religion. According to the fifth principle of Arya Samaj, 'All should perform their actions according to Dharma i.e. with the consideration of truth or untruth. Long back in human history, Rishi Dayanand came on the stage and asked people to accept what is scientific (true) and discard what is unscientific, as the human society in those times was dominated by all dogmatic religions and people were forced to accept what was advocated in their religion without any consideration of truth or untruth involved. The phrases like 'So far as Bible is concerned, the sun moves around the earth and so far as science is concerned earth moves round the sun' ruled the roost.

An advocate of co-existence

A great visionary saint Dayanand could realise in the middle of the 19th century itself the need for the principles of co-existence for the survival of humanity in the world. Today this idea is much talked about but nobody or no nation knows how to follow the principle of co-existence. In the 10th principle of Arya Samaj, Dayanand lays down the very fundamental underlying principles of co-existence. Accordingly, one individual person or nation should be free in abiding by the rules that concern one's own self-interest but an individual person or nation should not be free in abiding by the rules that concern the interests of the entire society or world. Through these lines, his message is clear. He is not against individual freedom, but he is against the freedom enjoyed by individual person or nation at the cost of others.

Awareness towards the preservation of Environment

Today the world is facing environmental hazard. The biological life is standing on the verge of extinction from this planet. Due to the depletion of ozone layer and growing pollution, global warming is increasing. Rishi Dayanand emphasised for the preservation of the environment. He was well aware that the human beings through their various activities are polluting the environment. According to him, it is the ardent duty of every individual to help preserve the environment. The activities for preserving environment were called by him as Yajña or Agnihotra. He does not want to introduce Yajña or Agnihotra as some religious tool or activity but as a tool to purify environment as advocated in the Vedas and Gita. He explains the aim of Yajña in the Ṛgvedādibhāṣya-bhūmikā as to purify the environment and precipitation of Rain.

An advocate of Education

Rishi Dayanand was the ardent advocate of education

to ensure the upliftment of human beings and their real freedom. He laid down the eighth principle of Arya Samaj as, 'We should diffuse knowledge and dissipate ignorance'. According to Romain Rolland, the eighth principle of Arya Samaj - 'to diffuse knowledge and dissipate ignorance' - has played a great part in the education of India. -----which seeks to resuscitate the energies of the race and to use at the same time the intellectual and technical conquests of the West. Thus, Rishi Dayanand was well aware of the fact that the progress of human race was not possible without proper education. Education is the power and strength of an Individual and a nation.

An advocate of Equal Status to women

Today's world is grappling for providing women with the equal status of men. Many women organisations have come up to safeguard the interests of women and to launch the tirade against gender bias and discrimination based on gender. Rishi Dayanand was the first person in the modern history of humankind who placed women at a respectable place, perhaps, at a higher place even than the men. He quotes Manusmṛti and observes yatra nāryastu pujyante, ramante tatra devatā, i.e. Gods reside there, where the women are respected.

To sum up it can be observed that Dayanand's contribution of 10 principles of Arya Samaj is not only the contribution to Arya Samaj or Indian society but also the contribution to the entire human race for its co-existence and ever existence with friendship and fraternity.

I have not come to preach any new dogma or religion, to establish a new order, or to be proclaimed a new Messiah or Pontiff. I have only published before my people the truth of the Vedic Wisdom, which had been hidden during the centuries of India's subjugation.

Maharshi Swami Dayanand Saraswati

INTRODUCTION

'Satyarth Prakash' (Light on True Meaning) is the Magnum Opus of Swami Dayanand Saraswati, the living embodiment of Vedic life and thought and the illustrious son of India who founded the Arya Samaj movement. It occupies a prominent place in the Classical, Religious and Philosophical literature of the world. Its main objective is to depict the true face of Hinduism and to set an agenda for reformation of world religions in the larger of interest of humanity. First 10 chapters deal with former and last chapters deal with the latter objective. It exposes the truth in its real sense away from religious dogmas and fundamentalism. It is, in fact, as immortal as the truth itself is.

It is the beacon light leading people and religious sects from darkness to light, irrationality to rationality, irreligion to religion, and nescience to science. It was aimed at reformation at all levels, individual, social, political, religious, educational, economic, environmental and moral. According to it, even the prevalent religions need to be reformed. It depicts the way of life as envisaged by the Vedas, which prevailed throughout the whole World until about 5000 years back when enlightenment, peace and prosperity were at the zenith of its glory.

It presents a charter of life at once sublime and noble. It contains principles and rules of conduct to all. In short, it makes people mould and better their lives on the lines, which were chalked out by the Vedas, and the pattern laid down by what is the best in ancient Vedic heritage, whose living symbol was the Swami himself.

Author's comments on the tenets and working of various religious denominations were made in good faith and were not motivated, as the author has envisaged, for injuring the susceptibilities of their adherents. He meant to highlight the true face of Dharma and prevent the perpetration of 'Adharma' in the name of 'Dharma'. In fact, it gave the incentive especially to the leaders of those faiths to revise their teachings and give them a rational tone. The object of the Maharshi in writing this work, to quote his own words, is as under:

> 'There is not the remotest idea to hurt the feelings of any person either directly or indirectly; but on the contrary, the book proposes that humans should distinguish truth from falsehood. Thus alone can the human race steadily advance on the path of happiness, since none but the preaching of truth is the mainstay for the improvement and advancement of the human family.'

It is widely read by the people living in India and abroad. This treatise was originally written in Hindi. It has been translated into all the principal regional languages of India as well as in English, French, German, Chinese and Burmese.

The present English translation is conspicuous for its richness of thought and plucking out the actual and factual intention of the original author in the most modern English terms. This edition is beneficial to both learned and laity, as it brings home the main theme in a very simple and lucid language and all technical aspects dealing with grammar and etymology have been cited under footnotes to serve the purpose of reference to the scholars.

The author finds this opportunity to thank Dr. Deen Badu Chandra of Atlanta Arya Samaj of America who persuaded him to carry out this noble cause.

Last but not the least the author does not want to fail to acknowledge the help in proof reading and modifying the language so as to suit a common reader rendered by his beloved wife Dr. Surinder Kaur, a senior scientist with DIPR, DRDO, Min. of Def. Govt. of India.

Principal (Dr.) Ravi Parkash Arya
1051, Sector-1, Rohtak-124001, Haryana (India)
Mob. +919313033917
vedicscience@rediffmail.com; vedicscience@gmail.com
https://vedic-sciences.com

PREFACE

By the Original Author

By the time, the first edition of this book 'Satyarth Prakash' was brought out, I was not much familiar with the Hindi language, as my mother tongue was Gujarati and I had my schooling through Sanskrit medium. Consequently, a lot of mistakes crept in the first edition. Now I have become well conversant with this language, as such the second edition has been brought out after laying suitable corrections following the rules of Hindi grammar. Although, this edition is conspicuous with a slight difference in the idioms, phraseology and construction of sentences as compared to the first edition, but the same was unavoidable in order to ensure the necessary improvement over the language keeping the original intent intact. Yes, the typographical errors of the first edition have not been allowed to surface in the present edition.

This book comprises of 14 chapters called SamullÈsas. The first 10 chapters form the first part and last four, the second part. The last two chapters and 'A Statement of my Beliefs' which could not form the part of the first edition have also been incorporated into the present edition.

Chapter I: deals with an exposition of various names of Īśvara (God).

Chapter II: deals with grooming and upbringing of a child.

Chapter III: deals with student life (*Brahmcharya*),

curriculum, a list of authentic and spurious books and a teaching methodology.

Chapter IV: deals with the institution of marriage and duties of family life.

Chapter V: deals with duties of retired life (Vānaprastha), and of a Peripatetic monk (Sannyāsa Aśrama).

Chapter VI: deals with Science of Governance (Rājadharma).

Chapter VII: deals with the subject of the Veda and God (Iśvara).

ChapterVIII: deals with the Creation, Sustenance and Dissolution of the Universe.

Chapter IX: deals with knowledge, ignorance, bondage and salvation.

Chapter X: deals with good and bad conduct, and food regimen.

Chapter XI: contains a critique of the various dogmas and religious sects prevalent in India.

Chapter XII: deals with the Cārvāka, Bauddha (Buddhist) and Jain sects.

Chapter XIII: deals with Christianity.

Chapter XIV: deals with Islam.

The book concludes with a special summary of Sanātana Vedic teachings of Aryans, which I endorse in Toto.

The main object behind the composition of this book is to highlight the truth. In other words, to highlight truth as truth and falsehood as falsehood is the main objective of this book. The truth is not constituted in overshadowing reality, but constituted in accepting things as they are.

A prejudiced person always tends to prove his false beliefs to be true and his rival's truth to be false. As such, he can never reach the truth. Hence, it is the bounden duty of all scholars to present the truth and falsehood in their real sense through their teachings, preaching and writings. They should also embrace truth and abhor falsehood in their own interest and contentment.

Although, the human being is well conversant with the contents of truth and falsehood, yet he inclines towards falsehood owing to his selfish motives, bigotry, prejudice and ignorance. This book has not been composed with the above intention. There is not the remotest idea to hurt the feelings of any person either directly or indirectly; but on the contrary, the book proposes that humans should distinguish truth from falsehood. Thus alone can the human race steadily advance on the path of happiness, since none but the preaching of truth is the mainstay for the improvement and advancement of the human family.

All errors and omissions, typographical or otherwise, will be rectified, as soon as they are pointed out, but no heed will be paid to any remark made out of bias and prejudice with the object of unnecessary criticism. Of course, any suggestion made in the interest of humanity at large will be incorporated after due verification of facts.

All religious sects have many learned scholars. Should those scholars accept without any prejudice the universal truths (commonly accepted truths by all religions) and abhor conflicting statements paving way for mutual co-existence, friendship and fraternity, the entire world will be benefited. The dissension among scholars kindles flames of discord among laity fostering distress and causing permanent damage to the happy times. This damage, which is so dear to the heart of selfish, has hurled humankind into the deepest depths of misery.

If any selfless person sets about the altruistic welfare, he faces opposition and embarrassment at the hands of persons motivated by selfish interests. Nevertheless, there is an old saying:

सत्यमेव जयते नानृतम्। सत्येन पन्था विततो देवयानः॥

satyameva jayate nānṛtaṁ, satyena panthā vitato devayānaḥ.

That is, truth always triumphs and not falsehood. Truth paves the way for learning.

Having firm faith into this adage, the enlightened one never wavers from his mission of altruistic welfare and revealing the true face of things.

It is one of the settled truth that

यत्तदग्रे विषमिव परिणामेऽमृतोपमम्।
yattadagre viṣamiva pariṇāme'mṛtopamam. Gītā

[Meaning] All actions targeted towards achieving (spiritual) knowledge and dharma appears to be poisonous, to begin with but turn into nectar finally.

Mindful of the above motive, this book has been composed.

After a careful perusal of its contents, and having known of its true intention, the readers are free to have their choice.

The whole merit of this book is that it accepts un-conflicting truth from all religious sects and rejects all sectarian and dogmatic views. Another merit of this book is that it has plucked out all unwelcome thoughts registered in all religious sects to the gaze of all (learned and laity), so that an atmosphere of mutual understanding and trust may be allowed to prevail.

Although I was born and brought up in Āryāvartta (India), yet do not defend the false beliefs and practices of the religious sects prevalent in this country, rather portray the facts in the true sense. I maintain the same type of attitude while dealing with other religions. So far as the question of human upliftment is concerned, I don't distinguish between foreign and indigenous population.

Had I been biased, I would have blindly defended what is indigenous and disapproved what are non-indigenous. However, this is unbecoming of a human being. Oppression of the weak is the animal tendency. If human beings take this liberty, they are no better than animals. The humanity demands the protection of weak. The persons who try to flourish at the cost of others are worst than animals.

The first eleven chapters (Sammullāsas) have been devoted to indigenous religious sects. The truth published in these chapters is in conformity with Vedas, and so acceptable to me. The views of Puraṇas and Tantras have been discredited, so worthy of being disapproved by all.

The twelfth chapter discusses the Chārvāka view, which is declining now a day. This (Chārvāka) resembles Jainism and Buddhism so far as atheism is concerned. The Chārvāka is atheistic of a high order; hence, it is necessary to check its activities and advancement. If mendacity is not checked in time, the fraud and corruption will have the heydey. The Buddhist and the Jain views have also been incorporated along with the Chārvāka in the twelfth Chapter laying emphasis on the points of both discord and accord.

The account of Buddhism is taken from texts like 'Dīpavañśa' and 'Sarvadarśana Saṅgraha'.

For the account of Jainism, following authorities have been referred to:

4 Basic Sūtras (texts): 1. Āvaśyaka Sūtra (Essential texts) 2. Viśeṣa Āvaśyaka Sūtra (Specifically essential texts) 3. Daśavaikālika Sūtra 4. Pākṣika Sūtra.

11 Aṅgas (Subsidiary texts): 1. Ācārāṅga Sūtra 2. Saḍāṇga Sūtra 3. Thāṇāṅga Sūtra 4. Samavāyāṅga Sūtra 5. Bhagavatī Sūtra 6. Jñātādharma Kathā Sūtra 7. Upāsaka Daśā Sūtra 8. Antagada Daśā Sūtra 9. Anuttara Ova-vai Sūtra 10. Vipāka Sūtra and 11. Praśna Vyākaraṇa Sūtra

12. Upāṅga (Sub-Subsiadiary texts): 1. Upavai Sūtra 2. Rāvap Seni Sūtra 3. Jīva-abhigama Sūtra 4. Pannagaṇā Sūtra 5. Jambu-dvipa Pannatī Sūtra 6. Canda Pannatī Sūtra 7. Sūra Pannatī Sūtra 8. Niriyāvalī Sūtra 9. Kappiyā Sūtra 10. Kapavadī Sayā Sūtra 11. Pūppyā Sūtra and 12. Pūpya Cūliyā Sūtra

5 Kalpa Sūtra (Kalpa Texts): 1. Uttara-Adhyana Sūtra 2. Niśītha Sūtra 3. Kalpa Sūtra 4. Vyavahāra Sūtra 5. Jīta Kalpa Sūtra

6 Chedas (Cheda Texts): 1. Mahā Niśītha Bṛhad Vācana Sūtra 2. Mahā Niśītha Laghu Vācana Sūtra 3. Madhyama Vācana Sūtra 4. Piṇḍa Nirukti Sūtra 5. Augha Nirukti Sūtra 6. Paryyūṣaṇā Sūtra

10 Payannā Sūtra (Payannā Texts): 1. Catussaraṇa Sūtra 2. Pañca Khāṇa Sūtra 3. Tadula Vaiyālika Sūtra 4. Bhakti Parijñāna Sūtra 5. Mahā Pratyākhyāna Sūtra 6. Candā Vijaya Sūtra 7. Gaṇī Vijaya Sūtra 8. Maraṇa Samādhi Sūtra 9. Devendra Stavana Sūtra and 10. Sansāra Sūtra. Nandī Sūtra and Yogoddhā Sūtra are also

considered authentic texts.

5 Pañcāṅgas: 1. Brief Commentaries on all the above-cited books 2. Etymological texts 3. Caraṇī (Poetical Expositions) 4. Bhāśya (Elaborate Commentaries). These four constitute sectional texts and all these four along with their texts are called Pañcāṅgas.

The Ḍhūnḍia sect of Jains does not recognize sectional texts. Many other texts in addition to the above are recognized by the Jains. The twelfth chapter has specifically been devoted to this sect.

The Jain texts have undergone numerous repetitions. Moreover, some of Jains have a tendency to disown their own book that falls into the hands of non-Jains or is found published by non-Jains. This is not justified since a text recognized by some Jain and disowned by another Jain cannot be termed as unauthentic. Of course, a book that finds no recognition ever in hands of a Jain can be termed as unauthentic, but there is no such text available as has ever been de-recognized by all Jains. Hence, our critique of Jain texts will hold good in case of only those who recognizes that particular text and not in the case of those who do not recognize the text.

Nevertheless, many Jains even while recognizing a text disown it when it is subjected to a controversy. This is the reason why the Jains keep their books secret and do not let others (non-Jains) have access to them. They are replete with such impossible speculations as could ever be answered by any Jain. The best answer, however, is the abhorrence of false beliefs or lie.

The thirteenth chapter has been devoted to the Christianity. Its followers hold the Bible to be their religious book. One may refer to 13th Chapter for detailed study of Christianity. Islamic views have been referred to in the fourteenth chapter. Its followers hold the Quran to be their religious book. The reader is advised to consult this chapter for detailed information on this subject followed by a brief summary of the Vedic views.

Whosoever will read his preconceived notions in this book, he will fail to decipher the actual intended sense of the original author. Four factors act as a help in deciphering the actual intended meaning of a text. They are:

1. Ākāṅkṣā: Correlation between speaker's intention and the words expressed.

2. Yogyatā: Compatibility between meaning and words.

3. Āsatti: Proper order of words expressed to convey a particular meaning and

4. Tātparya: Speaker's intention.

When a particular book is accessed mindful of the above factors, the intended meaning of the text is revealed to readers.

There are many prejudiced persons especially those obsessed with sectarian bias. They use to make surmises against the actual intention of the speaker. The sectarian bias does not allow them to think rationally and leads them to the disastrous path. Just as I take up the study of Purāṇas, Jain Texts, Bible, and Quran without any preconceived notion and try to pick out good points and discard bad points and strive, using the good points, for the progress, advancement and betterment of humankind. Others are also expected to follow suit.

The flaws of these religious sects have been briefly made public, so that our worthy readers may be able to distinguish between truth and falsehood, embracing the former and renouncing the latter. It is unbecoming of wise humans to create confusion among masses and mislead them to resort to violent acts like riots, terrorism and bloodshed. The ignorant are sure to misinterpret what is maintained here, but the wise will be able to realize the actual intention of the present author. I don't see my efforts go unrewarded while presenting my views here.

A sincere perusal of this book will certainly help redeem my efforts. It is the ardent duty of all men to continue to publish truth without any prejudice or preconceived notion. May the Omniscient, Omnipresent, All-Blissful, Ever-existing, Almighty God help further this noble cause by His divine grace.

No further elaboration is needed for wise.

Sd/-

(Swami) Dayanand Saraswati

Udaipur, State of Maharana Udai Singh,
Bright half of Bhadrapada Month,
1939 Vikram era, (Christian era 1882)

Though I was born in Aryavarta (India) and live in it, yet just as I do not defend the falsehood of the faiths and religions of this country, but expose them fully; in like manner, I deal with the religions of other countries. I treat the foreigners in the same way as my own countrymen, so far as the elevation of the human race is concerned.

Swami Dayanand Saraswati

CHAPTER 1

Now we begin to explain true meanings of the various Names of God.

The Exposition of Om and other Names of God

ओ३म् शन्नो मित्रः शं वरुणः शन्नो भवत्वर्य्यमा ।
शन्नऽइन्द्रो बृहस्पतिः शन्नो विष्णुरुरुक्रमः ।। ऋग्वेद, 1.90.9

Oṁ śanno mitraḥ śaṁ varuṇaḥ
śanno bhavatv aryyamā.
śanna'indro bṛhaspatiḥ śanno viṣṇur-urukramaḥ.

नमो ब्रह्मणे नमस्ते वायो त्वमेव प्रत्यक्षं ब्रह्मासि।त्वामेव प्रत्यक्षं बह्म्र वदिष्यामि ऋतं वदिष्यामि सत्यं वदिष्यामि तन्मामवतु तद्वक्तारमवतु। अवतु माम् अवतु वक्तारम् । ओ३म् शान्तिश्शान्तिश्शान्तिः ।।१।। तैत्तिरीय आरण्यक, 7.1

namo brahmaṇe namaste vāyo
tvam-eva pratyakṣaṁ brahma vadiṣyāmi
ṛtaṁ vadiṣyāmi satyaṁ vadiṣyāmi
tan-mām-avatu tad-vaktāram-avatu.
avatu mām avatu vaktāram
Oṁ śāntiś śāntiś śāntiḥ *Taittirīya Araṇyaka, 7.1*

"May you (Om) O God, Who is (Mitra), Friend of all, (Varuṇa) Holiest of all, and (Aryamā) Controller of the Universe, be gracious to us. May you (Indra) O Lord Almighty, (Bṛhaspati) the Lord of the Universe, the

Support of all, be gracious to us.

May you (Viṣṇu) O Omnipresent and (Urukrama) Omnipotent Being, be gracious to us."

"We salute you O Brahman! (Omnipresent one), O Vāyu! (the most Powerful Supreme Being). You alone are real Omniscient Brahman. I will call You, You alone, as true Brahman. You will as truly revealed in the Vedas, will I obey and preach. I will be truthful in words, deed and thought. You are my shelter. May You protect me, who speaks nothing but the truth?

Let there be Peace on earth! Let there be Peace in midsphere! Let there be Peace in the celestial sphere!

Here 'Oṁkāra' (Om) is the exclusive name of God. It is composed of three sounds 'A', 'U', 'M'. This one name represents many other names of God. For instance, Akāra (A) stands for Virāṭ, Agni and Viśva, etc. Ukāra (U) stands for Hiraṇyagarbha, Vāyu and Taijas, etc. Makāra (M) stands for Iśvara, Āditya and Prājña, etc. We find these names of God clearly mentioned in true Śāstras (Scientific treatises) like Vedas.

Question: Why aren't these names taken to mean other objects than God? Do they also mean universe and five gross elements like earth, etc. or deities like Indra, and herbs like green ginger in medical science?

Answer: Yes, they do, but they also mean God.

Question: Don't you take these words to mean exclusively deities?

Answer: No. What authority do you have to support such exclusive meaning?

Question: Deities are well known and most elevated.

That is why I take these words to mean them.

Answer: Isn't God well-known? Is there anyone superior to Him? Why don't you take these words to mean God as well? When God is well known and unmatched, how can anyone be superior to him? Therefore, your proposition is untenable. There are many inconsistencies in it. For instance, when a person cannot enjoy what is within his reach and keeps on craving for inaccessible, he cannot be called wise.

Suppose, if a hungry person shows a preference for food that is non-existent than that of existing one, he will not be considered as wise. The same thing holds true of you because you want to assign various names like Virāṭ, etc. to so-called deities whose existence is questionable instead of God whose existence is well known and supported by several authorities.

If you argue that, the meanings of these words should be determined by context. For example, if a servant is asked by his master to bring 'saindhava'. Here, a servant has to consider context before presenting 'saindhava' to his master, as the very word 'saindhava' has two meanings: 'horse' and 'salt'. If the master is to leave on a journey, the servant is naturally required to bring the horse, and if the master is taking his meals, the servant should bring salt. On the contrary, if the servant brings salt at the time of journey and horse at mealtime, he is sure to invite the fury of his master and be ridiculed as a fool. A wise takes the right decision at the right time and a fool does the reverse of it. This goes to prove that only a meaning referred by context is acceptable. All of us should accept and follow this principle of interpretation.

Other Vedic Authorities Supporting the above

hypothesis

The following authorities can be quoted from the Vedas and the Upaniṣads to support the above hypothesis.

ओं खम्ब्रह्म । यजु. 40.17

Oṁ kham brahma. *Yajurveda, 40.17*

Om is Omnipresent like space.

ओमित्येतदक्षरमुमत्रथमुपासीत। छान्दोग्य उपनिषत् 1.1.1

Om-ityetad-akṣaram-udgītham-upāsīta.

The Chāndogya Upaniṣad, 1.1.1

"He alone, Whose name is Om, Who is Immortal, is worthy of our adoration."

ओमित्येतदक्षरमिदं सर्वं तस्योपव्याख्यानम्।। माण्डूक्य 1.1

Om-ityetad-akṣaram idaṁ sarvaṁ tasyopa-vyākhyānam.

Māṇḍukya Up. 1.1

"Om is only the primary sound that denotes the name of God. Other names are secondary."

सर्वे वेदा यत्पदमामनन्ति तपांसि सर्वाणि च यद्वदन्ति ।
यदिच्छन्तो ब्रह्मचर्यं चरन्ति तत्ते पदं संग्रहेण ब्रवीम्योमित्येतत्।।

sarve vedā yat-padam āmananti
tapānsi sarvāṇi yad vadanti.
yadicchanto brahmacaryaṁ caranti
tatte padaṁ saṅgraheṇa bravimyomityetat.

Kathopaniṣad, 2.15

"Who is quoted by all the Vedas. For Whom all penances are undertaken and for Whose realization, the life of Brahmacharya (chastity) is led, He is called Om.

प्रशासितारं सर्वेषामणीयांसमणोरपि ।

रुक्माभं स्वप्नधीगम्यं विद्यात्तं पुरुषं परम्।।

praśāsitāraṁ sarveṣām aṇīyānsam aṇorapi.
rukm-ābhaṁ svapna-dhīgamyaṁ vidyāt-taṁ puruṣaṁ param.

Manusmṛti, 12.122

"He, Who is the Governor of all, subtler than the subtle, Self-effulgent like Gold, Who can be known through the controlled mind of Samādhi, is the Supreme Being."

एतमग्निं वदन्त्येके मनुमन्ये प्रजापतिम् ।
इन्द्रमेके परे प्राणमपरे ब्रह्म शाश्वतम्।।

etam agniṁ vadantyeke manum anye prajāpatim.
indram eke pare prāṇam apare brahma śāśvatam.

Manusmṛti, 12.123

"Some call Him Agni, because He is self-effulgent. Other knows Him by the name of Manu, because He is the embodiment of knowledge, and Prajāpati because He upholds all. Yet others call Him Indra, because He is the supreme lord of riches, rests Prāṇa, because He is the life force of all and others, again, call Him eternal Brahma because He is all-pervading."

स ब्रह्मा स विष्णुः स रुद्रस्स शिवस्सोऽक्षरस्स परमः स्वराट्।
स इन्द्रस्स कालाग्निस्स चन्द्रमाः।।

sa brahmā sa viṣṇuḥ sa rudras sa śivos so'akṣars sa paramaḥ svarāṭ sa indras sa kālāgnis sa candramā.

Kaivalya Upaniṣad, 1.8

"He is variously called as Brahmā, the creator of world; Viṣṇu, the All-pervading; Rudra, the reprimander of wicked; Śiva, the dispenser of good to all; Akṣara, the imperishable; Svarāṭ, the self-effulgent; Indra, the Lord of all riches; Kālāgni, the devourer of all (during decreation); and Candramā."

इन्द्रं मित्रं वरुणमग्निमाहुरथो दिव्यस्स सुपर्णो गरुत्मान् ।
एकं सद्विप्रा बहुधा वदन्त्यग्निं यमं मातरिश्वानमाहुः ।।

indraṁ mitraṁ varuṇam agnim
āhur atho divyas sa suparṇo garutmān.
ekaṁ sad-viprā bahudhā vadantygniṁ
yamaṁ mātariśvānamāhuḥ.

Ṛgveda, 1.164.46

"There is one reality and the same is called by various names by wise, according to various qualities; such as, Indra, Mitra, Varuṇa, Agni, Divya, the divine one; Suparṇa, the best upholder and perfect actor; Mātriṣvān, the mighty one like air; Garutmān, the majestic one."

भूरसि भूमिरस्यदितिरसि विश्वधाया विश्वस्य भुवनस्य धर्त्री ।
पृथिवीं यच्छ पृथिवीं दृँह पृथिवीं मा हिंसीः ।।

bhūrasi bhūmir-asyaditir-asi viśva-dhāyā viśvasya bhuvanasya dhartrī pṛthivīṁ yaccha pṛthivīṁ dṛṁha pṛthivīṁ mā hinsīḥ.

Yajurveda, 13.18.

"He is known by various names, such as Bhū, Bhūmi, Aditi, Viśvadhāyā, Pṛthivī."

Note: God is called Bhūmi because He is the germination ground of all creatures.

इन्द्रो मह्ना रोदसी पप्रथच्छव इन्द्रः सूर्य्यमरोचयत् ।
इन्द्रे ह विश्वा भुवनानि येमिर इन्द्रे स्वानास इन्दवः ।।

Indro mahanā rodasī paprathacchava indraḥ sūryamarocayat
Indra ha viśvā bhuvanāni yemira indre svānāsa indavaḥ. *Sāmaveda, 1588*

"He is Indra, the creator of light space and observer space, creator of stars, and all planets in the universe."

प्राणाय नमो यस्य सर्वमिदं वशे ।
यो भूतः सर्वस्येश्वरो यस्मिन्त्सर्वं प्रतिष्ठितम् ।।

prāṇāya namo yasya sarvamidaṁ vaśe.
yo bhūtaḥ sarvasyeśvro yasmintsarvaṁ pratiṣṭhtam.

Atharvaveda, 11.4.1

"We bow unto thee, O Prāṇa (God) - Who controls and governs the whole universe, Who is the master of entire creation, Who is inhabited by all."

The above-cited authorities support the view that God is primarily signified by the names like Om and no name of God is meaningless. The meaningless names are often come across in society, e.g. a poor man is found named as Dhanapati (Lord of riches). This argument leads to a conclusion that various names of God are given because of His various qualities, actions, and dispositions.

Thus, all the names of God are meaningful. For instance, He is called Om, because of his being a protector; Kham, because of his being All-pervading like space; Brahma, because of his being the Biggest one.

Here it may also be pointed out that the term 'Om' exclusively refers to God, as corroborated by the evidence of grammatical texts, Nirukta, Brāhmaṇas, and Sūtra Texts composed by seers. Here Agni and other names refer to God only when the context so requires or the attributive epithets indicate so. Wherever, prayer, adoration, meditation, omniscience, omnipresence, holy, eternity and creator-hood are attributed, God is referred to. In such references as,

ततो विराडजायत विराजो अधिपूरुषः ।

tato virāḍ ajāyata virajo'adhi pūruṣaḥ.

Yajurveda, 31.5

श्रोत्राद्वायुश्च प्राणश्च मुखादग्निरजायत ।

śrotrād vāyuś ca prāṇaś ca mukhād agnir ajāyata

Yajurveda, 31.12

तेन देवा अयजन्त।

tena devā ayajanta. *Yajurveda, 31.9*

पश्चाद्भूमिमथो पुरः ।

paścād bhūmim atho puraḥ. Yajurveda, *31.5*

तस्माद्वा एतस्मादात्मन आकाशः सम्भूतः। आकाशाद्वायुः। वायोरग्निः। अग्नेरापः। अद्भ्यः पृथिवी। पृथिव्या ओषधयः। ओषधिभ्योऽन्नम्। अन्नाद्रेतः। रेतसः पुरुषः। स वा एष पुरुषोऽन्नरसमयः।

tasmād vā etasmād ātmana ākāśaḥ sambhūtaḥ. ākāśād vāyuḥ. vāyor agniḥ. agner āpaḥ. adbhyaḥ pṛthivī. pṛthivyāḥ oṣdhayaḥ. oṣdhibhyo'annam. annād retaḥ. retasaḥ puruṣaḥ sa vā eṣa puruṣo'anna-rasa-mayaḥ.

Taittirīya, Upaniṣad, 5.3.1

The terms like virāṭ, puruṣa, deva, ākāśa, vāyu, agni, jala, bhūmi etc. should be taken to mean terrestrial objects, whenever, attributive epithets like created preserved, destroyed, less informed, materialistic, visible etc. are used. In context of these attributives, the above-cited terms (virāṭ, etc.) can never refer to God, since God is not subject to the process of creation and dissolution, etc. Above mantras relates to the context of creation, so the terms like Virāṭ quoted in the above mantras refer to terrestrial things rather than God. Similarly, whenever there is a use of attributive epithets like omniscient, etc., these very names denote God. When such words as denote desire, enmity, efforts, pleasure, pain, and finite knowledge are used, these very names will denote Jīva (individual soul). Now we shall quote hereunder such evidence as to show how the terms Virāṭ etc. signify God.

Exposition of different names of God

Virāṭ: The word virāṭ is derived from the root √ (rāj)ṛ 'to shine'[1] . God is called Virāṭ because He manifests multiform universe[2].

Agni: The word Agni is derived from root √(añc)u 'to move' or 'to worship'. The root signifying 'movement' is often interpreted as conveying three meanings: 'to know', 'to move' and 'to realize'. God is called Agni because He is knowledge incarnate, knowable, worshipful and worthy of being realized[3].

Viśva: The word Viśva is derived from the root √viś 'to enter', 'to reside'[4] . God is called Viśva because the entire universe resides in Him or He resides in the entire universe. The above names are represented by 'A' sound of 'Om' (AUM).

Hiraṇyagarbha: In Aitareya and Śatapatha Brāhmaṇas all luminary bodies are referred to as Hiraṇya. Light is also referred to as Hiraṇya. One who is the source and support of light and luminary bodies, viz. stars, is called Hiraṇyagarbha i.e. God. This is also substantiated by the following authority of Yajurveda (13.4).

---

1 prefix vi + √ rājṛ 'to shine+ suffix kvip.

2 यो विविधं नाम चराचरं जगद्राजयति प्रकाशयति स विराट्।

3 यो अंचु गतिपूजनयोः। अग, अगि, इण्,गत्यर्थक। गतेस्त्रयोऽर्थाः ज्ञानं गमनं प्राप्तिश्च। पूजनं नाम सत्कारः। योंऽचति अच्यतेऽगत्यंगत्येति वा सोऽयमग्निः।

4 विशन्ति प्रविष्टानि सर्वाण्याकाशादीनि भूतानि यसिमन् यो वा आकाशादि सर्वेषु भूतेषु प्रविष्टः स विश्व ईश्वरः।

हिरण्यगर्भः समवर्त्तताग्रे भूतस्य जातः पतिरेक आसीत् ।
स दाधार पृथिवीं द्यामुतेमां कस्मै देवाय हविषा विधमे ।।

hiraṇya-garbhaḥ sama-varttat-āgre
bhūtasya jātaḥ patir eka āsīt
sa dādhāra pṛthivīṁ dyām uta imāṁ
kasmai devāya haviṣā vidhema

[Meaning] Hiraṇyagarbha - the only Lord of the creation, existed in the beginning. He sustained the stars and the planets. Let us adore Him - the All-blissful one."

Thus, in the above stanza, Hiraṇyagarbha stands for God.

Vāyu: The word Vāyu is derived from the root √vā 'to move', 'to kill'[5] . God is called as Vāyu, as He is the life force and support of the universe, cause of its dissolution, and mightier than the mightiest[6].

Taijas: The word Taijas evolved as secondary derivative from the word Teja, derived from the root √tija 'to shine'. The God is called Taijas because He is resplendent and makes other luminary bodies shine. The above three names are represented by 'U' sound of 'Om' (AUM).

Īśvara: The word Īśvara is derived from root √Īśa 'to be powerful' [7] . One endowed with truth, rational knowledge, and infinite power is called Īśvara, i.e. God.

Āditya: The word Āditya is formed as a secondary derivative from the word 'aditi', derived from the root √do 'to decay'. God is called Āditya because he never

---

5 वा गति गन्धनयोः, गन्धनं हिंसनम्।

6 यो वाति चरऽचरंजगद्धरति बलिनां बलिष्ठः स वायुः।

7 ईष्टे सर्वैश्वर्यवान् वर्त्तते सः ईश्वरः।

dies or decays[8].

Prājña: The word Prājña evolved as a secondary derivative from the word Prajña, derived from the root √jña 'to know' prefixed by 'pra'. One endowed with perfect knowledge of universal behaviour is called Prājña, i.e. God. The above cited three names are represented by 'M' sound of 'Om' (AUM).

Just as three different names of God quoted above are represented by each of three sounds of 'Om' viz. A, U, and M, similarly, there are even other names of God signified by 'Om'.

The names-Mitra, Varuṇa- quoted in the mantra (*śanno mitraḥ.....*), also stand for God, because only the pre-eminent is subjected to be worthy of homage, adoration, prayer and meditation. He is the pre-eminent, who supersedes everyone else in respect of right ways, disposition, merit and action. Who is exceedingly superior to even the pre-eminent ones, is called Supreme Being. None was, is or will ever be equal to Him. When no one can equal Him, how can anyone supersede Him?

Neither material objects nor individual souls can ever possess such attributes of truth, justice, mercy, omnipotence, omniscience and other infinite powers, as possessed by God. Only a true and real can have disposition, merit and action that is true and real. Hence, humans should worship, adore and meditate none but God. Our divine learned men of yore, such as Brahmā, Viṣṇu, Mahādeva; lowly human beings called Daityas and Dānavas and ordinary humans in society believed in God

---

[8] न विद्यते विनाशो यस्य सोऽयमादितिः । अदितिरेव आदित्यः ।

alone and paid homage, adoration and meditation unto Him alone. We should all do the same. This subject will particularly be discussed in detail in chapter 9 that deals with salvation and meditation.

Question: Why the words like Mitra are not taken to mean their apparent meanings like 'friend' and the words like Indra, for the conventional deities?

Answer: It won't be proper to take them for their apparent meanings and conventional sense since a man can be friendly to one, unfriendly to another and still unconcerned about the third one. Therefore, the word 'Mitra' cannot primarily be taken to mean friend here. On the other hand, God is positively a Friend of all and is unfriendly or indifferent to none, something, which is an individual soul, can never be. Therefore, 'Mitra' is primarily taken to mean here God. Yes, in its secondary sense, it can also refer to a friend.

Mitra: The word Mitra is derived from the root √ñi(mid)ā 'to love'[9] . God is called Mitra because He loves all and worthy of being loved by all[10].

Varuṇa: The word Varuṇa is derived from root √vṛ 'to choose', 'to seek'[11]. One who is the refuge of seekers, and spirituals and sought after by them is called Varuṇa, i.e. God[12]. Varuṇa also means pre-eminent. Since God alone is Super pre-eminent entity, so He is called Varuṇa.

Aryamā: The word Aryamā is formed of two roots √ ṛ 'to go', 'to obtain' and of √(mā)ṅ 'to respect'. From first

---

9 ञिमिदा स्नेहने +क्र प्रत्यय

10 मेद्यति स्निह्यति वा स मित्रः।

11 √ vṛ 'to choose', 'to desire' + unan (Uṇādi suffix)

12 यः सर्वान् शिष्टान् मुमुक्षुन्धर्मात्मनो वृणोति अथवा शिष्टैर्मुमुक्षुभिर्धमात्मभिर्व्रियते वर्य्यते वा स वरुणः परमेश्वरः।

root √ṛ is derived Aryya and from second root √(mā)ṅ is derived mā, thus making it together aryya+mā=Aryyamā or Aryamā[13]. One, who rewards and honours truthful and lustful persons, and dispenses justice on merit in respect of good and bad deeds performed by different individuals is called Aryamā, that is God[14].

Indra: The word Indra is derived from root √idi 'to be powerful'.[15] The All-powerful one is called Indra that is God[16].

Bṛhaspati: The word Bṛhaspati is derived from root √pā 'to protect', preceded by Bṛhat[17]. One who is greatest among great, and governs the universes is called Bṛhaspati, i.e. God[18].

Viṣṇu: The word Viṣṇu is derived from the root √(viṣ)ḷ 'to pervade'[19]. God is named Viṣṇu, as He pervades entire universe, animate and inanimate[20].

Urukrama: The word Urukrama is constituted of two words uru+krama forming a Bahuvrīhi Compound. One who possesses great (uru) power (krama) is called Urukrama[21]. Because of his infinite power, God is called Urukrama. In view of the foregoing discussion, the meaning of the following verse from Ṛgveda can be read

---

13 √ṛ+yat (suffix) = Aryya, Aryya+maṅ+kanin (suffix) = Aryyamā

14 योऽर्य्यान् स्वामिनो न्यायधीशान् मिमीते मान्यान् करोति सोऽर्य्यमा।

15 इदि परमैश्वर्ये +रन् प्रत्यय।

16 य इन्दति परमैश्वर्यवान् भवति स इन्द्रः परमेश्वरः।

17 बृहत् + पा रक्षणे + डति प्रत्यय।

18 यो बृहतामाकाशादीनां पतिः स्वामी पालयिता स बृहस्पतिः।

19 √viṣḷ 'to pervade'+nu suffix

20 वेवेष्टि व्याप्नोति चराऽचरं जगत् स विष्णुः।

21 उरुर्महान् क्रमः पराक्रमो यस्य स उरुक्रमः।

as under:

ओ३म् शन्नो मित्रः शं वरुणः शन्नो भवत्वर्य्यमा ।
शन्नऽइन्द्रो बृहस्पतिः शन्नो विष्णुरुरुक्रमः ।।

Oṁ śanno mitraḥ śaṁ varuṇaḥ
śanno bhavatv aryyamā.
śanna'indro bṛhaspatiḥ śanno viṣṇur-urukramaḥ.

'May the Almighty God, the Omnipotent and Friend of all, bestow happiness. May He, the Pre-eminent one, grant well-being. May He, the Dispenser of Justice, grant us bliss. May He, the Lord of all riches, bless our prosperity. May He, the Support of all, bestow knowledge. May He, the Omnipresent one, bless us.

Brahma: The word Brahma is derived from the root √bṛha or bṛhi 'to increase'. One who is above all, greatest of all, and surpasses all in power is called Brahma, i.e. God.

A verse from Ṛgveda reads as follows:

नमो ब्रह्मणे। नमस्ते वायो। त्वमेव प्रत्यक्षं ब्रह्मासि। त्वामेव प्रत्यक्षं ब्रह्म वदिष्यामि। ऋतं वदिष्यामि। सत्यं वदिष्यामि। तन्मामवतु। तद्वक्तारमवतु। अवतु मामवतु वक्तारम्। ओ३म् शान्तिः शान्तिः शान्तिः।

namo brahmaṇe namaste vāyo; tvam-eva pratyakṣaṁ brahma vadiṣyāmi; ṛtaṁ vadiṣyāmi satyaṁ vadiṣyāmi; tan-mām-avatu tad-vaktāram-avatu; avatu mām avatu vaktāram. Oṁ śāntiś śāntiś śāntiḥ

[Meaning] We salute Brahman, the greatest of all and above all, the encompassor all. O Almighty! You are only true Brahman because You are Omnipresent and accessible to all. I shall act upon and preach to others what is your honest commandment in the Veda. I shall obey your commandments in thought, speech and action. Protect me. Protect me, the speaker of truth, so that I may never waver from your commandments, as your commandments are the real dharma (values to be followed by all) and else is adharma. Grant us peace at the spiritual (metaphysical) level, at the cosmic level and physical level.'

Here the word śānti has been repeated thrice. This indicates seeker's desire for harmony at metaphysical, astrophysical and physical levels. He wants to be free from metaphysical afflictions that relate to body and mind; physical afflictions caused by the proximity of physical things like a weapon, snake bite etc. and natural afflictions brought about by natural calamities.

Sūrya: There is a verse from Yajurveda, which reads as follows:

सूर्य आत्मा जगतस्तस्थुशश्च ।
sūrya ātmā jagats tasthuṣaś ca

In the above verse of Yajurveda, the term Jagat has been used to denote the animate world and tasthuṣaḥ inanimate world like earth, etc. God, being the life and light of the animate and inanimate worlds is called Sūrya.

Paramātmā: The word Ātmā is derived from the root √at 'to pervade'. One who pervades the universe of animate and inanimate things is called Ātmā[22]. God is called Paramātmā, because He is supreme of all individual souls, finest of all individual souls and matter particles including the sky. He is the life force of all beings[23].

Parameśvara: The word Parameśvara is formed of two words - Parama+Īśvara. The Resourceful one is called Īśvara. The greatest resourceful one and unmatched one

---

22 योऽतति व्याप्नोति स आत्मा ।

23 परश्चासौ आत्मा च य आत्मभ्यो जीवेभ्यः सूक्ष्मेभ्यः परोऽतिसूक्ष्मः स परमात्मा ।

is called Parameśvara[24].

Savitā: The Word Savitā is derived from root √(ṣu)ñ 'to extract' or √(ṣu)ṅ 'to deliver'[25]. He who creates the universe[26] is called Savitā, i.e. God.

Deva: The word Deva is derived from the root √(div)u 'to operate', 'desire to conquer', 'to work', 'to illuminate', 'praise', 'rejoice', 'be intoxicated', 'to sleep', 'worthy to be sought after', and 'to appreciate'[27]. Deva is one who makes the whole universe operate; one who desires to make the righteous win; one who provides all means to work; one who is self-effulgent and illuminates others; one who is worthy of praise, all-blissful, bestows happiness on others, punishes the inebriated ones; one who creates night for all creatures to sleep and dissolves the universe for souls to rest, worthy to be sought by all; one who is knowledge incarnate. Thus, Deva is the name of God, because all the above qualities can be attributed to God alone.

In other words, Deva is God Who operates Himself automatically and creates the whole universe without any outside help and He is a source of all universal operations[28].

Deva means invincible and one who conquers everyone[29]; one who knows all lustful and unjust acts[30];

---

24 य ईश्वरेषु समर्थेषु परमः श्रेष्ठः स परमेश्वरः।

25 षूञ् अभिषवे, षूङ् प्राणिगर्भविमोचने।

26 अभिषवः प्राणिगर्भविमोचनं चोत्पादनं। चराचरं जगत् सुनोति सूते वोत्पादयति स सविता परमेश्वरः।

27 दिवु क्रीडा-विजिगीषा-व्यवहार-द्युति-स्तुति-मोद-मद-स्वप्न -कान्ति -गतिषु

28 यो दीव्यति क्रीडति स देवः।

29 विजिगीषते स देवः।

one who illuminates all[31]; one who is worthy of praise and doesn't deserve condemnation[32].

One who is the embodiment of bliss and makes others feel blissful and alleviate their sufferings[33]. One who is full of Joy, devoid of sufferings, makes others rejoice and relieves them of sufferings[34]. One who keeps the entire creation in unmanifest form during the period of decreation/ dissolution[35]. He who has all his desires fulfilled and aspired by all seekers[36]. One who encompasses all and worthy to be appreciated by all is called Deva[37].

Kubera: The word Kuber is derived from the root √kubi 'to cover'[38]. One who encompasses all by virtue of His power all-pervasiveness is called Kuber[39], i.e. God.

Pṛthivī: The word Pṛthivī is derived from the root √pṛthu 'to spread'[40]. One who spreads this extensive universe is called Pṛthivī[41], i.e. God.

Jala: The word Jala is derived from root √jala 'to beat,

---

30 व्यवहारयति स देवः।

31 यश्च चराचरं जगत् द्योतयति।

32 यः स्तूयते स देवः।

33 यो मोदयति स देवः।

34 यो माद्यति स देवः।

35 यः स्वापयति सः देवः।

36 यः कामयते काम्यते वा स देवः।

37 यो गच्छति गम्यते वा सः देवः।

38 कुबि आच्छादने

39 यः सर्वं कुबति स्वव्याप्त्याच्छादयति स कुबेरो जगदीश्वरः।

40 पृथु विस्तारे

41 यः पर्थति सर्वं जगद्विस्तृणाति तस्मात् स पृथिवी।

to compress'[42]. God is called Jala, because He beats or punishes the wicked and compresses/coalesces the invisible atoms[43].

Ākāśa: The word Ākāśa is derived from the root √kāśṛ 'to illuminate' or 'to enlighten'[44]. One who illuminates or enlightens the entire world from all sides is called Ākāśa[45], i.e. God.

Anna, Annāda and Attā: The words anna, annāda or attā are derived from the root √ad 'to eat' or 'to absorb'. There is a reference from Taittirīya Upaniṣad (2.2; 3.10) which says:

अद्यतेऽत्ति च भूतानि तस्मादन्नं तदुच्यते। अहमन्नमहमन्नमहमन्नम्।
अहमन्नादोऽहमन्नादोऽहमन्नादः। अत्ता चराऽचरग्रहणात्।।

adyate'tti ca bhūtāni tasmād annaṁ taducyate. (2.2)
ahamannam ahamannam ahamannam.
ahamannādo'ahamannādo'ahamannādaḥ. (3.10)
attā carā'caragrahaṇāt.

(Vedānta Śāriraka Sūtra by Vyāsa, 1.29)

[Meaning] Anna is so called as it is eaten/ absorbed or it eats/ absorbs into Himself material world. God is called Anna, Annāda and Attā, because He contains in Himself the entire universe, animate or inanimate.

Three times repetition indicates the reverence to God. The seer wants to say that the entire world is born, live and perishes in God just as worms take birth, live and die in a fig fruit (Gular).

---

42 जल घातने

43 जलति घातयति दुष्टान्, संघातयति अव्यक्तपरमाण्वादीन् तद् ब्रह्म जलम्।

44 काशृ दीप्तौ

45 यः सर्वतः सर्वं जगत् प्रकाशयति स आकाशः।

Vasu: The word Vasu is derived from the root √vas 'to abide or dwell'[46]. One who dwells in all things, and is the abode of all is called Vasu, i.e. God[47].

Rudra: The word Rudra is derived from the root √rudir 'to shed tears' with ṇic suffix[48]. One who makes wicked shed tears is called Rudra, i.e. God[49].

It is said in the Śatapatha Brāhmaṇa of Yajurveda,

यन्मनसा ध्यायति तद्वाचा वदति, यद्वाचा वदति तत् कर्मणा करोति यत् कर्मणा करोति तदभिसम्पद्यते।।

yan-manasā dhyāyati tadvācā vadati, yadvācā vadati tat karmaṇā karoti, yat karmaṇā karoti tadbhi sampadyate.

> [Meaning] A man often says what he thinks, does what he says and reaps the fruits of what he does.

It proves that a soul reaps the fruit of its own deeds. A wicked is awarded punishment by God for his wicked acts. Since God makes the wicked shed tears, He, therefore, is called Rudra.

Nārāyaṇa: According to Manusmṛti (1.10), Nara is a name for both 'water' and 'soul'. Ayana means abode. As such, Nārāyaṇa will be the abode of them all. Therefore, God is called Nārāyaṇa. The verse reads as under:

आपो नारा इति प्रोक्ता आपो वै नरसूनवः।
ता यदस्यायनं पूर्वं तेन नारायणः स्मृतः।।

āpo nārā proktā āpo vai nara-sūnavaḥ
tā yad asyāyanaṁ pūrvaṁ tena nārāyaṇaḥ smṛtaḥ

---

46 वस निवासे

47 वसन्ति भूतानि यस्मिन्नथवा यः सर्वेषु वसति स वसुरीश्वरः।

48 रुदिर् अश्रुविमोचने + णिच् प्रत्यय

49 यो रोदयत्यन्यायकारिणो जनान् स रुद्रः।

Candra: The word Candra is derived from the root √cadi 'to be in bliss'[50]. One who is the embodiment of bliss and bestows bliss upon others is called Candra, i.e. God[51].

Maṅgala: The word Maṅgala is derived from the root √magi 'to move' with alac suffix[52]. One who is the embodiment of well being and cause of well-being for all souls is called Maṅgala, i.e. God[53].

Budha: The word Budha is derived from the root √budha 'to know'[54]. One who is the embodiment of intelligence and cause of intelligence for all beings is called Budha, i.e. God[55].

Śukra: The word Śukra is derived from the root √ī(śuc)ir 'to be pure' and 'to purify'[56]. One who is most pure and purifies others coming into his contact is called Śukra, i.e. God[57].

Śanaiścara: The word Śanaiścara is derived from the root √cara 'to move' and 'to eat' preceded by the word 'śanais'[58]. One who is easily accessible to all and forbearing is called Śanaiścara, i.e. God[59].

---

50 चदि आह्लादने

51 यश्चन्दति चन्दयति वा स चन्द्रः ।

52 मगि गत्यर्थक + अलच् प्रत्यय

53 यो मंगति मंगयति वा स मंगलः ।

54 बुध अवगमने

55 यो बुध्यते बोध्यते वा स बुधः: ।

56 ईशुचिर् पूतीभावे + क्र प्रत्यय

57 यः शुच्यति शोचयति वा स शुक्रः ।

58 शनैस्+चर गतिभक्षणयोः

59 यः शनैश्चरति स शनैश्चरः ।

Rāhu: The word Rāhu is derived from the root √raha 'to forsake'[60]. One who is extremely pure forsakes the wicked and saves others from wicked is called Rāhu, i.e. God[61].

Ketu: The word Ketu is derived from the root √kit 'to reside', 'to heal'[62]. One who is abode whole universe, free from all ailments and heals all seekers during the period of salvation is called Ketu, i.e. God[63].

Yajña: The word Yajña is derived from the root √yaj 'to replenish natural forces', 'to fuse or blend two or more things/elements to create a new one' and 'to help needy living beings'[64]. As per Śatapatha Brāhmaṇa, God is called Yajña[65], because He creates the material world by inducing fusion in molecules of matter and venerated by all learned persons[66]. God is so called (Yajña), as He was, at present and in future will be adored by all Ṛṣis and Munis right from Brahmā onwards by virtue of His Omnipresence.

Hotā: The word Hotā is derived from the root √hu 'to give and take'[67]. One who gives all souls what is worth giving and takes from them what is worth taking is called Hotā, i.e. God[68].

---

60 रह त्यागे

61 यो रहति परित्यजति दुष्टान् राहयति त्याजयति स राहुरीश्वरः।

62 कित निवासे रोगापनयने च

63 यः केतयति चिकित्सति वा स केतुरीश्वरः।

64 यज देवपूजासंगतिकरणदानेषु

65 यज्ञो वै विष्णुः।

66 यो यजति विद्वद्भिरिज्यते वा स यज्ञः।

67 हु दानाऽदानयोः, आदाने चेत्येके

68 यो जुहोति स होता।

Bandhu: The word Bandhu is derived from the root √bandh 'to hold' or 'to bind'[69]. One who holds and regulates the worlds together by his laws, so that they don't move out of their precincts and who supports, protects all the worlds and provides all means of happiness to all like that of a brother is called Bandhu, i.e. God[70].

Pitā: The word Pitā is derived from the root √pā 'to protect'[71]. God is called Pitā,[72] because He protects all. He is like a father who showers his blessings upon his children and wishes them all success, so does God.

Pitāmaha: One who is the father of fathers called Grandfather (Pitāmaha [73] . God, being so, is called Pitāmaha.

Parapitāmaha: One who is the father of ancestors is called Great Grandfather (Para-pitāmaha)[74]. God is the father of our forefathers, so called Parapitāmaha.

Mātā: Just as a kind and benevolent mother shower her blessings and good wishes on her children for their happiness and progress[75], so does God in respect of all created beings. Hence, He is called Mātā.

Āchārya: The word Ācārya is derived from the root

---

69 बन्ध बन्धने

70 यः स्वस्मिन् चराचरं जगद् बध्नाति बन्धुवद् धर्मात्मनो सुखाय सहायो वा वर्त्तते स बन्धु।

71 पा रक्षणे

72 यः पाति सर्वान् स पिता।

73 यः पितृणां पिता स पितामह।

74 यः पितामहानां पिता स प्रपितामहः।

75 यो मिमीते मानयति सर्वान् जीवान् स माता।

√cara 'to go', 'to eat' prefixed with āṅ[76]. One who helps individual beings inculcate good conduct and acquire all sorts of knowledge/sciences is called Ācārya. God being endowed with such a quality called Ācārya[77].

Guru: The word Guru is derived from the root √gṛ 'to pronounce, 'to sound'[78]. God is called Guru, as He pronounces Vedas containing all knowledge and prescribing true principles of creation and decreation[79]. He is preceptor even of preceptors born in the beginning of creation like Agni, Vāyu, Āditya and Aṅgirā[80].

Aja: The word Aja is derived from the root √aja 'to move', 'to throw' and √jani 'to evolve'[81]. God is called Aja because He combines all constituents of material creation in proper order and makes souls born in association with their proper physical bodies, yet remains unborn[82].

Brahmā: The word Brahmā is derived from the root √bṛha, bṛhi 'to increase or 'to expand'[83]. God is called Brahmā, as He causes the entire universe to expand after having created it[84].

Satya: There is a famous statement in Taittirīya

---

76 आङ्+चर् गतिभक्षणयोः

77 यः आचारं ग्राहयति, सर्वा विद्या बोधयति स आचार्य ईश्वरः।

78 गृ शब्दे

79 यो धर्म्यान् शब्दान् गृणात्युपदिशति स गुरुः।

80 स पूर्वेषामपि गुरुः कालेनानवच्छेदात्। योग दर्शन्, समाधिपाद, 26

81 अज गतिक्षेपणयों, जनि प्रादुर्भावे

82 योऽजति सृष्टिं प्रति सर्वान् प्रकृत्यादीन् पदार्थान् प्रक्षिपति, जानाति, कदाचिन्न जायते सोऽजः।

83 बृह् बृहि वृद्धौ

84 योऽखिलं जगन्निर्माणेन बृंहति वर्द्धयति स ब्रह्मा।

Upaniṣad that says:

'सत्यं ज्ञानमनन्तं ब्रह्म'
satyaṁ jñānam anantaṁ brahma.

[Meaning] God is called Satya, Jñāna and Ananta.

The three objects energy (matter), soul and God are three different causes of creation. They all are called sat by virtue of their imperishable nature. The God is most excellent among all the three imperishable causes, so He is called Satya[85].

Jñāna: God is called Jñāna (Repository of knowledge) because He knows all the worlds, animate and inanimate[86].

Ananta: God is called Ananta (Endless) because He is beyond the definition of dimensions or boundaries[87].

Brahma: God is called Brahma, because He is biggest of all[88].

Anādi: The word Anādi is formed of Ādi in the sense of Negative Determinative compound (Nañ Tatpuruṣa Samāsa). The word Ādi is derived from root √ḍudāñ 'to donate' with prefix āṅ[89]. Ādi (beginning) is that which has nothing to precede it, but followed by others[90] and that which is devoid of the first cause is called Anādi.

---

85 सन्तीति सन्तस्तेषु सत्सु साधु तत्सत्यम्।

86 यज्जानाति चराचरं जगत्तज्ज्ञानम्।

87 न विद्यतेऽन्तोऽवधिर्मर्यादा यस्य तदनन्तम्।

88 सर्वेभ्यो बृहत्त्वाद् ब्रह्म। तैत्तिरीय उपनिषद्

89 आङ्+डुदाञ् दाने

90 यस्मात् पूर्वं नास्ति परं चास्ति स आदिरित्युच्यते।

God, being devoid of first cause, is called Anādi[91].

Ānanda: The word Ānanda is derived root √ṭunadi 'to prosper' or 'to thrive' with āṅ prefix[92]. One who is the embodiment of bliss; all emancipated souls enjoy bliss in Him and who bestows happiness upon spiritual beings is called Ānanda, i.e. God[93].

Sat: The word 'Sat' is derived from root √asa 'to be'[94]. One who exists beyond the bounds of time and space is called Sat, i.e. God[95].

Cit: The word 'Cit' is derived from root √citi 'to know', 'to be conscious[96]. One who is the embodiment of knowledge or consciousness and makes all beings conscious of truth and falsehood is called Cit, i.e. God[97].

Saccidānanda: God is called so being attributed with the qualities of Sat (ever existence), Cit (consciousness) and Ānanda (bliss).

Nitya: One who is unchangeable and imperishable is called Nitya (Eternal). God being so, called Nitya.

Śuddha: The word Śuddha is derived from root √śundha 'to purify'[98]. One who is pure (free from all

---

91 न विद्यते आदिः कारणं यस्य सोऽनादिरीश्वरः।

92 आङ्+टुनदि् समृद्धौ

93 आनन्दन्ति सर्वे मुक्ता यस्मिन् यद्वा यः सर्वांजीवानानन्दयति स आनन्दः।

94 अस भुवि

95 यदस्ति त्रिषु कालेषु न बाध्यते तत्सद् ब्रह्म।

96 चिती संज्ञाने

97 यश्चेतति चेतयति संज्ञापयति सर्वान् सज्जनान् योगिनस्तच्चित्परं ब्रह्म।

98 शुन्ध शुद्धौ

impurities) and purifies all is called Śuddha, i.e God[99].

Buddha: The word Buddha is derived from the root √budha 'to know' with -kta suffix[100]. One who is Omniscient and makes others known is called Buddha, i.e. God[101].

Mukta: The word Mukta is derived from the root √(muc)ḷ 'to free'[102]. One who is free from all impurities, and frees seekers from suffering is called Mukta, i.e. God[103].

God is Nitya (Eternal), Śuddha (Pure), Buddha (Omniscient) and Mukta (Free from Impurities) by nature.

Nirākāra: The word Nirākāra is derived from the root √ḍu(kṛ)ñ 'to do' prefixed by nir and (ā)ṅ[104]. One who is formless and is never embodied is called Nirākāra, i.e. God[105].

Nirañjana: The word Nirañjana is derived from the root √(añj)u 'form', 'immoral conduct', 'ill-will', 'beyond the reach of sensory organs' prefixed by nir[106]. One who is formless, away from immoral conduct and ill-will; who is beyond the reach of senses is called Nirañjana, i.e.

---

99 यः शुन्धति सर्वान् शोधयति वा स शुद्ध ईश्वरः।

100 बुध अवगमने

101 यो बुद्धवान् सदैव ज्ञाताऽस्ति स बुद्धो जगदीश्वरः।

102 मुच्लृ मोचने

103 यो मुंचति मोचयति वा मुमुक्षून् स मुक्तो जगदीश्वरः।

104 निर्+आङ्+डुकृञ् करणे

105 निर्गत आकारात्स निराकारः।

106 निर्+अंजु व्यक्ति-म्लक्षण-कान्ति-गतिषु

God[107].

Gaṇapati/Gaṇeśa: The word Gaṇapati/Gaṇeśa is formed of two words Gaṇa+pati/Gaṇa+īśa. The word Gaṇa is derived from the root √gaṇa 'to enumerate'[108]. One who is the Lord or the protector of all material objects or living beings that can be subjected to enumeration is called Gaṇapati or Gaṇeśa, i.e. God[109].

Viśveśvara: One who is the head of universe is called Viśveśvara, i.e. God[110].

Kūṭastha: One who never undergoes a transformation in various operations of transformational nature even though He is instrumental behind them[111].

Devī: The word Devī has as many meanings as the word Deva. The God has denominations in all the three genders, e.g. Brahma (in neuter gender), Citi (in feminine gender) and Īśvara (in masculine gender). Deva is masculine denomination of Īśvara (God), Devī is feminine denomination like Citi. Hence, God is called by the name of Devī also.

Śakti: The word Śakti is derived from the root √(śak)ḷ 'to be able'[112]. One who is capable enough to create the whole universe is called Śakti, i.e. God[113].

Śri: The word Śri is derived from the root √(śri)ñ 'to

---

107 अंजनं व्यक्ति-र्म्लक्षणं कुकाम इन्द्रियैः प्राप्तिश्चेत्यस्माद्यो निर्गतः पृथग्भूतः स निरंजनः।

108 गण संख्याने

109 ये प्रकृत्यादयो जडा जीवाश्च गण्यन्ते संख्यायन्ते तेषामीशः स्वामी पतिः पालको वा।

110 यो विश्वमीष्टे स विश्वेश्वरः।

111 यः कूटेऽनेकविधव्यवहारे स्वस्वरूपेणैव तिष्ठति स कूटस्थः परमेश्वरः।

112 शक्लृ शक्तौ

113 यः सर्वं जगत् कर्त्तुं शक्नोति स शक्तिः।

serve'[114]. One who is served by the whole world, learned as well as ascetics is called Śri, i.e. God[115].

Lakṣmī: The word Lakṣamī is derived from the root √Lakṣa 'to see' and 'to mark'[116]. God is called Lakṣmī, since He observes the whole world, moveable and immoveable, giving it varied shapes and forms characterised by various salient features, e.g. human body characterized by eyes and nose; trees characterized by leaves, flowers, fruits and roots; different liquids and solids characterized by black, red and white colors; the material world characterized by clay, stone, Moon and Sun etc. He is splendour of splendid and cherished goal of Vedas and learned Yogis[117].

Sarasvatī: The word Sarasavtī is formed of word saras (derived from root √sṛ 'to go'[118]) with the denominative suffix -(mat)up+feminine suffix -ṅ(ī)p[119]. One who is endowed with immense knowledge, that is, knowledge of the application of relationship of different words with their objects is called Sarasvati, i.e. God[120].

Sarvaśaktimān: One who does not require the assistance of another in accomplishing His task, and who is capable of accomplishing His tasks by His Own means is called Sarvaśaktimān, i.e. God.

---

114 श्रिञ् सेवायाम्

115 यः श्रियते सेव्यते सर्वेण जगता विद्वद्भिर्योगिभिश्च स श्रीरीश्वरः।

116 लक्ष दर्शनांकनयोः

117 यो लक्षयति पश्यत्यंकते चिह्नयति चराचरं जगदथवा वेदैराप्तैर्योगिभिश्च यो लक्ष्यते स लक्ष्मी सर्वप्रियेश्वरः।

118 सृ गतौ

119 सरस्+मतुप्+ङीप्

120 सरो विविधं ज्ञानं विद्यते यस्यां चित्तौ सा सरस्वती।

Nyāyakārī: The word Nyāya is derived from root √(ṇi)ñ 'to obtain'. According to the commentary of Vātsyāyana on Nyāya Darśana, Nyāya means arriving at the truth with the help of eight kinds of means of cognition such as Direct Cognition (Pratyakṣa), Inference (Anumāna), Analogy (Upamāna) etc[121]. Nyāya also means dispensing dharma (Justice) without favour or fervour[122]. Since God dispenses Justice without favour or fervour innately, He is called Nyāyakārī[123].

Dayālu: The word Dayālu is derived from the root √daya 'to give', 'to go', 'to protect', 'to kill' and 'to take'[124]. One who instils fearlessness knows the difference between true and false sciences, protects the virtuous, and punishes the wicked is called Dayālu, i.e. God[125].

Advaita: Notion of duality is called dvitā or dvītaṁ and the same is known as Dvaita[126]. Non-duality is Advaita. God is called Advaita because He is distinguished for Oneness, Non-duality, i.e. devoid of second hostile personality or susceptibility of division in Him[127].

Nirguṇa: Guṇa is a quality that counts or a quality

---

121 प्रमाणैरर्थपरीक्षणं न्यायः।

122 पक्षपातराहित्याचरणं न्यायः।

123 न्यायकर्त्तुं शीलमस्य स न्यायकारीश्वरः।

124 दय दानगतिरक्षणहिंसादानेषु

125 दयते ददाति जानाति गच्छति रक्षति हिनस्ति यया सा दया, बह्वी दया विद्यते यस्य स दयालुः परमेश्वरः।

126 द्वयोर्भावो द्वाभ्यामितं सा द्विता द्वीतं वा सैव तदैव वा द्वैतम्, न विद्यते द्वैतं द्वितीयेश्वरभावो यस्मिंस्तदद्वैतम्।

127 सजातीयविजातीयस्वगतभेदशून्यं ब्रह्म।

that qualifies an object. One who is free from qualities of all inanimate things or animate beings is called Nirguṇa, i.e. God[128]. Guṇas here are constituted of three material qualities, viz. sattva, rajas and tamas; five sensory properties of five subtle elements, viz. sound, touch, colour, taste and smell; and the characteristic of living beings like imperfect knowledge, ignorance, passions and desires. The above Characteristic of God is substantiated by the authority of Upaniṣad. "He is beyond the sensory properties of sound, touch, colour, etc. [129]"

Saguṇa: One who is possessed of qualities is called Saguṇa[130]. God is called Saguṇa because He is possessed of such attributes as perfect knowledge, perfect bliss, purity and infinite power. Everything in this universe can be categorized both as Saguṇa (possessed of certain qualities) and Nirguṇa (devoid of certain other qualities). For instance, Earth is Saguṇa, being possessed of the sensory quality of smell and Nirguna, being devoid of qualities like passion and desire characteristic to animate beings. Similarly, God is Nirguṇa, being devoid of the qualities characteristic of material world and living beings and Saguṇa, being possessed of qualities of omnipresence, omniscience etc. In other words, there is no object in the world that can stand in isolation of the concept of Saguṇa and Nirguṇa. For example, a material object is called Nirguṇa so far as the qualities of living beings are concerned and Saguṇa as far as its own natural material qualities are concerned. The similar thing holds

---

128 गण्यन्ते ये ते गुणा वा यैर्गणयन्ति ते गुणाः, यो गुणेभ्यो निर्गतः स निर्गुण ईश्वरः।

129 अशब्दमस्पर्शमरूपमव्ययम्।

130 गुणैः सह वर्त्तते स सगुणः।

true in respect of God.

Antaryāmī: One who, by virtue of his quality of Omnipresence, governs and controls the entire universe, animate and inanimate, innately is called Antaryāmī[131], i.e. God.

Dharmarāja: Dharmarāja is one who always reflects Dharma (ethics, morality, truth, justice and righteousness) and reflected by Dharma and not otherwise[132]. God being so qualified called Dharmarāja.

Yama: The word Yama is derived from the root √yamu 'to control'[133]. One, who administers Law of Rewards for actions of all creatures and clears them of all sorts of injustice, is called Yama, i.e. God[134].

Bhagavān: The word Bhagvān is formed of the word Bhaga (derived from root √bhaja 'to serve') with denominative suffix ṣ(mat)up[135]. One who is endowed with all richness and worthy to be adored is called Bhagvān, i.e. God[136].

Manu: The word Manu is derived from the root √man 'to know'[137]. One who is endowed with true and perfect knowledge and worthy of being known and believed is called Manu[138], i.e. God.

---

131 अन्तर्यन्तुं नियन्तुं शीलं यस्य सोऽयमन्तर्यामी।

132 यो धर्मे राजते स धर्मराजः।

133 यमु उपरमे

134 यः सर्वान् प्राणिनो नियच्छति स यमः।

135 भज सेवायाम् + मतुप्

136 भगः सकलैश्वर्यं सेवनं वा विद्यते यस्य स भगवान्।

137 मन ज्ञाने

138 यो मन्यते स मनुः।

Puruṣa: The word Puruṣa is derived from root √pṛ 'to bring up' and 'to fill'. One who provides stuff (matter) for the whole universe and brings it up is called Puruṣa, i.e. God.

Viśvambhara: The word Viśvambhara is formed of word Viśva followed by the root √ḍu(bhṛ)ñ 'to uphold', 'to nurture'[139]. The God is called Viśvambhara, as He upholds and nurtures the world[140].

Kāla: The word Kāla is derived from the root √kala 'to count'[141]. One who counts and classifies all material objects and souls is called Kāla[142], i.e. God.

Śeṣa: The word Śeṣa is derived from the root √ (śiṣ)ḷ 'to survive'[143]. One who survives the cycle of creation and decreation is called Śeṣa[144], i.e. God.

Āpta: The word Āpta is derived from the root √(āp)ḷ 'to pervade'[145]. One who is accessible and accessed by all divine souls is called Āpta[146]. God is called Āpta being endowed with above qualities and free from fraud and deception.

Śaṅkara: The word Śaṅkara is formed of word 'Sam' followed by the root √ḍu(kṛ)ñ 'to do', 'to cause well

---

139 डुभृञ् धारणपोषणयोः

140 यो विश्वं बिभर्ति धरति पुष्णाति वा स विश्वम्भरो जगदीश्वरः।

141 कल संख्याने

142 कलयति संख्याति सर्वान् पदार्थान् स कालः।

143 शिष्लृ विशेषणे

144 यः शिष्यते स शेषः।

145 आप्लृ व्याप्तौ

146 यः सर्वान् धर्मात्मन आप्नोति वा सर्वैर्धर्मात्मभिराप्यते छलादिरहितः स आप्तः।

being'[147]. One who causes well-being and happiness is called Śaṅkara, i.e. God.

Mahādeva: The word Mahādeva is constituted of two words mahat+deva forming a Determinative (Tatpuruṣa) Compound. One who is distinguished among the greats, leader of the learned and illuminator of luminous objects is called Mahādeva[148], i.e. Great God.

Priya: The word Priya is derived of the root √(prī)ñ 'to gladden', 'to seek'[149]. One who gladdens divine souls, seekers of salvation, noble souls, and worthy of being sought after by all is called Priya[150], i.e. God.

Svayambhū: The word Svayambhū is constituted of the indeclinable particle Svayam followed by the root √bhu 'to be'[151]. One who is Self-existent, Self-sustained and never created by anyone else is called Svayambhū, i.e. God[152].

Kavi: The word Kavi is derived from the root √ku 'to sound'[153]. One who is Omniscient and Instructor of all sciences through Veda is called Kavi, i.e. God[154].

Śiva: The word Śiva is derived from the root √(śiv)u 'to cause welfare'[155]. One who is embodiment of

---

147 डुभृञ् धारणपोषणयोः

148 यो महतां देवः स महादेवः।

149 प्रीञ् तर्पणे कान्तौ

150 यः प्रीणाति प्रीयते वा स प्रियः।

151 स्वयं+भू सत्तयाम्

152 यः स्वयं भवति स स्वयम्भूरीश्वरः।

153 कु शब्दे

154 यः कौति शब्दयति सर्वा विद्याः स कविरीश्वरः।

155 शिवु कल्याणे

wellbeing and cause of the same is called Śiva, i.e. God.

In the foregoing pages, a hundred names of God have been explained, but there are innumerable others. The innumerable names of God are followed by His innumerable qualities, actions and dispositions.

Different qualities, actions and dispositions of God are represented by different denominations. Thus, the names quoted by me (Swami Dayanand Saraswati) are as a drop compared to the ocean. Innumerable qualities, actions and dispositions of God are registered in the Vedas and other Śāstras (Scientific treatises). Their study can make one enlightened about those denominations of God and other objects of creation.

Question: Why didn't you start your book with a maṅglācaraṇa (auspicious note for success, in the beginning, middle or end) as other authors do?

Answer: It is unbecoming of us. If one attempts auspicious notes, in the beginning, middle or end of one's work, the intervening parts of the book will stay inauspicious. The Sāṅkhya Philosopher says:

मंगलाचरणं शिष्टाचारात् फलदर्शनाच्छ्रुतितश्चेति ।
maṅgalācaraṇaṁ śiṣṭāchārāt phaladarśanāt śrutitaś cheti.

Maṅglācaraṇa (auspicious note) is just translating into action the just, unbiased and truthful commandments of God enjoined in the Vedas.

Thus Maṅglācaraṇa is nothing else but an honest attempt for truthful documentation from the beginning to end, rather than a conglomeration of jumbled up statements of auspicious and inauspicious nature. Here one can have a glance at the statement of Taittirīya

Upaniṣad (7.11):

यान्यनवद्यानि कर्माणि तानि सेवितव्यानि नो इतराणि।।
yāni anvadyāni karmāṇi tāni sevitavyāni no itarāṇi.

[Meaning] O dear ones! You should practice those deeds alone that are blameless and not others.

Hence, the following auspicious statements used to initiate the Modern writings are often considered false by learned scholars, as they are opposed to the Vedas and Books authored by Ṛṣis e.g.

'श्रीगणेशाय नमः', 'सीतारामाभ्यां नमः', 'राधाकृष्णाभ्यां नमः', 'श्रीगुरुचरणारविन्दाभ्यां नमः', 'हनुमते नमः', 'दुर्गायै नमः', 'वटुकाय नमः', 'भैरवाय नमः', 'शिवाय नमः', 'सरस्वत्यै नमः', 'नारायणाय नमः'

Śri Gaṇeśāya namaḥ (Salutations to Gaṇeśa)
Sitārāmābhyāṁ namaḥ (Salutations to Sitā and Rāma)
Radhākṛṣṇābhyāṁ namaḥ (Salutations to Rādhā and Krishna)
Śrigurucaraṇārvindābhyāṁ namaḥ (Salutations to the Lotus Feet of Guru)

Hanumate namaḥ (Salutations to Hanumāna)

Durgāyai namaḥ (Salutations to Durgā)

Vaṭukāya namaḥ (Salutations to a form of Śiva).

Bhairvāya namaḥ (Salutations to Bhairava)

Śivāya namaḥ (Salutations to Śiva)

Sarasvatyai namaḥ (Salutations to Sarasvatī)

Nārāyaṇāya namaḥ (Salutations to Narayaṇa)

The above-cited auspicious notes are nowhere attested while initiating the Vedas and other Śāstras authored by Ṛṣis. Books authored by Ṛṣis are initiated either with the note of 'Om' or 'Atha', e.g.

अथ शब्दानुशासनम् ।
atha śabdānuśāsanam

Now we begin the science of language.

Vyākaraṇa Mahābhāṣya

अथातो धर्मजिज्ञासा
athāto dharma jijñāsā

Now we begin an inquiry into dharma.

Pūrva Mimānsā

अथातो धर्मं व्याख्यास्यामः
athato dharma vyākhyāsyāmaḥ

Now we shall explain dharma.

Vaiśeṣika Darśana

अथ योगानुशासनम्
atha yogānuśāsanam

Now we begin the science of Yoga. *Yoga Darśana*

अथ त्रिविधदुःखात्यन्तनिवृत्तिरत्यन्तपुरुषार्थः ।
atha trividha duḥkhātyanta nivṛttir atyanta puruṣārthaḥ

Now we shall begin with the complete cessation of three types of sufferings that constitute the supreme purpose of life.

Sāṅkhya Darśana

अथातो ब्रह्मजिज्ञासा ।
athāto brahma jijñāsā

Now we shall begin an inquiry into Brahman.

Vedanta Darśana

ओमित्येतदक्षरमुद्गीथमुपासीत ।
Om ityetad akṣaram udgītham upāsīta

Meditate upon Om, the name of imperishable God.

Chāndogya Upaniṣad

ओमित्येतदक्षरमिद सर्वं तस्योपव्याख्यानम्।
Om ityetad akṣaram idaṁ sarvaṁ tasyopavyākhyānam

Om is imperishable God, rest explains His existence.

Māṇḍukya Upaniṣad

Similarly, other texts authored by various Ṛṣis and Munis commenced with the initials like 'Atha' and 'Om'. For example, Ṛgveda begins with agni as it's initial. Yajurveda begins with īṣe. Sāmaveda begins with agni, Atharvaveda with ye triṣaptāḥ pariyanti. We do not find any Vedic or ancillary texts initiated with the auspicious notes like Śri Gaṇeṣāya namaḥ. There is also a tradition to pronounce 'Hari Om' in the beginning of Vedas. This false and speculative idea has been inherited from the tradition of Tāntrikas and Paurāṇikas. Vedas and none of other Śāstras begin with the initial note of Hari. Hence, it is advisable to initiate a book with either 'Om' or 'Atha'. Thus, this chapter briefly discusses the Names of God. In the next chapter, we shall focus on the Education.

This brings to an end of the first chapter of Satyarth Prakash Dealing with Names of God Authored by Śrimad Dayanand Sarasvati.

It is perfectly certain that India never saw a more learned Sanskrit scholar, a deeper metaphysician, a more wonderful orator, and a more fearless denunciator of any evil, than Dayanand, since the time of Shankaracharya.

Madame Blavastsky

CHAPTER 2

Now we begin to elaborate on 'Grooming A Child'.

मातृमान् पितृमानाचार्यवान् पुरुषो वेद ।
mātṛmān pitṛmān ācāryavān puruṣo veda

Śatapatha Brāhmaṇa

[Meaning] Verily, that man can truly become a great scholar who is blessed with three good instructors, viz., father, mother, and teacher.

Blessed is that family and most fortunate is that child whose parents are spiritual/divine and learned. Mother is the greatest counsellor, caretaker and well-wisher of a child. No one can be as affectionate, loving and care as the mother to her children.

A child is said to be truly blessed only when his/her mother (*Mātṛmān)* is spiritual, learned and devout. Hail to that mother who instils moral, ethical and spiritual values to her child right from their conception until the completion of their education.

It is proper for parents that they should avoid the use of intoxicating substances, alcoholic drinks, decomposed and unhealthy food prejudicial to the intellectual growth of fetus (expected child) before, during and after pregnancy. They should use such nutritious foodstuffs like clarified butter (Ghee), milk, honey as are conducive to healthy growth of sperm and ovum.

They should follow the Vedic regimen for begetting quality offsprings.

The ideal period for conception lasts from the 5th day to 16th day after onset of the menstrual cycle, barring the first four days, as well as the 11th and 13th lunar day (if intervening the above period). Thus, 10 nights are most suitable for conception. After 16th day of the menstrual cycle, the couple should avoid sexual contact until the recurrence of the same dates in the subsequent menstrual cycle. When conception takes place, sexual contact should be avoided for one year.

Before a sexual contact, the husband and wife should be perfectly healthy, mutually happy, and free from all sorts of anxiety and tension. In the matter of diet and dress, they should follow diet and dress code as laid down in Charaka and Suṣruta (Ancient Indian books of medical science). In order to be healthy, one is required to practice the methods of conjugal harmony as suggested in *Manusmṛti.*

During pregnancy, an expectant mother needs to be strictly cautious as to her diet and dress. She should avoid sexual contact with her husband for one year after conception. Until the birth of the child, the mother should take a diet rich in substances conducive to physical and mental health, beauty, energy, mental peace and other good qualities.

After delivery, the newborn baby should be given a scented bath and its birth cord (umbilical cord) should be severed (cut off) carefully. Havan should be performed with pure clarified butter. Mother should also be given a proper bath, so that both baby and mother may soon grow hale and hearty. The child's mother should also be given good nutritious diet, to enrich the quality of breast milk.

The mother should breastfeed her child at least for the first six days, even if she is unable to do so. Thereafter a cow's milk may be engaged to breastfeed the child. It should, however, be ensured that the cow gets nutritious diet.

In case a cow is unaffordable, then a child can be fed with the milk of goat, diluted with an equal amount of water. Decoction of medicinal herbs promoting health, intelligence and energy may be added to the milk.

After delivery, mother and child should be moved to a decorated room open to fresh air. Both mother and child should be taken out for an in open fresh air.

In cases where neither cow nor milk from goat is available, the parents may do whatever they consider suitable in the given circumstances (in consultation with a physician). What is important to understand here is that child's body grows at the cost of his/ her mother's body, so mother's body becomes weaker each time she gives birth. In the event of weakness, it is best for mother not to breastfeed her child for a longer period. Medicinal ointments may be applied to the nipples of mother to check the flow of milk. This will rejuvenate the mother in the next month itself. Until then the husband should restrain his passions. Couples following this regimen will beget healthy offsprings enriched with velour, spirituality, divinity, intelligence and long life. They themselves will enjoy healthy long life. In order to beget superior quality of offsprings, the wife should observe vaginal contraction and maintain cleanliness and the husband should preserve his seminal fluid.

A mother should always impart best of instructions to her child so that he may grow into a good human being of good manners and never indulge into misconduct of any type. When the child begins to speak, the mother should ensure that the child articulates various sounds properly in terms of their proper place of articulation and articulator. For instance, the labial sound 'p' has lips both as place of articulation and articulator. It is pronounced from lips with the closeness of upper and lower lips.

The child should also be taught proper pronunciation of short, long and prolonged vowels. The child must be trained to speak in a sweet, deep-rooted, beautiful voice clearly audible in terms of sounds, syllables, mora, words, syntax, sentences and pronunciation pauses.

When the child begins to talk and understand a little, he/she must be taught a refined language and manners to address his/her parents, seniors, juniors, highly respected persons in society, rulers and scholars. He/she must also know how to conduct himself/herself in their presence, so that he/she may not be spotted for his/her unbecoming behavior and may command respect everywhere. Parents should strive to inculcate in their children self restrain, love for knowledge and good company.

Parents should help their children to grow in a way that they avoid wasting their precious time in unnecessary games, crying, joking, fighting, complaining, greed for material objects, envy, malice and other vices. They should be taught not to touch or rub the genitals, as it can cause loss of vital power and impotence besides soiling the hand.

The parents should try, in every possible manner, to instil in their children a sense of truthfulness, heroism, patience, cheerfulness and other such qualities.

When boys and girls attain the age of five, they should be taught the alphabet of their parental language and other foreign languages too. Thereafter the parents should make them commit to memory such mantras, ślokas (verses), aphorisms, prose passages, and poems as explain good maxims, spiritual and moral education, concept of God, conducting with parents, teachers, scholars, peripatetic monks, ruler, fellow citizens, family members, brothers, sisters and friends. All this is necessary for children so that they are not duped by cheats. People should also educate their children about ideas and practices that are opposed to science, morality and ethics and that lead to superstitions, so that they may not believe in false things like ghosts and spirits.

Hereunder the true meanings of BhÊta (deceased person) and Preta (mortal remains) are depicted with evidence from *Manusmṛti* (5.65)

गुरोः प्रेतस्य शिष्यस्तु पितृमेधं समाचरन्।
प्रेतहारैः समं तत्र दशरात्रेण शुद्ध्यति।।
guroḥ pretasya śiṣyastu pitṛmedhaṁ samācaran.
prtahāraiḥ samaṁ tatra daśarātreṇa śudhyati.

[Meaning] Guru (teacher) having been turned into preta (mortal remains), the pupil performing *pitṛmedha* i.e. cremation rites is purified in ten days together with other people who carry the preta (mortal remains) in the crematorium.

It is clear, then, that on being cremated, a person becomes bhūta (an entity of past). All those who were born, but are not currently living are called bhūta because they lived in past. This has been the conviction of all scholars right from BrahmÈ down to modern age. However, people who are victims of scepticism, bad company and bad habits are often tormented by fears of ghosts, spirits, goblins and fairies.

Try to understand, when a person dies, his soul attains another body and species under the eternal law of God in consonance with moral or immoral deeds performed by him. Can anyone violate this eternal law of God? Ignorant people who have never studied, heard or thought of medical and physical sciences, consider a person afflicted with a mental disease like lunacy and physical diseases like high fever caused by vitiation of all the three pathological factors of *Vāta*, *Pitta* and *Kapha* as possessed by ghosts and spirits. Instead of having such ailments treated through medication or diet regimen, these people trust in cheats, rogues, idiots, wicked, selfish, people indulging in lowly professions, and fall a victim of tantric rites like trickery, quackery, leftover food, tying charm-threads, amulets and yantras, false magic chants and incantations. They waste their money and bring misery and suffering to their children prolonging the diseases, which could have been treated otherwise.

Unwise people who are well-off, when approach these wicked unethical and selfishly motivated so-called tantric people for medical investigation of mental diseases of their near and dear ones, they cheat them in the name of possession by some ghosts or evil spirit and warn them of fatal consequences, if some preventive tantric measures are not taken in time. Thus, they extort handsome amount of money from them in the name of mystic chants and magic rites.

Similarly, when some astrologer is approached, he investigates the mental problem as affliction by malevolent stars and suggests propitiatory rites like śānti pāṭha, japa, prayer, charity to cure him and to avoid any risk of life.

Question: Well, tell me Mr. Astrologer! The sun and other celestial bodies are lifeless like this earth. They cannot do anything except radiating light and heat. Do you think that these celestial bodies are living conscious beings that can harm us on being angry and bestow comfort and happiness on being propitiated?

Answer: Isn't it due to the influence of stars that the rulers and common people are experiencing pleasure and pain.

Questioner: Oh no! It is all due to moral and immoral acts.

Answerer: Is Astrology a pseudo-science?

Questioner: The part that deals with astronomy, mathematics, algebra and geometry is true science, but the part that deals with Astrology is a pseudo-science.

Answerer: Is then horoscope useless?

Questioner: Yes it is. In fact, it shouldn't be called horoscope but 'horror-scope', because the birth of a child brings happiness to the family, but the horoscope cast horrors. Horoscope is generally read to parents with a happy note but ends with a pal of gloom when reading between the lines. The parents are made to pay a huge amount for the propitiation of maleficent stars. Thus, the innocent people fall a victim of these wicked astrologers and destined to live a life of misery without any fault of theirs.

Similar is the case of Śītalā mātā (name of a deity that causes smallpox), charms and chants. These are also nothing but downright frauds and quackery. Should anyone claim that if he prepared a talisman or charmed thread consecrated by a chant, his deity or Peer (Muslim saint) would ward off all problems and hurdles coming on his way? Instead of being taken in by the words of such persons, it is better to challenge them by asking whether their charms and chants save people from death, the laws of God, and the law of *karma*. Many children, including their own, had died despite their talisman, charms and chants. Can they themselves evade death by using their amulets? This would render these fraudulent people speechless and they will realize that their tricks would not succeed.

Therefore, it behoves all of us to do away with all kinds of false and superstitious practices. Instead, we should never leg behind to graciously serve those eminent scholars who are virtuous benefactors of humankind and teach various sciences without prejudice or bias to all.

Those who practice frauds, alchemy, sorcery, tantric rituals of killing, charming, distracting mind and bewitchment, etc. should be considered extremely vile. Children in their early age should be counselled about these fraudulent practices, so that they may not fall a prey to imposters and suffer from their entrapment.

Students should also be taught about benefits of celibacy and staying away from perverted sexual activities. A celibate person gains in health, strength, energy, intellect and consequently feels happy. To be able to live a life of celibacy, a student is required to avoid reading, listening obscene stories and viewing obscene pictures, company of licentious people, contemplating lustful ideas, staring at women, meeting them in a secluded place, engaging in conversation with them and fingering or laying hand on them. Only then, a student is able to acquire best quality education and complete mastery over spiritual and material knowledge.

The lack of sperm counts and vital humour cause impotence and such a person is called as the ruiner of the family line. One who suffers from *Prameha* (diseases in which sperms and vital humour of the body pass out through urine) becomes physically weak, resulting in loss of physical lustre, intellect, courage, boldness, patience, energy, velour and such other good qualities.

Parents must advise their teenage children that if they forego the precious opportunity to acquire a good education, spiritual knowledge and preserve their vital energy, they will never find a chance to have it again in this life.

The children must be made to understand by parents that so long as they (parents) own their domestic responsibilities, they (children) have the excellent opportunity to pursue their studies, physical health. Parents can impart their children similar other instructions to transform them into ideal citizens. That is why the author of Śatapatha Brāhmaṇa lays emphasis on the expressions 'mātṛmān' and 'pitṛmān'. The meaning thereby, the mother acts as the instructor of child right from birth until the 5th year of age. Father is supposed to execute his responsibility of instructing a child from the 6th year onward to the 8th year, while from 9th year onward the education of a child is taken care of by the teacher in Gurukuls or schools, as the case may be. As such, it is the bounden duty of parents to have their sons and daughters admitted to educational institutions staffed by learned ideal teachers.

Those children alone become scholarly, cultured, well educated whose parents do not observe leniency in the matter of educating them, rather reprimand them whenever necessary. In this regard, the author of Mahābhāṣya (8.1.8) remarks as under:

सामृतैः पाणिभिर्घ्नन्ति गुरवो न विषोक्षितैः ।
लालनाश्रयिणो दोषास्ताडनाश्रयिणो गुणाः ।।
sāmṛtaiḥ pāṇibhir ghnanti gurvo na viṣokṣitaiḥ
lālanā-śrayiṇo doṣās tāḍanā-śrayiṇo guṇāḥ

[Meaning] Those parents and teachers who reprimand children, when necessary, are, in fact, giving them a drink of nectar compared to those who show undue affection. Undue affection is as if a poison fed to the children. Actually, undue affection spoils children, whilst reproofing makes them virtuous.

Children should also be trained to feel pleased when reprimanded, and feel uneasy when fondled. Nevertheless, parents and teachers should take utmost care that they should not harbour malice or jealousy while reprimanding them. They should only make of show of anger while being kind in their heart.

In addition to regular academic education, youngsters should be taught to stay away from vices of stealing, adultery, lethargy, negligence, intoxication, false speech, violence, cruelty, jealousy, malice and undue attachment.

They should also be taught to conduct themselves truthfully.

Just convince the youngsters that the image once damaged due to theft, adultery, and false speech cannot be improved throughout life. Similarly, if you are not able to keep up your words, your image is tarnished permanently. Therefore, you should try to be true to your words and honour the commitment made to someone or else no one will ever trust you.

One should not be too egoistic. VidurnĪti says:

अभिमानः श्रियं हन्ति ।

abhimānaḥ śriyaṁ hanti

[Meaning] Too much ego strips one of his grace and possessions.

So, one should not be egoistic. Deception, fraud, and ungratefulness bring pain even to the person who harbours them, what to say of others against whom they are aimed.

Deception and fraud are actions different from what they actually appear and satisfying one's own interest at the cost of others. Ungratefulness is not to feel oblige or not to be thankful for the help rendered.

A child should not lose his temper or use harsh words, rather cultivate speech that promotes peace and harmony. He should avoid useless talk, and speak what is required of him. He should respect his elders. When elders approach, a child should stand and wish 'Namaste', and offer them higher seat than what he occupies. During mass gatherings, he should occupy a seat that befits his status, so that he may never be asked to surrender his seat in favour of his elders.

The youngster should never be hostile to others. Even after having acquired riches, he should acquire virtues and abandon vices. He should keep the good company and avoid bad company. He should be ready to serve his parents and teachers.

The *Taittirīya Upaniṣad* (*Śikṣāvalli*, 11), says:

यान्यस्माकं सुचरितानि तानि त्वयोपास्यानि नो इतराणि।
yānyasmākaṁ sucaritāni tāni tvayopāsyāni no itarāṇi.

[Meaning] Only our righteous act and conduct should be followed, not others.

The purport of above statement is that parents and teachers should always instruct their children and students to follow truth and only those actions of theirs, which are righteous and not wicked.

Youngsters should promulgate and propagate whatever truth is revealed to them. They should never trust a hypocrite and a person of immoral acts and obey as per their convenience those commands of their parents and teachers that are directed towards virtuous actions. The teachers should further explain to students the meanings of what their parents made them learn by heart such verses as focus on dharma (moral and ethical values and duties), knowledge and good conduct and the texts like *Nighaṇṭu, Nirukta, Aṣṭādhyāyī*, aphorisms and Veda-mantras. God should be worshipped according to the characteristics explained in the First Chapter.

With regard to outfits and diet, they should conduct themselves in a way that can contribute to their health, knowledge and strength. They should eat a little less than their appetite, and abstain from meat, liquors and other intoxicants.

They should never enter unknown deep waters lest they suffer trouble from aquatic creatures or other objects (such as crocodiles), or even drowned if they don't know how to swim. Manu (4.129) also says, "Never bathe in unknown waters".[156]

Manu (6.46) further says:

दृष्टिपूतं न्यसेत्पादं वस्त्रपूतं जलं पिबेत्।
सत्यपूतां वदेद्वाचं मनःपूतं समाचरेत्।।
dṛṣṭipūtaṁ nyaset pādaṁ vastrapūtaṁ jalaṁ pibet
satyapūtāṁ vadedvācaṁ manaḥpūtaṁ samācaret.

[Meaning] Watch your steps as you walk, drink filtered clean water, speak the truth and think well before you act.

The famous Chāṇakya says:

माता शत्रुः पिता वैरी येन बालो न पाठितः।
न शोभते सभामध्ये हंसमध्ये वको यथा ।।
mātā śatruḥ pitā vairī yena bālo na pāṭhitaḥ
na śobhate sabhā-madhye hansamadhye bako yathā.

[Meaning] Parents who don't educate their children are their enemies. They lose their graceful status among scholars, like a heron among swans.

In fact, it is the paramount duty, greatest dharma and a matter of glory for parents to provide the supreme education to their children in terms of knowledge, *dharma* and civilization.

We have briefly discussed here the issue of Child Education. This is more than enough for the wise to understand.

---

156 नाविज्ञाते जलाशये

This brings to an end of the second chapter of Satyarth Prakash dealing with Education of Child Authored by - Śrimad Dayanand Sarasvati

"The man who resolves, to stick to the truth at all costs, steadily rises in virtues. When his virtues raise his reputation and prestige, he becomes all the more a devotee of truth. This devotion to truth becomes an unerring source of power and greatness."

Swami Dayanand Saraswati

CHAPTER 3

Now we begin to explain Formal Education (methods of learning and teaching in Brahmacarya Āśrama).

In the present chapter, we shall discuss the methodology of formal education. It is the paramount duty of parents, teachers and relatives to equip their children with the ornaments of best spiritual knowledge, highest education, good qualities, actions, and disposition.

The wearing of jewellery made of gold, silver, pearls, rubies, diamonds, etc. adds no beauty to the soul. Jewels only arouse vanity, sensual passion and fear of thieves, and an invitation to death. There are many examples where children wearing ornaments invited their death at the hands of scoundrels seeking to grab their jewellery.

It is said,

विद्याविलासमनसो धृतशीलशिक्षाः
सत्यव्रता रहितमानमलापहाराः ।
संसारदुःखदलनेन सुभूषिता
ये धन्या नरा विहितकर्मपरोपकाराः ।।
vidyā-vilāsa-manaso dhṛt-śīla-śikṣāḥ
satya-vratā rahita-māna-mal-āpahārāḥ

sansāra-duḥkha-dalanena subhūṣitā
ye dhanyā narā vihita-karma-paropakārāḥ

[Meaning] "Blessed are those men and women who are passionate about knowledge; who are educated and possess sweet and amiable tempers; who have taken a vow of truthfulness; who are devoid of vanity and impurity; who are known for alleviating the suffering of whole world; who are engaged in altruistic welfare activities as prescribed by the Vedas."

Boys and girls, when they attain the age of 8 years, should be sent to their respective schools. In no case, they should be allowed to be taught by teachers or teachress of immoral conduct. Only those teachers are qualified to teach who are thoroughly knowledgeable and imbued with moral and ethical values.

Parents should first have done investiture ceremony of their children (male and female) and then have them sent to their respective schools.

Educational institutions should be located in an area isolated from the humbug of cities. There should be a distance of at least three to four miles between the educational institutions meant for male and female students respectively. Those educational institutions that are meant for female students should be staffed with female teachers and support staff and those meant for male with male teachers and support staff. Not even a 5-year-old child of opposite sex should be allowed to be admitted in an educational institution of opposite sex.

As long as they are at the stage of Brahmacārī or Brahmachārī (student life), they should abstain from the following eight forms of sex:

Staring at opposite sex

Fingering or laying hands on opposite sex

Meeting with a person of opposite sex privately

Speaking to opposite sex in private

Obscene remarks

Foreplay

Focus on sexual thoughts

Sexual intercourse

The teachers should ensure that students are kept away from the above-mentioned activities so that they are able to cultivate perfect knowledge, highest education, good manners, and amiable temperament physical, mental and spiritual health, thus augmenting happiness throughout life.

The schools should be situated at a distance of 8 miles from the residential sectors. All students should be treated equally; no matter whether a student is a prince or princess, he comes from a poor or rich family. While in school, all should lead a life of austerity. The students or their parents should not see each other or correspond with them so that they can devote their full time to studies unconcerned about the worldly affairs. Students should always be accompanied by their teachers while on an outing, so that they may not indulge in immoral activities or become lethargic or indolent.

The *Manusmṛti* (7.152) lays down a norm:

कन्यानां सम्प्रदानं च कुमाराणां च रक्षणम् ।।

kanyānāṁ sampradānaṁ ca kumārāṇāṁ ca rakṣaṇam

[Meaning] "Both state and society should enact a law

making it compulsory for parents to send their children (both male and female) to school either after the 5th or 8th year. There should be a provision of penal action for keeping children back home after this age."

The first investiture (*Upanayana*) ceremony should take place at home, and the second in the school family. Parents and teachers should teach Gāyatrī Mantra to the children with its meanings. The mantra reads as under:

ओ३म् भूर्भुवः स्वः । तत्सवितुर्वरेण्यं भर्गो देवस्य धीमहि ।
धियो यो नः प्रचोदयात् ।।

Om bhūr bhuvaḥ svaḥ.
tatsavitur vareṇyaṁ bhargo devasya dhīmahi
dhiyo yo naḥ pracodayāt *Yajurveda, 36.3*

The term Om has already been explained in the first chapter. The meaning of three Mahāvyāhṛtis is now explained. Bhū is prāṇa (inhalation). God is called Bhū because he is the breath of the whole universe, animate and inanimate, dearer than life itself and Self-existent. Bhuvaḥ is apāna (exhalation). God is called Bhuvaḥ because He is immune of all sufferings and alleviates the sufferings of all those who seeks Him (His refuge). Svaḥ is vyāna (all-pervading life force). God is called vyāna because He is the All-pervading life force of the diverse universe and upholder of all the things in it. All these three words are taken from Taittirīya Āraṇyaka.

(Savituḥ)[157] Of One Who creates the whole universe and bestows all riches. (Devasya)[158] Of One Who gives all comforts and is sought after by all, (vareṇyam)[159]

---

157 यः सुनोत्युत्पादयति सर्वं जगत् स सविता तस्य

158 यो दीव्यति दीव्यते वा स देवः ।

159 वर्त्तुमर्हम्

Who is worthy to be accepted or pre-eminent, (bhargaỈ) Who is pure and purifier and All Conscious (tat) that Brahman (dhĪmahi) we meditate on, so that (yaỈ) He (pracodayāt) can direct (naḥ) our (dhiyaḥ) intellects to embrace virtues and abandon vices. Based on aforementioned explanations, the above *mantra* can be translated as under:

[Meaning] O God! You are Ever Existing, All Conscious and All-Bliss. You are Ever Pure, Ever-Wise, and Ever free by nature. You are Unborn, Eternal and Formless. You are Omniscient, Sustainer, Ruler and Creator of the Universe. You are Beginningless, Nourisher or Support of all. You are All Pervading and All-Compassionate spirit. O Creator, Bestower of all riches and comforts, we meditate on Your pure, purifying and All Conscious nature, so that, O Almighty! You can direct our intellects to embrace virtues and abandon vices. The God endowed with above qualities alone deserve our worship and adoration because there is no one above Him or equal to Him.[160]

O, people! Let us meditate upon the Pure and Conscious nature of God Who is All-Powerful, Ever Existing, All Conscious, All Bliss, Ever Pure, Ever-Wise, Ever free, All-Compassionate, Dispenser of Justice, Not afflicted by the cycle of life and death, Formless, Omniscient, Support of all, Protector, Creator, Nourisher

---

160 हे परमेश्वर! हे सच्चिदानन्दस्वरूप! हे नित्यशुद्धबुद्धमुक्तस्वभाव! हे अज निरंजन निर्विकार! हे सर्वान्तर्यामिन्! हे सर्वाधार! जगत्पते सकलजगदुत्पादक! हे अनादे! विश्वम्भर सर्वव्यापिन्! हे करुणामृतवारिधे! सवितुर्देवस्य तव यदों भूभुर्वः स्ववरेण्यं भर्गोऽस्ति जद्वयं धीमहि दधीमहि धरेमहि ध्यायेम वा कस्मै प्रयोजनायेत्यत्राह। हे भगवन् ! यः सविता देवः परमेश्वरो भवन्नस्माकं धियः प्रचोदयात् स एवास्माकं पूज्य उपासनीय इष्टदेवो भवतु नातोऽन्यं भवत्तुल्यं भवतोऽधिकं च कंचित् कदाचिन्मन्यामहे।

of all, Endowed with all riches, Embodiment of Purity and Worthy to be sought after so that The God Who prevails our intellect and soul may guide us to stay away from immoral acts and to follow the path of morality and ethics. He alone is adorable because there is no one above Him or equal to Him. He alone is our Father, Ruler, Judge and Bestower of happiness and comforts.

After being taught Gāyatrī mantra, youngsters should be trained in Sandhyopāsanā (meditation to be observed at twilight hours) with its preliminaries that include snāna (bath), ācamana (sipping water) and prāṇāyāma (breath control exercise).

1. Bath is prescribed first because it cleans outer body parts and ensures physical health. In this regard, Manu (5.109) says:

अद्भिर्गात्राणि शुध्यन्ति मनः सत्येन शुध्यति।
विद्यातपोभ्यां भूतात्मा बुद्धिर्ज्ञानेन शुध्यति।।
adbhir gātrāṇi śudhyanti manaḥ satyena śudhyati
vidyātapobhyāṁ bhūtātmā buddhir jñānena śudhyati.

[Meaning] Outer body parts are cleansed by water, Mind is cleansed by truth, individual soul by knowledge and austerity (power of enduring sufferings on the way of conducting dharma) and intellect by rational thinking.

Therefore, the bath is a must before breakfast.

2. Prāṇāyāma (breath control) is the second next requirement of Sandhyopāsanā (meditation to be observed at twilight hours). It is said in Yoga Śāstra (2.28) by Patañjali:

प्राणायामादशुद्धिक्षये ज्ञानदीप्तिराविवेकख्यातेः।।
prāṇāyāmād aśuddhi-kṣaye jñāna-dīptir āvivekakhyāteḥ.

[Meaning] The practice of Prāṇāyāma leads to the elimination of impurities of mind and soul and seeker gradually becomes enlightened ultimately attaining the goal of emancipation.

Manu (6.71) says:

दह्यन्ते ध्मायमानानां धातूनां च यथा मलाः ।
तथेन्द्रियाणां दह्यन्ते दोषाः प्राणस्य निग्रहात् ।।
dahyante dhmāyamānānāṁ dhātūnāṁ ca yathā malāḥ
tathendriyāṇāṁ dahyante doṣāḥ prāṇasya nigrahāt

[Meaning] Impurities of mind and senses are eliminated through Prāṇāyāma (the practice of breath control), just as impurities of gold like metals are eliminated when they are melted in the fire.

The method of Prāṇāyāma is explained in Yoga Śāstra (1.34) as:

प्रच्छर्दनविधारणाभ्यां वा प्राणस्य ।
pracchardana-vidhāraṇābhyāṁ vā prāṇasya.

[Meaning] Mind is controlled by exhalation and inhalation of breath.

Just as foods and liquids are expelled out of the body through vigorous vomiting, similarly, forcefully exhale and hold the breath as long as possible by contracting the anus upwards. Until the time anus is contracted upwards, one can manage to hold breath outside even for a longer period. When discomfort is felt, gradually inhale. Repeat this process (forceful exhalation and gradual inhalation) as long as you desire and possibly, you can do it. Don't forget to recite Om in this whole process. This stabilizes the mind and purifies the soul.

There are four types of Prāṇāyāmas, Bāhya Viśaya (externally oriented) and Ābhyantara (internally oriented), Stambhavṛtti (stilled) and Bāhyābhyāntarākṣepī (counter breathing).

Bāhya Viśaya (externally oriented): Holding breath out as long as possible.

Ābhyantara (internally oriented): Holding the breath in as long as possible.

Stambhavṛtti (stilled): When the breath is neither exhaled nor inhaled, but stilled as it is.

Bāhyābhyāntarākṣepī (Kumbhaka): To hold after exhalation and inhalation. Holding breath after inhalation is called internal kumbhaka and holding breath after exhalation is called Bāhya Kumbhaka (external Kumbhaka).

Kumbhaka helps control both the breaths (exhalation and inhalation) which ultimately brings mind and senses under control.

Breath control adds to the body energy and sharpens intellectual power that one can easily comprehend even the most difficult and abstruse concepts.

It helps increase organic fluid (seminal fluid) in the human body, which, in turn, stabilizes the mind and generates physical power, valour, self-restrain. It also promotes quick grasping power.

The practice of Yoga is equally advisable and applicable even to the women folk. They (boys and girls) should be instructed on how to eat food, wear outfits and conduct themselves properly among juniors and seniors.

3. The Ācamana (Sipping of water) is the third requirement of Sandhyopāsanā (meditation to be observed at twilight hours) which is also called Brahma Yajña. The first act in this procedure is Ācamana, which consists in sipping as much water as can pass through the

throat and reach the chest area while sipped from the middle of the palm. On being sipped, ācamana water relieves the throat of some of the Kapha (phlegm) and the Pitta (bile).

The second act is Mārjana, which consists of sprinkling water on the face and other parts of the body with the tips of the index and middle fingers. This act removes drowsiness. If a person doesn't feel drowsy, or if water is not available, this act can be done away with.

The third act is recitation of mantras pertaining to Prāṇāyāma (breath control) , Manasā Parikramā (mental circumambulation [161] and Upasthāna (communion) [162]

---

161 The famous Manasā Parikramā mantras are:

1. *Oṁ prācī dig agnir adhipatir asito rakṣitādityā iṣavaḥ. tebhyo namo'dhipatibhyo namo rakṣitṛbhyo nama iṣubhyo nama. ebhyo astu. yo'smān dveṣṭi yaṁ vayaṁ dviṣmas taṁ vo jambhe dadhmaḥ.* (*AV.* 3.27.1)

2. *Oṁ dakṣiṇā dig indro'dhipatis tiraścir ājī rakṣitā pitara iṣavaḥ. tebhyo namo'dhipatibhyo namo rakṣitṛibhyo nama iṣubhyo nama ebhyo astu. yo'smān dveṣṭi yaṁ vayaṁ dviṣmas taṁ vo jambhe dadhmaḥ.* (*AV.* 3.27.2)

3. *Oṁ pratīcī dig varūṇo'dhipatiḥ pṛdākū rakṣitānnam iṣavaḥ. tebhyo namo'dhipatibhyo namo rakṣitṛbhyo nama iṣubhyo nama ebhyo astu. yo'smān dveṣṭi yaṁ vayaṁ dviṣmas taṁ vo jambhe dadhmaḥ.* (*AV.* 3.27.3)

4. Om udīcī dik somo'dhipatiaḥ svajo rakṣitāśanir iṣavaḥ. tebhyo namo'dhipatibhyo namo rakṣitṛbhyo nama iṣubhyo nama ebhyo astu. yo'smān dveṣṭi yaṁ vayaṁ dviṣmas taṁ vo jambhe dadhmaḥ. (*AV.* 3.27.4)

5. *Oṁ dhruvā dig viṣṇur adhipatiḥ kalmāṣagrīvo rakṣitā virudha iṣavaḥ tebhyo namo'dhipatibhyo namo rakṣitṛbhyo nama iṣubhyo nama ebhyo astu. yo'smān dveṣṭi yaṁ vayaṁ dviṣmas taṁ vo jambhe dadhmaḥ.* (*AV.* 3.27.5)

6. *Om ūrdhvā dig bṛhaspatir adhipatiḥ śvitro rakṣitā varṣam*

followed by Mantras relating to Īśvara stuti, prārthanā, and upasanā (i.e. mantras leading to glorification, prayer and meditation of God)[163] ending the whole procedure

---

iṣavaḥ.tebhyo namo'dhipatibhyo namo rakṣitṛbhyo nama iṣubhyo nama ebhyo astu. yo'smān dveṣṭi yaṁ vayaṁ dviṣmastaṁ vo jambhe dadhmaḥ. (AV. 3.27.6)

162 *Om udvayaṁ tamasas pari svaḥ paśyanta uttaram. devatrā sūryyam aganma jyotir uttamam.* (*Yajurveda*, 35.14)

Om udu tyaṁ jātavedasaṁ devaṁ vahanti ketavaḥ. dṛśe viśvāya sūryam. (*Yajurveda*, 33.31)

Om citraṁ devānām udagād anīkaṁ cakṣur mitrasya varūṇsyāgneḥ.

āprā dṛyāvāpṛthīvī antarikṣaṁ. sūrya ātmā jagatasthu ṣaśca svāhā. (*Yajurveda*, 7.42)

Oṁ taccakṣur devahitaṁ purastācchukram uccarat. paśyem śaradaḥ śataṁ jīvema śaradaḥ śataṁ śṛṇuyāma śaradaḥ śataṁ prabravāma śaradaḥ śatamadīnāḥ syāma śaradaḥ śataṁ bhūyaśca śaradaḥ śatāt. (*Yajurveda*, 36.34)

163 *Oṁ viśvāni deva savitarduritāni parāsuva. yad bhadraṁ tanna ā suva.* (*Yajurveda*, 30.3)

Oṁ hiraṇyagarbhaḥ samavarttatāgre bhūtasya jātaḥ patireka āsīt. sa dādhār pṛthivīṁ dyāmutemāṁ kasmai devāya haviṣā vidhema. (*Yajurveda*, 13.4)

Oṁ ya ātmadā baladā yasya viśva upāsate praśiṣaṁ yasya devāḥ. yasyacchāyā'mṛtaṁ yasya mṛtyuḥ kasmai devāya haviṣā vidhema. (*Yajurveda*, 25.13)

Oṁ yaḥ prāṇato nimiṣato mahitvaika idrājā jagato babhūva. ya īśe asya dvipadaścatuṣpadaḥ kasmai devāya haviṣā vidhema. (*Yajurveda*, 25.11)

Oṁ yena dyaur ugrā pṛthivī ca driḍhā yena svaḥ stabhitaṁ yena nākaḥ. yo antarikṣe rajaso vimānaḥ kasmai devāya haviṣā vidhema. (*Yajurveda*, 32.6)

Oṁ prajāpate na tvad etānyanyo viśvā jātāni paritā bahūva. yat kāmās te juhumas tanno astu vayaṁ syāma patayo

with Aghamarṣaṇa mantras (prayer for exoneration from immoral acts).[164] This Sandhyopāsanā should be performed in a secluded place with a concentrated mind. In this regard, we may quote Manusm,ti (2.104):

अपां समीपे नियतो नैत्यकं विधिमास्थितः ।
सावित्रीमप्यधीयीत गत्वारण्यं समाहितः ।।

apāṁ samīpe niyato naityakaṁ vidhimāsthitaḥ.
sāvitrīmapyadhīyīta gatvāraṇyaṁ samāhitaḥ.

[Meaning] Having repaired to the forest, sit close to waters with a concentrated mind. Perform your daily meditation, recite the Gāyatrī mantra, understanding its meaning and act accordingly.

It is, however, best to perform Sandhyā since birth.

Second is Devayajña, which is performed in the form of Agnihotra and attending to scholars. Sandhyā and Agnihotra both are performed at sunrise and sunset, the only two twilight hours. One should devote at least one hour daily to Sandhyā meditation. Just as Yogis meditate upon God in Samādhi (contemplation), similarly, one

---

rayīṇām. (*Ṛgveda*, 10.121.10)

Oṁ sa no bandhurjanitā sa vidhātā dhāmāni veda bhūvanāni viśvā. yatra devāḥ amṛtamānaśānās tṛtīye dhāmannadhyairyanta. (*Yajurveda*, 32.10)

Om agne naya supathā rāye'asmān viśvāni deva vayunāni vidvān. yuyodhyasmajjuhurāṇameno bhūyiṣṭhāṁ te namauktiaṁ vidhema. (*Yajurveda*, 40.16)

164 *Om ṛtañca satyañcābhīddhāttpaso'dhyajāyata.*
tato rātryajāyata tataḥ samudro arṇavaḥ.

samudrād arṇvād adhi saṁvatsaro'jāyata.
ahorātrāṇi vidadhad viśvasya miṣato vaśī

sūryyācandramasau dhātā yathā pūrvam akalpayat.
divañca pṛthivīñcāntarikṣam atho svaḥ. (*Ṛgveda*, 10.121.10)

should perform Sandhyā meditation. The proper time for Agnihotra is after sunrise and before sunset.

For performing Agnihotra, a Vedī (fire-altar) is required. This Vedī can be made on a base either of metal (copper) or clay having a shape of an inverted pyramid. Its height should be 9 to 12 inches. It should be 9 square inches or 12 square inches at the open top and 3 square inches or 4 square inches at the bottom so that the base is one-fourth of the size of the top.

Let pieces of quality wood like Sandal, Palāśa (Buica Frondosa) or Mango, cut to fit the size of Vedī, be laid therein, fire be kindled in the centre and more pieces of wood be placed over the fire.

In addition, we need a praṇitā pot, a cup-like container for water.

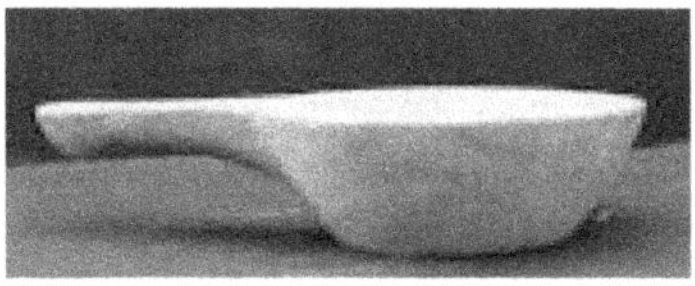

Prokṣaṇī pot, a spoon like a vessel to dip water to wash hands.

Ājya sthāli, a pot to heat and hold clarified butter.

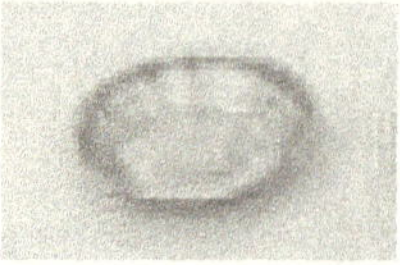

Camasā, a spoon made of gold, silver or wood.

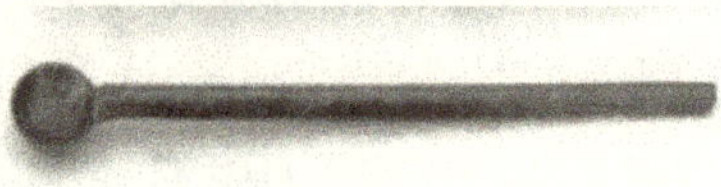

Let the clarified butter be properly melted and closely examined for any impurity.

Afterwards, Homa be performed with the following mantras:

ओं भूरग्नये प्राणाय स्वाहा।
भुवर्वायवेऽपानाय स्वाहा। स्वरादित्याय व्यानाय स्वाहा।
भूर्भुवः स्वरग्निवाय्वादित्येभ्यः प्राणापानव्यानेभ्यः स्वाहा।।
Oṁ bhūr agnaye prāṇāya svāhā.
Oṁ bhūr vāyave'pānāya svāhā.
Oṁ svrādityāya vyānāya svāhā.
Oṁ bhūr bhuvaḥ svar-agni-vāyavādityebhyaḥ prāṇ-apān-vyānebhyaḥ svāhā.

One oblation of ghee should be offered by reciting each of the above-cited mantras. If more oblations are required to be offered, then following mantras can be recited:

विश्वानि देव सवितर्दुरितानि परासुव। यद्भद्रं तन्न आ सुव ।।

ओ३म् भूर्भुवः स्वः । तत्सवितुर्वरेण्यं भर्गो देवस्य धीमहि ।
धियो यो नः प्रचोदयात् ।।
viśvāni deva savitar duritāni parāsuva.
yad bhadraṁ tanna āsuva. *(Yajurveda, 30.3)*
Om bhūr bhuvaḥ svaḥ.
tatsavitur vareṇyaṁ bhargo devasya dhīmahi
dhiyo yo naḥ pracodayāt *(Yajurveda, 36.3)*

The words 'Om', Bhū, 'Prāṇa' and others are the names of God. They have been explained above in chapter one. The word 'svāhā' means the words you speak must coincide with information in your mind, and not otherwise. Human beings should learn the virtue of doing altruistic welfare from God Who created the various objects of the world for the welfare of all living beings.

The advantage of Agnihotra is given below in Question and Answer form:

Question - What is the advantage of Homa?

Answer- It is a proven fact that polluted air and water cause diseases, which in turn cause suffering to living beings. On the other hand, pure air and water cause good health resulting into happiness. (Agnihotra purifies atmosphere).

Note: Here Maharishi Dayanand wants to say that *Agnihotra* helps to undo the effect of pollution. Now, this finding of Maharishi Dayanand Sarasvati has been proved by Laboratory experiments conducted on *Agnihotra* and Microbes. It has been proved that Agnihotra renders pathogenic bacteria (disease producing) polluting air and water to non-pathogenic ones.

Question- I think Sandal paste if applied to the body and clarified butter if taken in meals will be more beneficial than if they are destroyed by burning into the fire?

Answer- That only shows your ignorance of Science of Chemistry. It is one of the cardinal principles that nothing is ever lost. You must have noticed that a person standing some distance away from the place of Agnihotra can smell a fragrance of sweet substance offered into the fire of Agnihotra. In the same way, a person can smell foul odours coming from foul substances being burnt. This alone proves that a sweet substance put into the fire is not destroyed, but, becomes rarefied and is carried by air to distant places where it frees the air from its pollutants.

Note: Modern scientific experiments have proved that when something is burnt into the fire it transforms into its gaseous form increasing in volume. This increase in the volume of liquid substances on being changed into gaseous state due to heating has been calculated by modern scientists (particularly in the context of the transformation of liquid waters into vapours) by a factor of nearly 1000.[165]

Question- Well if that's the case, keeping saffron, musk, camphor, scented flowers and perfumed oils. etc. in the house will serve the same purpose.

Answer- The scent doesn't have the power to disinfect the air from pathogens. It is the Agnihotra fire alone, which is able to free the air from pathogenicity.

The antiseptic and antibiotic effects of the smoke of yaj¤a have also been examined by conducting laboratory experiments. It has been found that the smoke emitted by Yaj¤a is a powerful antibiotic in nature. Nautiyal et. al (2007)[166] conducted a study on Agnihotra. He found

---

[165] Cf. Mason (1978 : 77) cited in *Vedic Meteorology*, by Dr. Ravi Prakash Arya, published by Indian Foundation for Vedic Science, Delhi, 2006, p.22

[166] *Journal of Ethnopharmacology*, Volume 114, Issue 3, December 2007, Pages 446-451

elimination of the aerial pathogenic bacteria due to Agnihotra smoke. It was observed during an experiment that one-hour treatment of Agnihotra smoke on aerial bacterial population caused over 94% of the decrease in bacterial counts and ability of Agnihotra to disinfect the air and make environment cleaner was maintained up to 24 hours in the closed room. It was also found that pathogenic bacteria remained absent in the open room even after 30 days of performing Agnihotra which indicates the bactericidal potential of the Agnihotra.

A preliminary experiment was carried out to study the effect of Agnihotra on the bacterial population in a room where Agnihotra was performed. For this study, two rooms of equal dimensions (13¼' x 8' x 11') were selected. In both rooms, the fire was prepared from dried cow dung cakes in copper pyramids and the basal reading of a number of microorganisms in both the rooms was taken by exposing blood agar plates at four corners of the room for 10 minutes. This was done exactly half an hour before Agnihotra time. Agnihotra was performed exactly at sunset in one of the rooms. Bacterial counts were taken again in both the rooms in a similar manner at half hour intervals. Thus, readings were taken in both the rooms up to two hours after the performance of Agnihotra. It was quite interesting to note that microbial counts in the room where Agnihotra was performed were reduced by 91.4% whereas the room where the only fire was generated did not show appreciable changes in the microbial counts. This leads one to think that it was the process of Agnihotra that was responsible for the reduction of bacterial counts and not the mere presence of fire.[167]

Question - If air and water are disinfected by the performance of Agnihotra, then what is the purpose of reciting mantras during Agnihotra?

Answer - Mantras are recited because they elaborate the utility of performing *Agnihotra.* Secondly, recitation helps memorization of Mantras, study and preservation of Vedic texts.

Question - Is it unethical and immoral not to perform *Agnihotra*?

Answer - Yes it is. Because human beings are constantly polluting air and water through their biological and physical activates causing affliction of diseases and sufferings to others. This amounts to an unethical and immoral act. This act of polluting the atmosphere can be undone by disinfecting atmosphere through *Agnihotra* to an extent either equal to or more than the pollution has been created.

The overall result of the *Agnihotra* is that the desirable substances can be inhaled through the nostrils by all. This mechanism of intake, as opposed to oral intake (in the liquid and solid form), is more efficient by a factor of several hundred. Nevertheless, this doesn't mean that a person should avoid taking nutritious food like ghee (cow ghee) etc. Taking nutritious food like ghee is, although, essential for maintaining physical and mental health, but *Agnihotra* is even more essential.

Question- How many āhutis (oblations) should a person offer to the Agnihotra fire and in what quantity?

---

[167] http://www.homatherapypoland.org/agnihotra-and-microbes-laboratory-experience-dr-arvind-d-mondkar-msc-phd-micro

Answer- Each person should offer at least sixteen āhutis of Havan sāmagrī (oblation material) and at least one āhuti of ghee weighing approximately (six māsā) six grams. However, bigger the amount better it is. This was the reason, leading Aryas including great leaders, Ṛṣis, Maharṣis, Kings, Emperors used to take pride in performing Agnihotra and encouraged others to follow suit. As long as Agnihotra was widely practised, the great nation of Āryāvartta (India) had immunity from diseases and full of contentment and happiness. It can regain its glory if this practice is resumed.

The two Yajñas have been explained in detail here. Brahma Yajña or Sandhyopāsanā is restricted to the job of learning, teaching, glorification, prayer and meditation of God, whereas Devayajña consists in Agnihotra. Students in Brahmacarya Āśram, however, are required to perform Brahmayajña and Agnihotra.

The issue of entitlement of investing Yajñopavīta (eligibility of teaching) has been ordained in Suśruta (Sūtrasthāna, chapter 2) as under:

ब्राह्मणस्त्रयाणां वर्णानामुपनयनं कर्तुमर्हति राजन्यो द्वयस्य वैश्यो वैश्यस्यैवेति। शूद्रमपि कुलगुणसम्पन्नं मन्त्रवर्जमनुपनीतमध्यापयेदित्येके।

brāhmaṇas trayāṇāṁ varṇānām upanayanaṁ kartum arhati rājanyo dvayasya vaiśyo vaiśyasya eveti. śudram api kula-guṇasamapannaṁ mantavarjam an-upanītam adhyāpayedityeke.

[Meaning] A person coming from a profession of Brahmaṇa (intellectual community) can teach (invest Yajñopavīta to) students of three personality types i.e. Brahmaṇa (having an intellectual bend of mind), Kṣatriya (interested in martial arts and physical exercises) and Vaiśya (interested in marketing). A person coming from Kṣatriya (defence) profession can teach students of Kṣatriya (defence) and Vaiśya (mercantile) personality types. A person coming from the profession of Vaiśya (mercantile class) can teach a student of Vaiśya (mercantile) personality type only. A student having good antiquates even though endowed with Śudra personality type (interested in production and service providing work) should also be taught all scientific treatises except Mantra Saṅhitās (Mantra portion of Vedic Saṅhitas) without being invested with Yajñopavīta. This is the view of some authorities.

Note: Here it is significant to understand that the names Brāhmaṇa, Kṣatriya, Vaiśya and Śudra described in Vedic literature don't signify castes, rather psychological personality types. A child endowed with sharp intellect and spiritual traits was identified as Brāhmaṇa personality type. A child endowed with good physique, boldness, valour and fighting nature was identified as Kṣatriya personality type. A child dominant with a business bent of mind and trading abilities was identified as a Vaiśya personality type and a child with dull mind showing no interest for studies, but having an inclination towards production and service sector was identified as Śudra personality type. It has been noticed that Śudra bend of mind takes the least interest in spiritual studies, so their Upanayana has been denied by some authorities. In fact, an investiture ceremony was directly related to the teaching of Vedas. Only highly intelligent and spiritually oriented selected students used to study Vedas, as it took 12 years to complete the study of one Veda including its Upaveda, Brāhmaṇa, Āraṇyaka, Upaniṣad and other subsidiary sciences. Therefore, it was not easy for each student to study Vedas.

By the time, the children enter the age between five and eight years, they should be sent to their respective schools, girls to girls' school and boys to boys' school.

The following period as ordained in Manusmṛti (3.1) may be followed to initiate studies.

षड्त्रिंशदाब्दिकं चर्य्यं गुरौ त्रैवैदिकं व्रतम्।
तदर्धिकं पादिकं वा ग्रहणान्तिकमेव वा।।

ṣaṭ-triñśad ābdikaṁ caryya gurau trai-vaidkaṁ vratam
tadardhikaṁ pādikaṁ vā grahaṇāntikam eva vā.

[Meaning] Three periods have been prescribed for the study of three Vedas. The first period is of 36 years- 12 years for each Veda. The second period is of 18 years, i.e. 6 years for each Veda and the third period is of 9 years, i.e. 3 years for each Veda. As such a student is required to observe Brahmacharya either for 44 years, keeping in view of highest time frame of 36 years+8 years of childhood; or for 26 years, keeping in view of time frame of 18 years+8 years of childhood; or for 17 years, keeping in view the lowest time frame of 9 years+8 years of childhood.

According to the *Chāndogya Upaniṣad* (3.16), Brahmacharya phase can be divided into three categories- youngest, middle and highest.

Youngest *Brahmacharya* (*Vāsava Brahmacharya*):

पुरुषो वाव यज्ञस्तस्य यानि चतुर्विंशति वर्षाणि तत्प्रातःसवनं चतुर्विंशत्यक्षरा गायत्री गायत्रं प्रातःसवनं तदस्य वसवोऽन्वायत्ताः प्राणा वाव वसव एते हीदँ सर्वं वासयन्ति।।१।।

puruṣo vāva yajñas. tasya yāni caturviṁśati varṣāṇi tatprātaḥ savanaṁ. caturviṁśatyakṣarā gāyatrī. gayatraṁ prātaḥ savanaṁ. tad asya vasavo'nvāyattāḥ. prāṇā vāva vasava. ete hīdaṁ sarvaṁ vāsayanti. (1)

[Meaning] A person is verily a yajña. 24 years of Brahmacharya is like morning offerings. Gāyatrī metre has 24 syllables. Morning offerings are made with mantras composed in Gāyatrī metre. The vasus (life-sustaining factors) are linked to this offering. Prāṇas (bio-energy of the body) are vasus because they sustain the entire metabolism of the body.

A person is a combination of body, mind and soul. The body is nourished by food and water. The soul resides in the body. The life of a person is yajña in a sense that he should inculcate moral and ethical values and perform good deeds. To achieve this objective, it is incumbent on his part to observe celibacy for 24 years and acquire Vedic knowledge and quality education. Even after getting married, he should not indulge in sensual pleasures. By virtue of this discipline, his bio-energy nourishes him and he embodies all good qualities.

तञ्चेदेतस्मिन् वयसि किञ्चिदुपतपेत्स ब्रूयात्प्राणा वसव इदं मे प्रातःसवनं माध्यन्दिनं सवनमनुसन्तनुतेति माहं प्राणानां वसूनां मध्ये यज्ञो विलोप्सीऽयेत्युद्धैव तत एत्यगदो ह भवति।।२।।

tañ ced etasmin vayasi kiñcid upatapet. sa brūyāt prāṇā vasava. idaṁ me prātaḥ savanaṁ mādhyandinaṁ savanaṁ anu saṁ tanute ti. māhaṁ prāṇānāṁ vasūnāṁ madhye yajño vilopsīyeti. uddhaiva tat etyagado ha bhavati. (2)

[Meaning] In this age, whoever treats himself in the fire of knowledge (endows him with knowledge), his bio-energy acts as vasu (the support of his life) for him. Let this morning offering (24 years of Brahmacharya) continue over to midday offering (44 years of Brahmacharya). Let my life not be broken off in the midst. If this body is kept healthy, it will become invulnerable to all sort of diseases.

In the youngest type of Brahmacharya, a student should bear in mind that if he should maintain Brahmacharya (celibacy), then his body and mind would remain healthy and strong and his bio-energy would generate excellent personality traits. Thus, more and more such conditions may be created in society as are conducive to maintain Brahmacharya. Nevertheless, it can be observed that if a person starts married life after the age of 24 years, he will not, obviously, then be susceptible to diseases and will live disease fee life for 70-80 years.

Middle Brahmacharya (Raudra Brahmacarya)

अथ यानि चतुश्चत्वारिँशद्वर्षाणि तन्माध्यन्दिनसवनं चतुश्चत्वारिंशदक्षरा त्रिष्टुप् ॰ त्रैष्टुभं माध्यन्दिनं सवनं तदस्य रुद्रा अन्वायत्ताः प्राणा वाव रुद्रा एते हीदं सर्वं रोदयन्ति।।३।।

atha yāni catuś-catvāriñśad-varṣāni tan mādyandin savanaṁ. catuś-catvāriñśad-akṣarā triṣṭup, traiṣṭubhaṁ mādhyandin savanaṁ. tad asya rudrā anvāyattāḥ. prāṇā vāva rudrā. ete hīdaṁ sarvaṁ rodayanti.

[Meaning] The 44 years of Brahmacharya is like midday offering. Triṣṭup metre has 44 syllables. Midday offerings are made with mantras composed in the Triṣṭup metre. The rudras are linked to this offering. Prāṇas (bio-energy of the body) is verily the rudras, because people starts weeping when they leave the body.

The middle Brahmacharya spans over to 44 years. If a person observes celibacy up to 44 years to study Vedas, his bio-energy, senses, mind, and soul become so healthy and strong that he is able to punish wicked persons and protect good ones.

तं चेदेतस्मिन्वयसि किञ्चिदुपतपेत्स ब्रूयात्प्राणा रुद्रा इदं मे माध्यन्दिनं सवनं तृतीयसवनमनुसन्तनुतेति माहं प्राणाना रुद्राणां मध्ये यज्ञो विलोप्सीऽ येत्युद्धैव तत एत्यगदो ह भवति।।४।।

taṁ ced etasmin vayasi kiñcid upatapet. sa brūyāt prāṇā rudrā. idaṁ me mādhyandinaṁ savanaṁ tṛtīya savanaṁ anu saṁ tanute ti. māhaṁ prāṇānāṁ ridrāṇāṁ madhye yajño vā vilopsīyeti. uddhaiva tat etyagado ha bhavati.

[Meaning] In this age, whoever treats himself in the fire of knowledge (endows himself with knowledge), (let him know that) his bio-energy is rudra that makes people weep while leaving the body. Let this midday offering (44 years of Brahmacharya) continue over to the third (evening) offering (48 years of Brahmacharya). Let my life not be broken off in the midst (in between). If this body is kept healthy, it will be invulnerable to all sort of diseases.

If one does penances until 44 years of his age, it will be called middle Brahmacharya. The bio-energy of the body makes him powerful enough to resist onslaughts of wicked persons and to champion the cause of virtue. A teacher should advise his students, 'O students! it is in your interest to prolong Brahmacharya (celibacy). Just as I endow moral and ethical values and perform excellent deeds while observing celibacy; just as I graduated from my teacher's school in a perfectly healthy state, I encourage you to follow suit.'

Highest Brahmacharya (Āditya Brahmacharya)

अथ यान्यष्टाचत्वारिंशद्वर्षाणि तत्तृतीयसवनमष्टाचत्वारिंशदक्षरा जगती जाग-तं तृतीयसवनं तदस्यादित्या अन्वायत्ताः प्राणा वावादित्या एते हीदं सर्वमाददते।।५।।

atha yāni aṣṭā-catvāriñśad-varṣāni tat tṛtīya savanam. aṣṭā-catvāriñśad-akṣarā jagatī, jāgataṁ tṛtīya-savanaṁ. tad asyādityā anvāyattāḥ. prāṇā vāva ādityā. ete hīdaṁ sarvaṁ ādadate.

[Meaning] The 48 years of Brahmacharya (celibacy) is like third evening offering. Jagatī metre has 48 syllables. Evening offerings are made with mantras composed in Jagatī metre. The Ādityas are linked to this offering. Prāṇas (bio-energy of the body) are verily the Ādityas, because they enable the body to receive all knowledge.

The third highest type of Brahmacharya lasts up to 48 years of age. Brahmacharya of 48 years is equal to Jagatī metre consisting of 48 syllables. The harmonized bio-energy of the body makes one capable of acquiring all sciences.

तं चेदेतस्मिन् वयसि किञ्चिदुपतपेत्स ब्रूयात् प्राणा आदित्या इदं मे तृतीयसवनमायुरनुसन्तनुतेति माहं प्राणानामादित्यानां मध्ये यज्ञो विलोप्सीयेत्युद्धैव तत एत्यगदो हैव भवति।।६।।

taṁ ced etasmin vayasi kiñcid upatapet. sa brūyāt prāṇā ādityā. idaṁ me tṛtīya savanaṁ āyuranu saṁ tanute ti. māhaṁ prāṇānāṁ ādityāṇāṁ madhye yajño vā vilopsīyeti. uddhaiva tat etyagado ha bhavati.

[Meaning] In this age, whoever treats himself in the fire of knowledge (equips himself with knowledge), let him know that his bio-energy is Āditya (capable of acquiring all knowledge). Let this third offering (48 years of Brahmacharya) continue over to full length of life (400 years). Let my life not be broken off in the midest (in between). If this body is kept healthy, it will be invulnerable to all sort of diseases.

The teachers and parents who want their students or children live an austere life in order to acquire knowledge inculcate moral and ethical values should educate them about the same (living an austere life). The children and students thus educated become capable of maintaining Brahmacharya of the highest level (48 years) and prolonging their life up to full span, i.e. 400 years. Those who don't let this Brahmacharya go waste, they live a disease free life and become worthy of attaining dharma (knowledge, moral and ethical values), artha (necessities of life), kāma (fulfilment of spiritual and worldly desires) and mokṣa (emancipation).

The human body undergoes four stages of evolution. In this regard, Suśruta (Sūtra-sthāna, 35.25) observes as under:

चतस्रोऽवस्थाः शरीरस्य वृद्धिर्यौवनं सम्पूर्णता किञ्चित्परिहाणिश्चेति। आषोडशाद् वृद्धिः। आपञ्चविशतेर्यौवनम्। आचत्वारिशतः सम्पूर्णता। ततः किञ्चित्परिहाणिश्चेति।

catasro'vasthāḥ śarīrasya vṛddhir yauvanaṁ sampūrṇatā kiñcit parihāṇiś ceti. āṣoḍaśād vṛddhiḥ. āpañcaviṁśater yauvanam. ācatvāriṁśataḥ sampūrṇatā. tataḥ kiñcit parihāṇiś ceti.

[Meaning] Body undergoes four stages of evolution-growth, youthhood, maturity and decay. Growth begins from 16th year onward, youthhood from 25th year onward, maturity begins from 40th year onward and from then on there is gradual decay.

Growth: the First stage of evolution is called a stage of growth that begins from 16th year onward. During this stage all dhātus i.e. physical evolutes like rasa (a thick liquid produced in stomach as a result of digestion), rakta (blood), mānsa (muscles), meda (fat), asthi (bone), majjā (marrow), śukra (reproductive fluid or semen) of the body grow.

Youthhood: Second stage of evolution is youth hood that begins from the 25th year of age.

Maturity: the Third stage of evolution is maturity that

begins from the 40th year of age. All dhātus are now fully mature and reach saturation point during this period.

Decay: Afterwards, there is gradual decay resulting in loss of dhātus in sleep and perspiration.

The best time for marriage, therefore, is the 40th year, or even better, the 48th year.

Question- Does this rule of Brahmacharya (celibacy) apply equally to both men and women?

Answer- No. If a man observes celibacy for 25, 30, 36, 40, 44 and 48 years, the corresponding age for a woman is 16, 17, 18, 20, 22, 24 years respectively. In other words, a man of 25 can marry to a woman of 16 years, a man aged 30 years can marry to a woman of 17 years and so on. This rule holds good in case of those men and women who want to get married. This, however, is recommendable to those yogī (divine) men and women who are perfectly learned, unblemished and exercise control over their senses. It is an extremely difficult task to restrain the flow of carnal desires and keep senses under control.

Following guidelines have been laid down for teachers and taught in Taittirīya Upaniṣad (7.9)

ऋतं च स्वाध्यायप्रवचने च। सत्यं च स्वाध्यायप्रवचने च। तपश्च स्वाध्यायप्रवचने च। दमश्च स्वाध्यायप्रवचने च। शमश्च स्वाध्यायप्रवचने च। अग्नयश्च स्वाध्यायप्रवचने च। अग्निहोत्रं च स्वाध्यायप्रवचने च। अतिथयश्च स्वाध्यायप्रवचने च। मानुषं च स्वाध्यायप्रवचने च। प्रजा च स्वाध्यायप्रवचने च। प्रजनश्च स्वाध्यायप्रवचने च। प्रजातिश्च स्वाध्यायप्रवचने च।

ṛtaṁ ca svādhyāya-pravacane ca. satyaṁ ca svādhyāya-pravacane ca. tapaśca svādhyāya-pravacane ca. śamaśca svādhyāya-pravacane ca. agnayaśca svādhyāya-pravacane ca. agnihotraṁ ca svādhyāya-pravacane ca. atithayaśca svādhyāya-pravacane ca. mānuṣaṁ ca svādhyāya-pravacane ca. prajā ca svādhyāya-pravacane ca. prajanaśca svādhyāya-pravacane ca. prajātiśca svādhyāya-pravacane ca.

[Meaning] The process of teaching and learning may be carried out based upon right and truthful conduct, righteous act, restraining external senses from wicked acts and mind (the internal sense organ) from vices. The process of teaching and learning may be carried out having sound knowledge and making good use of electricity, Āhavanīya and other fires. While conducting teaching and learning, one should not forget to perform Agnihotra or Atithi yajña (serving learned scholars or peripatetic monks). This process of teaching and learning can be carried out by fulfilling all human obligations. (No human obligation is hurdle on the way of learning and teaching process). The process of teaching and learning can be accomplished even by fulfilling one's obligations towards children or subjects, procreation and pupils.

In addition to above guidelines, observance of both Yamas (social regulations) and Niyamas (personal regulations) is also said to be of paramount importance for students. Manu (4.204) here observes:

यमान् सेवेत सततं न नियमान् केवलान् बुधः।
यमान्पतत्यकुर्वाणो नियमान् केवलान् भजन्।।
yamān seveta satataṁ na niyamān kevalān budhaḥ
yamān patatyakurvāṇo niyamān kevalān bhajan.

[Meaning] A wise man should constantly observe not only the Niyamas (personal disciplinary regulations), but also the Yamas (social disciplinary regulations). Anyone who observes Niyamas (personal disciplinary regulations) alone and disregards the Yamas (social disciplinary regulations), cannot progress in life.

There are five types of Yamas (social disciplinary regulations).

तत्रहिंसासत्यास्तेयब्रह्मचर्यापरिग्रहा यमाः ।

tatra ahinsā-satya-asteya-brahmacarya-aparigrahā yamāḥ. *(Yogadarśana, 2.30)*

[Meaning] Ahinsā (giving up enmity), Satya (truthfulness in speech and action), Asteya (non-stealing in thought, speech and action), Brahmacharya (abstaining from illicit relationships), Aprigraha (free from voracity).

These Yamas are to be observed always.

Similarly, there are five Niyamas (personal disciplinary regulations). They are:

शौचसन्तोषतपःस्वाध्यायेश्वरप्रणिधानानि नियमाः ।

śauca-santoṣa-tapaḥ-svādhyāyeśvara-praṇidhānāni niyamāḥ. *(Yogadarśana, 2.32)*

Śauca (physical cleansing through bath etc.), Santoṣa (contentment with whatever earned by hard work), Tapa (not to back out from righteous acts even in difficult times), Svādhyāya (to keep oneself engaged in learning, teaching) and Iśvarapraṇidhāna (dedicate oneself to the devotion of God).

Both Yamas and Niyamas are to be observed. Observance of Niyamas alone disregarding Yamas doesn't lead to progress (upliftment or emancipation), rather paves the way for regress (reeling down the cycle of life and death).

For acquisition of knowledge the need of desire is underlined in Manusmṛti (2.2):

कामात्मता न प्रशस्ता न चैवेहस्त्यकामता।
काम्यो हि वेदाधिगमः कर्मयोगश्च वैदिकः।
kāmātmatā na praśastā na caivehāstyakāmatā
kāmyo hi vedādhigamaḥ karmayogaś ca vaidikaḥ.

[Meaning] Excessive desire is not appreciable, but the total lack of desire is also not possible. It is desire alone that leads one to acquire the knowledge of the Veda and perform deeds as ordained in the Vedas.

Further, the author (Manusmṛti, 2.28) sets up criteria of a Brāhmī state (or Brāhmaṇaship) for seeking knowledge and God. He cites all those factors that lead one to Brāhmī state or Brāhmaṇaship as under:

स्वाध्यायेन व्रतैर्होमैस्त्रैविद्येनेज्यया सुतैः।
महायज्ञैश्च यज्ञैश्च ब्राह्मीयं क्रियते तनुः।।
svādhyāyena vratair homais traividyenejyayā sutaiḥ
mahāyajñaiś ca yajñaiś ca brāhmīyaṁ kriyate tanuḥ

[Meaning] Following factors lead an individual to Brahmī state (wherein one seeks knowledge and Brahman) transforming himself/herself into a Brāhmaṇa (seeker of knowledge and Brahma) worthy to acquire Vedic knowledge and seek God's grace. The factors are 1. Learning and teaching of all sciences, 2. observing vows of celibacy and truth, 3. performing Agnihotra etc., accepting truth, abandoning untruth and sharing true sciences, 4. following three-fold Vedic path of action, meditation and knowledge, 5. performing fortnightly allegorical rituals like Darśeṣṭi (new moon ritual) and Pūrṇamāseṣṭi (full moon ritual), 6. procreating superb progeny, 7. discharging five daily duties towards acquisition of knowledge, purifying atmosphere, serving parents and guest scholars or saints and feeding animals living in surrounding area, 8. performing Śrauta yajñas (allegorical rituals exposing various aspects of universal creation) and developing science and technology.

All the above factors are mandatory to transform an individual into a Brāhmaṇa personality (the seeker of knowledge and Brahman).

The significance of restraining senses is highlighted by Manu (2.88):

इन्द्रियाणां विचरतां विषयेष्वपहारिषु ।
संयमे यत्नमातिष्ठेद्विद्वान् यन्तेव वाजिनाम्।।
indriyāṇāṁ vicharatāṁ viṣayeṣvapahāriṣu,
saṁyame yatnamātiṣṭhedvidvān yanteva vājinām.

[Meaning] As a skilful charioteer keeps his horses under control, even so, should a person, by all means, try to keep his senses - which are apt to lead both mind and soul into the pursuit of wicked objects - under complete control.

Because (Manu. 2.93)-

इन्द्रियाणां प्रसंगेन दोषम् ऋच्छत्यसंशयम् ।
सन्नियम्य तु तान्येव ततः सिद्धि नियच्छति।।
indriyāṇāṁ prasaṁgena doṣam ṛchchhatyasaṁśayam,
sanniyamya tu tānyeva tataḥ siddhi niyachchhati.

[Meaning] A person is sure to commit mistakes under the sway of his senses. Success can be achieved only when the senses are restrained.

Further, it is said by Manu (2.97):

वेदास्त्यागश्च यज्ञाश्च नियमाश्च तपांसि च।
न विप्रदुष्टभावस्य सिद्धि गच्छन्ति कर्हिचित्।।
vedāstyāgaścha yajñāścha niyamāścha tapāṁsi cha,
na vipraduṣṭabhāvasya siddhi gachchhanti karhichit.

[Meaning] Study of Veda, the sacrifice of all worldly things, the performance of Yajñas, observance of five Niyamas (mentioned above), austerities- none of these can ever bring success to a wicked and corrupt person who has no control over his senses.

Here under the clarification about the break in studies of Vedas, the performance of Havana etc. is given by referring to Manu (2.205-206).

वेदोपकरणे चैव स्वाध्याये चैव नैत्यके।
नानुरोधोऽस्त्यनध्याये होममन्त्रेषु चैव हि।।

नैत्यके नास्त्यनध्यायो ब्रह्मसत्रं हि तत्स्मृतम्।
ब्रह्माहुतिहुतं पुण्यम् अनध्यायवषट्कृतम्।।

vedopakaraṇe chaiva svādhyāye chaiva naityake,
nānurodho'styanadhyāye homamantreṣu chaiva hi.

naityake nāstyanadhyāyo brahmasatraṁ hi tatsmṛtam,
brahmāhutihutaṁ puṇyam anadhyāyavaṣaṭkṛtam.

[Meaning] Anādhyāya (Break or holiday) is not prescribed in the study of Vedas and other Śāstras, the performance of daily duties like Pañca-mahāyajñas (five great yajñas) and recitation of Havana mantras.

The daily routine work cannot be ceased, as we never cease to breathe. This is ordained by God. An Agnihotra performed with the oblations offered to God even on holiday brings prosperity.

To sum up, just as lying is always associated with immorality and speaking truth with morality, in the same way, there is always a prohibition (anādhyāya) for bad acts and sanction (non-prohibition) for virtuous acts.

There is a secret tip for youngsters in Manusmṛti (2.121), which reads as under:

अभिवादनशीलस्य नित्यं वृद्धोपसेविनः।

चत्वारि तस्य वर्द्धन्त आयुर्विद्या यशो बलम्।।
abhivādanaśīlasya nityaṁ vṛddhopasevinaḥ,
chatvāri tasya varddhanta āyurvidyā yaśo balam.

[Meaning] A student who is humble, well behaved and shows respect to scholars and elderly persons and always ready to offer his unstinted services to them gains in life span, knowledge, name, fame and strength.

Those who are devoid of the above qualities remain deprived of these benefits.

The obligations of teachers and students are mentioned in the Manusmṛti (2.159-160) as under:

अहिंसयैव भूतानां कार्यं श्रेयोऽनुशासनम्।
वाक् चैव मधुरा श्लक्ष्णा प्रयोज्या धर्ममिच्छता।।

यस्य वाङ्मनसे शुद्धे सम्यग्गुप्ते च सर्वदा।
स वै सर्वमवाप्नोति वेदान्तोपगतं फलम्।।
ahisayaiva bhūtānāṁ kāryaṁ śreyo'nuśāsanam,
vāk chaiva madhurā ślakṣaṇā prayojyā dharmamichchhatā.

yasya vāṅmanase śuddhe samyaggupte cha sarvadā,
sa vai sarvamavāpnoti vedāntopagataṁ phalam.

[Meaning] It is obligatory on the part of teachers (and students) that they should guide everybody to the path of happiness and salvation without any malice to one and all. One who wants to promote dharma (morality and human values) should use speech that is sweet and gentle.

A person whose speech and thoughts are pure and ever perfectly guarded gains essence of Vedas as a reward.

The identity of a real learned scholar (Brāhmaṇa) is given in Manusmṛti (2.162) as under:

सम्मानाद् ब्राह्मणो नित्यमुद्विजेत विषादिव।
अमृतस्येव चाकाङ्क्षेदवमानस्य सर्वदा।।
sammānād brāhmaṇo nityamudvijeta viṣādiva,
amṛtasyeva chākāṅkṣedavamānasya sarvadā.

[Meaning] That scholar alone is said to possess true knowledge of the Veda and God, who develops an aversion for honours and awards as if it were poison, develops liking for dishonours or non-honours as if it were nectar.

The gain of knowledge is equated to austerity in Manusmṛti (2.164)

अनेन क्रमयोगेन संस्कृतात्मा द्विजः शनैः।
गुरौ वसन् सञ्चिनुयाद् ब्रह्माधिगमिकं तपः।।
anena kramayogena saṁskṛtātmā dvijaḥ śanaiḥ,
gurau vasan sañchinuyād brahmādhigamikaṁ tapaḥ.

[Meaning] In this way, a male or female student duly invested with Yajñopavīta (sacred thread) and living under the watchful eye of his teacher, should gradually accumulate the austerity in the form of Vedic knowledge.

The significance of Vedic knowledge is highlighted in Manusmṛti (2.168).

योऽनधीत्य द्विजो वेदमन्यत्र कुरुते श्रमम्।
स जीवन्नेव शूद्रत्वमाशु गच्छति सान्वयः।।
yo'nadhītya dvijo vedamanyatra kurute śramam,
sa jīvanneva śūdratvamāśu gachchhati sānvayaḥ.

[Meaning] A scholar (invested with Yajñopavīta, the symbol of Vedic knowledge) who abandons the study of Veda and applies his energies elsewhere, soon falls from the status of Brāhmaṇaship (scholarship) with the entire family and joins status of Śudras (laymen devoid of

Vedic, spiritual and material knowledge).

Note: Here it is emphasized that knowledge acquisition is the continuous life long process. As soon as a person abandons the study, he no longer enjoys the status of being a scholar or Brāhmaṇa.

Some other do's and don'ts have been laid down for students in Manusmṛti (2.177-180).

वर्जयेन्मधुमांसञ्च गन्धं माल्यं रसान् स्त्रियः ।
शुक्तानि यानि सर्वाणि प्राणिनां चैव हिसनम् । ।177 । ।

varjayenmadhumāṁsañcha gandhaṁ mālyaṁ rasān striyaḥ,
śuktāni yāni sarvāṇi prāṇināṁ chaiva hisanam.

अभ्यंगमञ्जनं चाक्ष्णोरुपानच्छत्रधारणम् ।
कामं त्रफ़ोधं च लोभं च नर्त्तनं गीतवादनम् । ।178 । ।

abhyaṁgamañjanaṁ chākṣaṇorupānachchhatradhāraṇam,
kāmaṁ traphodhaṁ cha lobhaṁ cha narttanaṁ gītavādanam.

द्यूतं च जनवादं च परिवादं तथानृतम् ।
स्त्रीणां च प्रेक्षणालम्भमुपघातं परस्य च । ।179 । ।

dyūtaṁ cha janavādaṁ cha parivādaṁ tathānṛtam,
strīṇāṁ cha prekṣaṇālambhamupaghātaṁ parasya cha.

एकः शयीत सर्वत्र न रेतः स्कन्दयेत्क्वचित् ।
कामाद्धि स्कन्दयन् रेतो हिनस्ति व्रतमात्मनः । ।180 । ।
ēkaḥ śayīta sarvatra na retaḥ skandayetkvachit,
kāmāddhi skandayan reto hinasti vratamātmanaḥ.

[Meaning] A student must avoid alcohol, meat perfumes, garlands, condiments, physical contact with opposite sex, all fermented foods and violence to all living beings.

A student must also avoid anointing the body parts with creams and oils, applying collyrium into eyes, use of outlandish dress items. A student must avoid lust, anger, greed, public dancing, singing and music.

A student must also avoid gambling, discussion on a particular person, backbiting, lying, seeing an opposite sex with lustful eyes, embracing a person belonging to opposite sex, and hurting others.

A student must not sleep lonely. He must avoid sexual stimulation of genitals leading to ejaculation. If a student allows ejaculation because of sexual urge, he violates the vow of celibacy.

The text of an address to be given by Āchārya to his students at the time of graduation/convocation ceremony is given in Taittirīya Upaniṣad (Śikṣā Valli, 11) which reads as under:

वेदमनूच्याचार्योऽन्तेवासिनमनुशास्ति। सत्यं वद। धर्मं चर। स्वाध्यायान्मा प्रमदः। आचार्य्याय प्रियं धनमाहृत्य प्रजातन्तुं मा व्यवच्छेत्सीः। सत्यान्न प्रमदितव्यम्। धर्मान्न प्रमदितव्यम्। कुशलान्न प्रमदितव्यम्। स्वाध्यायप्रवचनाभ्यां न प्रमदितव्यम्। देवपितृकार्य्याभ्यां न प्रमदितव्यम्।।१।। मातृदेवो भव। पितृदेवो भव। आचार्य्यदेवो भव। अतिथिदेवो भव। यान्यनवद्यानि कर्माणि तानि सेवितव्यानि नो इतराणि। यान्यस्माकं सुचरितानि तानि त्वयोपास्यानि नो इतराणि।।२।।

vedamanūchyāchāryo'ntevāsinamanuśāsti, satyaṁ vada, dharmaṁ chara, svādhyāyānmā pramadaḥ, āchāryyāya priyaṁ dhanamāhṛtya prajātantuṁ mā vyavachchhetsīḥ, satyānna pramaditavyam, dharmānna pramaditavyam, kuśalānna pramaditavyam, svādhyāyapravachanābhyāṁ na pramaditavyam, devapitṛkāryyābhyāṁ na pramaditavyam. mātṛdevo bhava, pitṛdevo bhava, āchāryyadevo bhava, atithidevo bhava, yānyanavadyāni karmāṇi tāni sevitavyāni no itarāṇi। yānyasmākaṁ sucharitāni tāni tvayopāsyāni no itarāṇi.

ये के चास्मच्छ्रेयांसो ब्राह्मणास्तेषां त्वयासनेन प्रश्वसितव्यम्। श्रद्धया देयम्। अश्रद्धया देयम्। श्रिया देयम्। ह्रिया देयम्। भिया देयम्। संविदा देयम्।।३।।

ye ke chāsmachchhreyāṁso brāhmaṇāsteṣāṁ tvayāsanena praśvasitavyam, śraddhayā deyam, aśraddhayā deyam, śriyā deyam, hriyā deyam, bhiyā deyam, saṁvidā deyam.

अथ यदि ते कर्मविचिकित्सा वा वृत्तविचिकित्सा वा स्यात् ये तत्र ब्राह्मणाः समदिर्शनो युक्ता अयुक्ता अलूक्षा धर्मकामाः स्युर्यथा ते तत्र वर्त्तेरन्। तथा तत्र वर्त्तेथाः।।४।।

atha yadi te karmavichikitsā vā vṛttavichikitsā vā syāt ye tatra brāhmaṇāḥ samadirśano yuktā ayuktā alūkṣā dharmakāmāḥ syuryathā te tatra vartteran, tathā tatra varttethāḥ.

एष आदेश एष उपदेश एषा वेदोपनिषत्। एतदनुशासनम्। एवमुपासितव्यम्। एवमु चैतदुपास्यम्।।५।।

ēṣa ādeśa ēṣa upadeśa ēṣā vedopaniṣat, ētadanuśāsanam, ēvamupāsitavyam, ēvamu chaitadupāsyam.

[Meaning] Having completed the Vedic teachings, the Principal instructs his students as follows: Speak the truth. Follow the path of Dharma (moral and ethical values). Don't be careless in your studies and teachings. Having completed your Vedic studies while living a chaste life, express your gratitude to your teacher with the gift of his choice and enter into married life so that the family line is not broken or interrupted. Never be careless enough to discard truth, dharma (human values), physical health, skills, the habit of learning and teaching, serving scholars and elderly persons.

Show respect to your mother, father, teacher and

guests (peripatetic monks). Perform only such righteous, truthful, blameless acts as promoting happiness and not others. Follow only our good practices and not others.

Sit in the company of pre-eminent scholars in our midst. Do trust them alone. You must do charity by all means whether you believe in charity or not. Charity must be done with grace, modesty, fearing from God and even with a promise to repeat it in future.

If you ever have a doubt regarding a particular act or conduct, then consult and follow those scholars, irrespective of a yogi or laymen, who are impartial, kind hearted, lovers of dharma.

This is the commandment. This is the instruction. This is the end result of the study of Vedas. This is worth to be followed. Follow this. Conduct yourself only in this manner.

Manu (2.4) says that human behaviour is a conditioned response.

अकामस्य क्रिया काचिद् दृश्यते नेह कर्हिचित्।
यद्यद्धि कुरुते किञ्चित् तत्तत्कामस्य चेष्टितम्।।
akāmasya kriyā kāchid dṛśyate neha karhichit,
yadyaddhi kurute kiñchit tattatkāmasya cheṣṭitam.

[Meaning] No action is performed without an urge of desire behind it. Whenever an action is performed, it is impelled by some desire.

It must be borne in mind that even the dilation or contraction of eyes cannot take place unconditionally. This proves that every action is a conditioned response because the performer has his own motive to perform a particular action.

आचारः परमो धर्मः श्रुत्युक्तः स्मार्त्त एव च।
तस्मादस्मिन्सदा युक्तो नित्यं स्यादात्मवान् द्विजः।।

āchāraḥ paramo dharmaḥ śrutyuktaḥ smārtta ēva cha,
tasmādasminsadā yukto nityaṁ syādātmavān dvijaḥ.

आचाराद्विच्युतो विप्रो न वेदफलमश्नुते।
आचारेण तु संयुक्तः सम्पूर्णफलभाग्भवेत्।।
āchārādvichyuto vipro na vedaphalamaśnute,
āchāreṇa tu saṁyuktaḥ sampūrṇaphalabhāgbhavet.

[Meaning] Moral and ethical conduct is the highest virtue prescribed in the tradition of Śrutis (Vedas) and Smṛtis (Dharmaśāstras or books prescribing a code of conduct for various persons in a society). As such, a scholar who exercises self-restraint always conducts himself morally and ethically.

A scholar devoid of moral and ethical conduct never enjoys the fruit of bliss produced from the dharma (inculcation of moral and ethical values) as prescribed in Veda. On the other hand, if a scholar conducts morally and ethically, he enjoys all sorts of comforts and happiness.

योऽवमन्येत ते मूले हेतुशास्त्रश्रयाद् द्विजः।
स साधुभिर्बहिष्कार्यो नास्तिको वेदनिन्दकः।।
yo'vamanyeta te mūle hetuśāstraśrayād dvijaḥ,
sa sādhubhirbahiṣkāryo nāstiko vedanindakaḥ.

[Meaning] A scholar who denigrates Veda or the texts authored by seers in conformity with the Veda is an atheist and worthy to be expelled by the virtuous people.

On the question of deciding the criteria of Dharma and Adharma, Manu (2.12) says:

श्रुतिः स्मृतिः सदाचारः स्वस्य च प्रियमात्मनः।
एतच्चतुर्विधं प्राहुः साक्षाद्धर्मस्य लक्षणम्।।
śrutiḥ smṛtiḥ sadāchāraḥ svasya cha priyamātmanaḥ,
ētachchaturvidhaṁ prāhuḥ sākṣāddharmasya lakṣaṇam.

[Meaning] Criteria of dharma is decided based on four factors, namely Vedas, Dharmaśāstras (like Manusmṛti), good conduct, and what is allowed by conscious of oneself.

Dharma is the conduct associated with fair justice, recognition of truth and derecognition of falsehood. On the contrary, adharma is associated with unfair justice, derecognition of truth and recognition of falsehood.

Who is qualified to realize dharma is clarified in Manusmṛti (2.13) as under:

अर्थकामेष्वसक्तानां धर्मज्ञानं विधीयते।
धर्मं जिज्ञासमानानां प्रमाणं परमं श्रुतिः ।।
arthakāmeṣvasaktānāṁ dharmajñānaṁ vidhīyate,
dharmaṁ jijñāsamānānāṁ pramāṇaṁ paramaṁ śrutiḥ.

[Meaning] The knowledge of dharma is attained by those who are not allured by wealth and sensual pleasures. The Veda is the prime authority to determine dharma.

Teachers should instil the aforementioned teachings into their pupils. Education should not be a prerogative of intellectuals only, rather the rulers, other administrators, traders/ merchants, producers/ labourers/ service providers must also be educated, otherwise, the growth of institutions of learning, dharma, governance and business will be thwarted. Scholars, educationists, academicians in a state remain confined to the activities of research and dissemination of knowledge, whereas rulers/ administrators, merchants/ traders, producers/ labourers/ service providers add to the economic growth of a state. Here, however, it may be reminded that for want of a proper Accreditation and Assessment State Agency, standard of education and research may deteriorate. As such, the state is required to be intelligent enough to monitor the progress of teaching and research. The teaching and research in a state are funded by the tax levied from the citizens engaged in administration, business/trading, services and production. Under the circumstances, it is mandatory that public in a state be well educated to see that their money allocated to teaching and research doesn't go waste. In this way, we may put into place a system of mutual check and balance involving intellectuals and other people overseeing each other. If the rules and regulations of a state are contributed by intellectuals, the teaching and research activities of the intellectuals are funded by other people in the state. So the education and dharma (moral and ethical values) must be promoted among all the citizens regardless of varṇa (personality types and professional classes), gender, colour or creed.

The teaching and learning process must be subjected to a proper assessment. There may be five means of assessment.

First of all, the Accreditation and Assessment Agency must assess that whatever is learnt or taught in the name of education is consistent with the Nature, Attributes and Actions of God and the Vedas.

Secondly, it is to be assessed that the teaching of various sciences and subjects is taking place in conformity with the natural laws. For example, if somebody teaches that a child is born without the union of parents, it would be contrary to the laws of nature.

Thirdly, it is to be assessed that a teacher is a learned man, truthful, unprejudiced and endowed with moral and ethical values.

Fourthly, it must be ascertained by the assessment agency that a teaching faculty is guided by the principle of Self-Judgment (what is good for you is good for others and what is painful for you is painful for others) in the dictates of knowledge.

Fifthly, the assessment of research and teaching must be made according to eight means of cognition (acquisition of knowledge):

Pratyakṣa Pramāṇa (Perception)
Anumāna (Inference)
Upamāna (Analogy)
Śabda (Authority)
Aitihya (History)
Arthāpatti (Deductive reasoning)
Sambhava (Probability)
Abhāva (Absence)

Now we shall explain the above means of cognition as delineated in the First and Second Chapter of Nyāya Darśana.

5.1 Pratyakṣa Pramāṇa (Perception)

इन्द्रियार्थसन्निकर्षोत्पन्नं ज्ञानमव्यपदेश्यमव्यभिचारिव्यवसायात्मकं प्रत्यक्षम्।

न्याय० 1.1.

indriyārthasannikarṣotpannaṁ jñānamavyapadeśyam-avyabhichārivyavasā-yātmakaṁ pratyakṣam.

[Meaning] The proximity of sensory organs with their stimuli leads to perception. If cognition is (avyapdeśyaṁ) derived from words, (avyabhichārī) or has an element of doubt, and (avyavasāyātmakaṁ) not definite, it can no longer be a called a perception. It should

Perception is the first means of cognition. It takes place from the stimulus (audition, touch, vision, taste, olfaction) coming in direct contact (without the intervention of some other object) with sensory organs (ear, skin, eyes, tongue, nose) and sensory organs contacting mind and mind contacting the self. However, the perception ceases to be a perception if it is derived from words. For example, if one says, Bring me water. The cognition of water produced by the word 'water' cannot be taken as a perception until and unless it is produced from actual and contact of water with the eyes. The perception ceases to be a perception if it is temporary. For example, a mistaken perception of a pillar for a human figure during the dark cover of night is not permanent, but it is going to change surely in the light of the sun. This perception can no longer be called a perception. Similarly, the perception ceases to be a perception, if it is not definite and has an element of doubt at any stage. Suppose, if one expresses doubt about water or white clothes spread out to dry while seeing a river sand from a distance or if one is not able to ascertain properly about the presence of Devadatta or Yajnadatta while seeing from a distance, his perception doesn't fall into the category of perception.

Anumāna (Inference)

अथ तत्पूर्वकं त्रिविधमनुमानं पूर्ववच्छेषवत्सामान्यतो दृष्टञ्च ।।
न्यायदर्शन (न्याय.), 1.1.5

atha tatpūrvakaṁ trividhamanumānaṁ pūrvavachchheṣavatsāmānyato dṛṣṭañcha.

Nyāya Darśana (N.D.), 1.1.5

[Meaning] Inference is followed by perception. It is of three types. (pūrvavat) First, one based upon the cause, the second one is (śeṣavat) based upon effect and the third one is (sāmānyato dṛṣṭaṁ) based on the common experience.

Anumāna (inference) always follows perception. If two things are perceived together at a certain time and place, recurrence of either of them at another place and time gives one to infer the existence of the missing one. For instance, in our daily life, we perceive together father and son, fire and smoke, pleasure and pain caused by our karmas (actions). Whenever we are faced to see a child alone, we can easily infer the existence of his father based on our experience. Similarly, we can infer fire when coming across a smoke. The scenario of pleasure and pain the current life gives one to infer the past life.

The inference is of three kinds. First, one is based upon the cause, i.e. the effect is inferred based on cause. For example, the inference of rain (effect) based on clouds (cause), the inference of progeny (effect) based on marriage (cause), and inference of wisdom of students (effect) based on their study (cause).

The second one is based upon effect, i.e. cause is inferred on the basis of effect. For example, inference of rain (cause) on the basis of flood (effect), inference of father (cause) on the basis of child (effect), inference of creator (cause) on the basis of creation (effect), inference of good and bad deeds (cause) on the basis of pleasure and pain (effect),

Third, one is based on common experience. For example, from our common experience, we know that we cannot reach our destination without making a move. The same experience holds good in case of others too. Anumāna (inference) is composed of two words, anu (to follow) + māna (to infer). Thus, anumāna is that which is inferred followed by a perception. For instance, without the perception of smoke, the unseen agni cannot be inferred.

Upamāna (Analogy)

प्रसिद्धसाधर्म्यात्साध्यसाधनमुपमानम्। न्यायदर्शन, 1.1.6

Prasiddhasādharmyātsādhyasādhanamupamānam.
N.D. 1.1.6

[Meaning] (upamānaṁ) Analogy is (sādhanaṁ) means of identifying (sādhyaṁ) an unknown object or thing based on a (sādharmyāt) resemblance of (prasiddha) a well-known object or thing.

The thing, which is required to be known, is called Sādhya (to be known), and that which becomes the means of this knowledge from some kind of likeness/resemblance between the two is called Sādhana (means). Upamāna (Analogy) is the means of identification of an unknown thing from its resemblance (likeness) to another known thing.[168]

For Example, a man says to his servant, "Go bring Vishnumitra (unknown) who resembles Devadatta (well known). The servant identifies Vishnumitra based on the resemblance of Devadatta. Similarly, the information of resemblance of Cow (well know) to Neelgai (unknown antelope) helps one to identify Neelgai in the jungle.

Śabda (Authority)

आप्तोपदेशः शब्दः । न्याय० 1.1.7
āptopadeśaḥ śabdaḥ. N.D. 1.1.7

[Meaning] Instructions of a Ṛṣi or thorough scholar who is spiritual, righteous, truthful, endowed with helping attitude, hardworking and having complete control over his senses can be taken as an authority.

Āptas are those Ṛṣis or thorough scholars who are spiritual, righteous, endowed with helping attitude, truthful, hardworking and have complete control over

168 उपमीयते येन तदुपमानम्।

their senses. They share their best knowledge ranging from worldly objects to God and experiences with other human beings with the sole motive of elevating their lives. Instructions of such scholars and the Vedas, the instructions of God, Who is known a Perfect Āpta, can be taken as authority, a means of cognition.

Aitihya (History)

न चतुष्ट्वमैतिह्यार्थापत्तिसम्भवाभावप्रामाण्यात्। न्याय० 2.2.7

chatuṣṭvamaitihyārthāpattisambhavābhāvaprāmāṇyāt.

N.D. 2.2.7

[Meaning] The means of cognition are not restricted to four, because Aitihya (History), Arthāpatti (Deduction), Sambhava (Probability) and Abhāva (Absence) are also categorized as means of cognition.

Historical accounts relating to a person, place, thing, natural phenomena or otherwise are also taken as means of cognition.

Arthāpatti (Cause-Effect Syllogism)

Arthāpatti may also help in cognition. Arthāpatti is a cause-effect syllogism. The conclusion is derived based on cause and effect statement. The basic of this syllogism type is: If 'a' is the cause of 'b', then there is no 'b' without 'a'. This may be illustrated as under:

Major premise: Every effect has a cause.

Minor Premise: Rain is caused by clouds.

Conclusion: There can be no rain without clouds

Sambhava (Nomological Possibility)

Sambhava (nomological possibility) is also enumerated as one of the means of cognition. Sambhava (nomological possibility) is a possibility under the currently obtained laws of nature. Nomological possibility counteracts the logical possibility or metaphysical possibility.

Most philosophers since David Hume (1711-1776) have held that the laws of nature are metaphysically contingent - that there could have been different natural laws than the ones that actually obtain. If so, then it would not be logically or metaphysically impossible, for example, for you to travel to Alpha Centauri in one day; it would just have to be the case that you could travel faster than the speed of light. But of course there is an important sense in which this is not possible; given that the laws of nature what they are, there is no way that you could do it. Travelling faster than the speed of light may be logically possible, but nomologically impossible. Similarly birth of a child without parents, raising a dead person, lifting a mountain, causing a stone to float on the sea surface, smashing the moon into pieces, horns on a man's head, the marriage of two people born to sterile women are nomologically impossible under the currently obtained laws of nature. Although their logical or metaphysical possibility may be not be ruled out.

Abhāva (Absence)

Abhāva (absence of a stimulus already experienced) is also counted as one of the means of cognition. Just as the presence of a stimulus act upon a receptor or sense organ, similarly absence of a stimulus already experienced by an individual also act upon our receptors or sense organs. That is why we often hear a negative response from the individuals. For instance, glass is missing. Today we did not hear the same old music. The smell of an incense stick has stopped coming. I would like to eat mango, etc. These types of responses by individuals support the hypothesis of an abhāva or 'absence of an already experienced stimulus' as a means of cognition.

One can infer the presence of thing at a place other than assigned to it due to Abhāva means of cognition. Suppose a person was ordered to bring the elephant from the elephant house. Finding elephant absent in the elephant house, he may bring it from another place it was present. For him, Abhāva also acts as a means of cognition.

The above-explained eight means of cognition can be summed up into four major categories. Aitihya (History) can be studied under Śabda (Authority), and Arthāpatti (Cause-Effect Syllogism), Sambhava (Nomological Possibility), and Abhāva (Absence) can be studied under Anumāna (Inference).

It is only by these five means of assessment that the teaching and research activities of the various educational institutions can be monitored for the quality (right or wrong) check up.

Having delineated with epistemological aspect (means of acquisition of knowledge) as prescribed in Nyāya philosophy, now the ontological aspect (constituents of the universe) as prescribed in Vaiśeṣika Darśana (philosophy) will also be taken into account. According to Vaiśeṣika philosophy (1.1.4), the main constituents of the universe which are necessary to be known for unravelling the mystery of the creation/universe are categorized into six kinds. They are:

धर्मविशेषप्रसूताद् द्रव्यगुणकर्मसामान्यविशेषसमवायानां पदार्थानां साधर्म्यवैधर्म्याभ्यां तत्त्वज्ञानान्निःश्रेयसम्।

dharmaviśeṣaprasūtād dravyaguṇakarmasāmānyaviśeṣ-asamavāyānāṁ padārthānāṁ sādharmyavaidharmyābhyāṁ tattvajñānānniḥśreyasam.

[Meaning] The knowledge of similarities and dissimilarities between six fundamental entities originated with different physical and metaphysical properties leads to perfection/emancipation. Those six fundamental entities are: (1) Dravyas (physical, and metaphysical substance) (2) Guṇas (physical and metaphysical properties of various Dravyas) (3) Karmas (Motions/actions) associated with various Dravyas (4) Sāmānya (commonality) (5) Viśeṣa (distinctness) and (6) Samavāya (inherence).

The first category is called 'Dravya', which is classified further into nine types. (the *Vaiśeṣika Darśana*, 1.1.5).

पृथिव्यापस्तेजोवायुराकाशं कालो दिगात्मा मन इति द्रव्याणि।

pṛthivyāpastejovāyurākāśaṁ kālo digātmā mana iti dravyāṇi

[Meaning] Dravyas are nine: Earth, Water, Fire, Air, Space, Time, Direction, Soul and Mind.

Dravya in the *Vaiśeṣika Darśana* (1.1.15) is defined as under:

क्रियागुणवत्समवायिकारणमिति द्रव्यलक्षणम्।

kriyāguṇavatsamavāyikāraṇamiti dravyalakṣaṇam,

[Meaning] Dravya is defined as something in which motion/action and a physical or metaphysical property reside inherently.

Dravya inherits both motion and property (physical or metaphysical) or property alone. Of the nine dravyas mentioned above, six of them - Earth, Water, Fire, Air, Mind and Soul- possess both motion and property. The other three dravyas - Space, Time and Direction- are devoid of motion but possess some physical or metaphysical property. In fact, there is a cause and effect relationship between dravayas and their motions or properties. In other words, dravyas came into being first followed by motions and properties in them.

The *Vaiśeṣika Darśana* (2.1.1) defines Earth (solid mass) as under:

रूपरसगन्धस्पर्शवती पृथिवी ।

rūparasagandhasparśavatī pṛthivī.

[Meaning] Pṛthivī (Earth or solid mass) is something, which is endowed with physical properties of sight, taste, smell, and touch.

The properties of sight, taste and touch are due to its predecessors like fire, water and air respectively present in them.

व्यवस्थितः पृथिव्यां गन्धः ।

vyavasthitaḥ pṛthivyāṁ gandhaḥ.

[Meaning] Smell is Earth's unique inherent property.

Similarly, taste is the unique inherent property of waters (flowing mass), while sight is the unique inherent property of fire (glowing mass), touch is the unique inherent property of air (blowing mass) and the sound is the unique inherent property of space (vibrating mass).

Āpa (waters) are defined in Vaiśeṣika Darśana (2.1.2) as under:

रूपरसस्पर्शवत्य आपो द्रवाः स्निग्धाः ।

rūparasasparśavatya āpo dravāḥ snigdhāḥ.

[Meaning] Waters are endowed with physical properties of sight, taste and touch. They are also endowed with fluidity and softness.

Taste is the unique inherent property of waters, while sight, touch are due to their predecessors like fire and air present in them.

In addition to above, āpa (waters) have coldness as their inherent property (*Vaiśeṣika Darśana*, 2.1.2).

अप्सु शीतता।

apsu śītatā.

[Meaning] Waters have cool touch.

Teja (fire) is defined as under (*Vaiśeṣika Darśana*, 2.1.3)

तेजो रूपस्पर्शवत्।

tejo rūpasparśavat

[Meaning] Fire has sight and touch as inherent properties.

Sight is the unique inherent property of Teja (fire), while touch is due to its predecessor 'air' present in it.

Vāyu (Air) is defined (Vaiśeṣika Darśana, 2.1.4) as under:

स्पर्शवान् वायुः।

sparśavān vāyuḥ.

[Meaning] Air is endowed with the property of touch.

Heat and cold in the air are due to the presence of fire and waters respectively.

None of the above-cited properties like sight, taste, smell and touch are associated with Ākāśa (space).

The *Vaiśeṣika Darśana* (2.1.5) had it as:

त आकाशे न विद्यन्ते। .

ta ākāśe na vidyante

[Meaning] These properties (sight, taste, touch, and smell) are not associated with space.

Sound is the unique inherent property of Ākāśa. [Now the question arises as to what is the sign of Space] The sign of space has been described in Vaiśeṣika Darśana (2.1.20) as under:

निष्क्रमणं प्रवेशनमित्याकाशस्य लिंगम्।
niṣkramaṇaṁ praveśanamityākāśasya liṁgam.

[Meaning] Exit and entrance are the sign of Ākāśa (space).

[Here one may raise a question. If Ākāśa or Bhūtākāśa (space with active energy) is the first dravya to originate from Ātman (chidākāśa) followed by air, fire, water and earth in sequence, then according to the principle of cause and effect, sound, the property of space would have transferred to the successive dravyas (effects). For instance, the property of air (touch) transferred to fire, water and earth. Similarly, the property of fire (sight) transferred to water and earth and the property of water (taste) transferred to earth. Nevertheless, the property of Ākāśa did not transfer to dravyas originating in succession. The answer is that the principle of cause and effect doesn't apply in the case of Ākāśa. The property of Ākāśa never transfers to its successive products/effects like air, fire, water and earth. It may be taken as an exception. This fact is upheld by Vaiśeṣika philosopher (2.1.5) as:

कार्य्यान्तराप्रादुर्भावाच्च शब्दः स्पर्शवतामगुणः।

kāryyāntarāprādurbhāvāchcha śabdaḥ sparśavatām-aguṇaḥ.

[Meaning] Since the sound is not detected in the effects (dravyas) like earth, water, fire and air, the same is not the property of above dravyas (earth, water, fire and air) possessing the property of touch.

However, the sound is the unique inherent property of Ākāśa.

'Time' is defined in Vaiśeṣika Darśana (2.2.6) as under:

अपरस्मिन्नपरं युगपच्चिरं क्षिप्रमिति काललिंगानि ।

aparasminnaparaṁ yugapachchiraṁ kṣipramiti kālaliṁgāni.

[Meaning] Time is characterized by the notions of apara (new/young), para (old), yugapat (at the same time), chira (late), kṣipra (immediately).

It is further explained (Vaiśeṣika Darśana, 2.1.5) that 'time' is the cause of all effects.

नित्येष्वभावादनित्येषु भावात्कारणे कालाख्येति ।

nityeṣvabhāvādanityeṣu bhāvātkāraṇe kālākhyeti.

[Meaning] The notion of time is not associated with the eternal/imperishable things, but it is associated with perishable things only. As such, 'time' is described as a cause of all effects.

Dik (preferred direction) in Vaiśeṣika Darśana (2.2.10) is defined as follows:

इत इदमिति यतस्तद्दिश्यं लिंगम् ।

ita idamiti yatastaddiśyaṁ liṁgam.

[Meaning] Direction is characterized by the notions of 'to the east', 'to the south', 'to the west', 'to the north', up etc.

The method of determination of a particular direction is highlighted very beautifully in Vaiśeṣika Darśana (2.2.14 -16). It says:

आदित्यसंयोगाद् भूतपूर्वाद् भविष्यतो भूताच्च प्राची। एतेन दिगन्तरालानि व्याख्यातानि।

ādityasaṁyogād bhūtapūrvād bhaviṣyato bhūtāchcha prāchī, ētena digantarālāni vyākhyātāni.

[Meaning] The eastern direction is determined based on sunrise. The phenomenon of sunrise is taking place since the beginning of creation. It took place in the past, it will also continue to take place in future as it takes place now.

Similarly, one may determine the southern, western and northern directions. The direction opposite to sunrise is west. A man facing the direction of rising sun has a south (dakṣiṇa) on his right (dakṣiṇa) and north (uttara) on his left.

Through this, the sub-directions or intervening directions are explained.

Intervening directions are named as:

The South- East is known as Āgneyī.

North-West is known as Nairṛti.

North-West is known as Vāyavī.

Northeast is known as Aiśānī.

Now we shall deal with characteristics of Ātmā as given in Nyāya Darśana (1.1.10) and Vaiśeṣika Darśana (3.2.4). Nyāya Darśana says:

इच्छाद्वेषप्रयत्नसुखदुःखज्ञानान्यात्मनो लिंगमिति।

ichchhādveṣaprayatnasukhaduḥkhajñānānyātmano liṁgamiti.

[Meaning] Tendency of attachment, detachment, efforts, pleasure, pain and knowledge are the visible signs of Ātman or soul.

Vaiśeṣika Darśana (3.2.4) upholds

प्राणाऽपाननिमेषोन्मेषजीवनमनोगतीन्द्रियान्तिर्वकाराः
सुखदुःखेच्छाद्वेषप्रयत्नाश्चात्मनो लिंगानि।

prāṇā'pānanimeṣonmeṣajīvanamanogatīndriyāntirvakār āḥ sukhaduḥkhechchhādveṣaprayatnāśchātmano liṁgāni.

[Meaning] Exhalations, inhalations, eye reflexes, life, cognition (mind's movement towards senses), Intersensory reactions (e.g. excitement of taste at the sight of a mango), sensations of hunger and thrust, physical ailments, pleasure, pain, attachment, detachment and efforts are the signs of soul.

Mind, the ninth dravya is defined as under:

युगपज्ज्ञानानुत्पत्तिर्मनसो लिंगम्।

yugapajjñānānutpattirmanaso liṁgam.

[Meaning] The characteristic of Mind is that it cannot allow two cognitions to take place at the same time.

The foregoing is the description of nature and characteristics of Dravyas. We shall now take up the second category of constituents called Guṇas (physical and metaphysical properties of Dravyas). They are described in Vaiśeṣika Darśana (1.1.6) as under:

रूपरसगन्धस्पर्शाः संख्याः परिमाणानि पृथक्त्वं संयोगविभागौ परत्वाऽपरत्वे बुद्धयः सुखदुःखे इच्छाद्वेषौ प्रयत्नाश्च गुणाः।

rūparasagandhasparśāḥ saṁkhyāḥ parimāṇāni pṛthaktvaṁ saṁyogavibhāgau paratvā'paratve buddhayaḥ sukhaduḥkhe ichchhādveṣau prayatnāścha guṇāḥ.

[Meaning] Colour, taste, smell, skin-sensation, saṅkhyā (numerical values), parimāṇa (different dimensions), separableness, opposites like union and division, remoteness and proximity, pleasure and pain, desire and aversion, Buddhi (power of differentiation or discrimination), efforts, gurutva (state of heaviness or solid mass), dravtva (liquid state) and sneha (viscous state), sanskāra (potential, kinetic/speed and psychic energy), dharma (moral and ethical values), adhrma (immoral and unethical acts) and sound- these are 24 properties of various dravyas.

Guṇas (properties of dravya) are defined in the *Vaiśeṣika Darśana* (1.1.6) as under:

द्रव्याश्रय्यगुणवान् संयोगविभागेष्वकारणमनपेक्ष इति गुणलक्षणम्।

dravyāśrayyaguṇavān saṁyogavibhāgeṣvakāraṇaman-apekṣa iti guṇalakṣaṇam

[Meaning] Guṇa (property is that which resides in a Dravya, which has no property of its own, which never cause things to unite or divide and exist independently of another property.

Nature of sound and other properties is described hereunder:

श्रोत्रेपलब्धिर्बुद्धिनिर्ग्राह्यः प्रयोगेणाऽभिज्वलित आकाशदेशः शब्दः।

śrotrepalabdhirbuddhinirgrāhyaḥ prayogeṇā'bhijvalita ākāśadeśaḥ śabdaḥ

[Meaning] Sound is that which acts upon ears or say heard by ears and realized by intellect and expressed through speech. It resides in Ākāśa (space). (Mahābhāṣya, 1.1.1)

Similarly, colour is perceived by eyes, taste by the tongue, smell by nose, skin sensation by skin.

Numerical values are those, which are subjected to counting

Parimāṇa is characterized by size and weight

Separableness is going apart from each other

Union is coming together

Division is breaking of union into several parts

Remoteness is far distance

Proximity is closeness

Pleasure is joy

Pain is misery

Desire is attachment

Aversion is detachment

Buddhi is power of differentiation or discrimination

Efforts is the input of strength for various pursuits

Gurutva is gravitation

Dravatva is liquid state

Sneha is viscous state

Sanskāra is energy- potential, kinetic and psychic energy

Dharma signifies moral and ethical values

Adharma signifies immoral and unethical values

The third category comprises of Karma (motion) which is described in the *Vaiśeṣika Darśana* (1.1.7) as under:

उत्क्षेपणमवक्षेपणमाकुञ्चनं प्रसारणं गमनमिति कर्माणि ।

utkṣepaṇamavakṣepaṇamākuñchanaṁ prasāraṇaṁ gamanamiti karmāṇi.

[Meaning] Ascension, dissension, contraction, expansion and locomotion (like coming, going, rotating etc.) are called karmas (motions).

Karma (motion) is characterized in the *Vaiśeṣika Darśana* (1.1.17) as under:

एकद्रव्यमगुणं संयोगविभागेष्वनपेक्षकारणमिति कर्मलक्षणम्।

ēkadravyamaguṇaṁ saṁyogavibhāgeṣvanapekṣakāraṇ-amiti karmalakṣaṇam

[Meaning] Motion is that which resides in any one dravya, which has no property of its own and independently cause things to unite or divide.

The fifth category called Sāmānya (common) is described in the *Vaiśeṣika Darśana* (1.1.18) as under:

द्रव्यगुणकर्मणां द्रव्यं कारणं सामान्यम्।

dravyaguṇakarmaṇāṁ dravyaṁ kāraṇaṁ sāmānyam

[Meaning] Dravya (material or metaphysical susbtance) is the material or inherent cause of all other dravyas, the attribute inherited by the dravyas and motion exhibited by dravyas.

For instance, the thread is the cause of white cloth flying in the air. As such, the thread factor is not common to cloth alone, but it is common even to the colour of cloth (attribute) and any motion exhibited by cloth.

The concept of Sāmānya (common) is further illustrated as under (*Vaiśeṣika Darśana*, 1.1.23):

द्रव्याणां द्रव्यं कार्यं सामान्यम्।

dravyāṇāṁ dravyaṁ kāryaṁ sāmānyam

[Meaning] The phenomenon of effect is common to all the dravyas proceeded from various causative dravyas.

The philosopher wants to say that all the various dravyas proceeded from various causes, share but one thing in common and that is that they are all effects.

The fourth category of constituents called Viśeṣa (distinct) is described in the *Vaiśeṣika Darśana* (1.2.5) as under:

द्रव्यत्वं गुणत्वं कर्मत्वञ्च सामान्यानि विशेषाश्च।

dravyatvaṁ guṇatvaṁ karmatvañcha sāmānyāni viśeṣāścha.

[Meaning] Beingness of dravya (physical and spiritual entities), guṇa (qualities/properties) and karma (motion/action) is both general and individual (special).

For instance, the beingness of dravya is common to all dravyas and beingness of dravya separates dravyas from guṇas and karmas. So, it is both general and special.

The concept of 'common' and 'distinct' requires discriminatory power.

सामान्यं विशेष इति बुद्ध्यपेक्षम्।

sāmānyaṁ viśeṣa iti buddhyapekṣam.

[Meaning] The notion of generalization and individuality is subject to the intelligence of the observer.

For instance, human-ness is common to all human beings, but it distinguishes humans from animals. Similarly, masculinity is common to all men but distinct to women, while femininity is common to all women, but distinct to men. Likewise, Brahmaṇa-hood, Kṣatriya-hood, Vaiśya-hood and Śudra-hood are both common and distinct.

The sixth called Samavāya (base) is explained in the

Vaiśeṣika Darśana (7.2.26) as under:

इहेदमिति यतः कार्यकारणयोः स समवायः।

ihedamiti yataḥ kāryakāraṇayoḥ sa samavāyaḥ.

[Meaning] The relation of 'this is in that' is called inherence relation. For example, the manufacturing of cloth depends upon threads; here threads are the cause and the cloth their effect. The threads are inherent in cloth. So, the relationship between cause and effect is called an inherence relationship.

In other words, the relationship between effect and cause is known as Samvāya (inherence).

There are two types of relationships between various objects-eternal and temporary. The relationship between cause and effect, whole and parts, action and agent, substance and attribute, class and individual is inherence/eternal or inseparable in nature. The relationship other than the inherence or eternal one is known as temporary. The substances other than cited above may join or combine in a temporary way.

While emphasizing upon the knowledge of the seven fundamental entities for understanding the mystery of creation, the Vaiśeṣika philosophy (1.1.4) talks about their sādharmya (similarities) and vaidharmya (dissimilarities). Here the term sādharmya (similarity) is explained in the *Vaiśeṣika Darśana* (1.1.9) as follows:

द्रव्यगुणयोः सजातीयारम्भकत्वं साधर्म्यम्।

dravyaguṇayoḥ sajātīyārambhakatvaṁ sādharmyam

[Meaning] A particular Dravya and Guṇa (property) often cause (produce) a dravya or guṇa of the same class. This tendency is known as Sādharmya (Similarity).

For instance, the Earth will give rise to an earthen pot

of the same quality. Similarly, the blue coloured thread will give rise to blue coloured cloth. This tendency is known as sādharmya. The reverse of it is known as vaidharmya.

Since the entire creation is the result of cause and effect. The phenomenon of cause and effect is elucidated further as:

कारणभावात्कार्यभावः। वैशेषिक दर्शन (वै० द०) 4.1.3

kāraṇabhāvātkāryabhāvaḥ.

Vaiśeṣika Darśana (V.D.) 4.1.3

[Meaning] An effect pre-supposes a cause.

न तु कार्याभावात्कारणाभावः। वै० द० 1.2.2

na tu kāryābhāvātkāraṇābhāvaḥ. *V.D. 1.1.2*

[Meaning] The absence of effect doesn't signify the absence of cause.

कारणाऽभावात्कार्याऽभावः। वै० द० 1.2.1

kāraṇā'bhāvātkāryā'bhāvaḥ. *V.D. 1.2.1*

[Meaning] No effect is possible without a cause.

कारणगुणपूर्वकः कार्यगुणो दृष्टः। वै० द० 2.1.24

kāraṇaguṇapūrvakaḥ kāryaguṇo dṛṣṭaḥ. *V.D.* 2.1.24

[Meaning] Effect inherits the qualities of its cause.

Some more technical terms useful in understanding thc Self and creation are defined here. First of all Parimāṇa is defined

अणुमहदिति तस्मिन्विशेषभावाद्विशेषाभावाच्च। वै० द० 7.1.11

aṇumahaditi tasminviśeṣabhāvādviśeṣābhāvāchcha.

[Meaning] Smaller and greater are relative terms. When two things are juxtaposed, one with comparatively reduced size is known as smaller and another with comparatively bigger size is known as greater. Thus, the smallness and greatness is defined in terms of relative presence of object or thing of reduced size and absence of an object or thing of reduced size.

For instance, a tetra-atomic molecule is smaller than lice, but greater than dia-atomic molecule. Similarly, a mountain is smaller than earth, but greater than a tree.

The next technical term 'sat' or 'sattā' (existence) is defined as under:

सदिति यतो द्रव्यगुणकर्मसु सा सत्ता। वै० द० 1.2.7

saditi yato dravyaguṇakarmasu sā sattā.

[Meaning] The term sat applied to dravya, guṇa and karma points out to their existence. Existence is common to all three.

भावोऽनुवृत्तेरेव हेतुत्वात्सामान्यमेव। वै० द० 1.2.4

bhāvo'nuvṛttereva hetutvātsāmānyameva.

[Meaning] Existence is applied to all dravyas, guṇas (attributes) and karmas (motions). Hence, it falls in the category of sāmānya (common).

Existence is the feature of dravyas that exist. Now non-existence is described. Non-existence is of five kinds.

Prāgabhāva (Prebirth absence)

Pradhvaṁśābhāva (Non-existence after annihilation)

Anyonyābhāva (Reciprocal non-existence)

Atyantābhāva (Absolute non-existence)

Sansargābhāva (Associative non-existence)

Prāgabhāva (Non-existence prior to birth):

क्रियागुणव्यपदेशाभावात्प्रागसत्। वै० द० 9.1.1

kriyāguṇavyapadeśābhāvātprāgasat.

[Meaning] Motion and quality are absent from any effect (object) that has not come into existence. So, the absence of motion and quality in an object before its production is called 'pragabhāva' (prebirth absence).

Note: A particular effect presupposes a particular cause and not all causes. Any material object or a thing has only two states: cause and effect. In its causal form, the material object remains non-existent, it comes into existence after transforming into effect. When a particular object or thing transforms into effect, it is qualified with some certain attributes and actions. Thus an existence of an object or a thing is known only by the attributes or actions associated with it. For want of any action or attribute, an object will remain non-existent or say in its causal form. For instance, a piece of cloth or a pot did not exist before they were made. This non-existence of a piece of cloth or a pot before their birth/formation is called Prāgabhāva.

Pradhvaṁśābhāva (Postmortal absence)

सदसत्। वै० द० 9.1.2

sadasat

[Meaning] The effect in existence, becomes (asat) absent after its destruction, just as a manufactured pot becomes absent after its destruction. This phenomenon is known as 'dhvansābhāva' (post-mortal absence)

For example, when a jar is broken, it ceases to exist.

Anyonyābhāva (Mutual or Reciprocal Absence)

सच्चासत्। वै० द० 9.1.4
sachchāsat

[Meaning] Even present objects are absent mutually or reciprocally. For instance, the cloth is absent from the pot and the pot from the cloth. In a similar way, a cow is absent in relation to horse and a horse in relation to cow. This is called Anyonyābhāva (mutual absence)

Atyantābhāva (Absolute non-existence)

यच्चान्यदसदतस्तदसत्। वै० द० 9.1.5

yachchānyadasadatastadasat

[Meaning] Absolute non-existence is different from all the above-mentioned three forms of non-existence. That which can never exist is called as Absolute non-existence.

Horns to a human being, flower in a sky and child to a barren woman are the examples of Absolute non-existence.

Sansargābhāva (Temporal or Spatial non-existence)

नास्ति घटो गेह इति सतो घटस्य गेहसंसर्गप्रतिषेधः। वै० द० 9.1.10

nāsti ghaṭo geha iti sato ghaṭasya gehasaṁsarga-pratiṣedhaḥ

[Meaning] Pot is not in the house, in this way denial of conjunction of an existing pot with the house describes a spatial category of atyantābhāva (spatial non-existence/absence). In view of it, some of the Ācharyas also categorize it as sāmayikābhāva (temporal absence) i.e. absence at a particular time and not thereafter.

In other words, non-existence of a thing in a particular place and time, while it exists at another place and time, is called temporal or spatial non-existence.

Thus having to delineate upon the concept of existence and non-existence/absence, the difference between vidyā (knowledge) and avidyā (ignorance) is discussed.

इन्द्रियदोषात्संस्कारदोषाच्चाविद्या। वै० द० 9.2.10

indriyadoṣātsaṁskāradoṣāchchāvidyā.

Meaning] Due to the problem of sense organs and sanskāras (information retained in mind), a person is attracted to the perishable visible world.

तद्दुष्टमज्ञानम्। वै० द० 9.2.11

tadduṣṭaṁ jñānam

[Meaning] Knowledge of vikṛti (material world) is avidyā.

अदुष्टं विद्या। वै० द० 9.2.12

aduṣṭaṁ vidyā

[Meaning] Knowledge of Brahman and the immaterial world is vidyā.

पृथिव्यादिरूपरसगन्धस्पर्शा द्रव्याऽनित्यत्वादनित्याश्च। वै० द० 7.1.2

pṛthivyādirūparasagandhasparśā dravyā'nityatvādanityāścha.

[Meaning] Properties of sight, taste, smell and touch are non-eternal when attributed to effects like Earth, Water, Fire, and Air, as they are non-eternal in their effect form, but the same properties assume eternity when attributed to causes of Earth, Water, Fire and Air, as Earth, Water, Fire and Air in causal form are eternal.

एतेन नित्येषु नित्यत्वमुक्तम्। वै० द० 7.1.3.

ētena nityeṣu nityatvamuktam.

[Meaning] Nevertheless, the same properties of sight, taste, smell and touch assume eternity when attributed to causes of Earth, Water, Fire and Air, as Earth, Water, Fire and Air in causal form are eternal.

At this stage, one can raise a question as to how to distinguish an eternal from non-eternal? The answer is:

सदकारणवन्नित्यम्। वै० द० 4.1.1

sadakāraṇavannityam.

[Meaning] The existing entity having no material cause for its creation is called *nitya.* Prakṛti, Time, Space, Mind, and Soul are all *nitya* entities.

Similarly, the effects that pre-suppose a material cause are known as non-eternal[169].

What are the means of knowledge? This question is dealt herewith.

अस्येदं कार्यं कारणं संयोगि विरोधि समवायि चेति लैंगिकम्। वै० द० 9.2.1

asyedaṁ kāryaṁ kāraṇaṁ saṁyogi virodhi samavāyi cheti laiṁgikam

[Meaning] Knowledge is gained through the means of effect, cause, concomitance, opposite thought, and inherence.

Examples are:

Effect as a means to knowledge: Effect is the means to reach its cause, e.g. son is a means to reach his father.

Cause as a means to knowledge: Cause also acts as the means to reach its effect, e.g. rainfall is often signalled by the dark clouds.

Inherence/concomitance as a means to knowledge: Inherence is also the means to knowledge, e.g. skin and body are concomitant- they always exist together. As such, skin is the means to the body.

---

169 सत्कारणवदनित्यम्।

Inference as a means to knowledge: The attributes exist in dravyas inherently. The relation between qualifier (quality/attribute) and qualificand (dravya) is called as inherence. Inherence (or inherent relation) is also one of the means to knowledge. In the relation of inherence, qualifier (attribute) is the means to understand the existence of qualificand (dravya), e.g. sound acts as the means to understand the existence of space, touch to air. Knowledge (attribute of the soul) is the means to understand the existence of the soul. Movement (the attribute of God) is the means to understand the existence of God.

Inherence of multiple qualifiers as a means to knowledge: When there is more than one qualifier associated with a qualificand, one qualifier becomes the means to the knowledge of co-qualifiers. For example, Earth (qualificand) has five qualifiers (attributes) like the smell (its independent attribute), taste (inherited from waters), sight (inherited from fire), touch (inherited from the air) and sound (inherited from space). In this case, one qualifier (smell) becomes the means to know its co-qualifiers- sound, taste, sight and touch inherited by the earth. Similarly, a qualifier (taste) becomes the means to know its co-qualifiers-sight, touch and sound inherited in waters. The qualifier (sight) becomes the means to know co-qualifiers- touch and sound inherited by fire, so on and so forth.

Opposite thought as the means to knowledge: Opposite thought also acts as the means to knowledge. To clarify it, the occurrence of an event/phenomenon suggests non-occurrence of that event/phenomenon. Similarly, non-occurrence of a phenomenon or event suggests the occurrence of that event or phenomenon. For example, the occurrence of rain also suggests non-occurrence of the same and vice verse (non-occurrence of rain suggests the occurrence of rain).

State of Pervasion: Vyāpti (state of pervasion) is defined in the *Saṅkhya Sūtra* (29, 31, 32) as under:

नियतधर्मसाहित्यमुभयोरेकतरस्य व्याप्तिः ।
आधेयशक्तियोग इति पञ्चशिखः । सांख्यसूत्र, 5. 29

niyatadharmasāhityamubhayorekatarasya vyāptiḥ,
ādheyaśaktiyoga iti pañchaśikhaḥ, sāṁkhyasūtra

[Meaning] Vyāpti (state of pervasion) is invariable concomitance of hetu /sādhana (means/known) and sādhya (end/to be known), in the case of both or either of them.

It is significant to know here is that pervaded (means/known) cannot exist without pervader (to be known). For example, pervaded smoke (means/known) cannot exist without pervader fire (end/to be known), but pervader fire may exist even without pervaded smoke. As such, pervaded smoke is always the means to know its pervader fire, but fire may not act as the means to know smoke.

According to some authorities, the pervaded one sometimes exists by itself, through its own power.

निजशक्त्युद्भवमित्याचार्याः । सांख्यसूत्र, 5.30

nijaśaktyudbhavamityāchāryāḥ. Sāṁkhyasūtra, 5.30

[Meaning] According to some authorities, the pervaded (smoke) can also exist without the help of pervader (fire).

For example, smoke when carried away by the wind to a distance place exists without its pervader, the fire. Therefore, for the state of pervasion, the invariable concomitance of pervaded (smoke) and pervader (fire) is not necessary. As such, vyāpti (state of pervasion) can be defined even without invariable concomitance between pervaded (vyāpya) and pervader (vyāpaka). In this condition, also pervaded (smoke) may suggest the existence of pervader (fire) somewhere else, if not exactly at the place of smoke.

There is another viewpoint of Pañcaśikha Ācārya. Accordingly, vyāpti (the state of pervasion) may be defined as the relationship of the locus (adhāra) and located (ādheya).

आधेयशक्तियोग इति पञ्चशिखः । सांख्यसूत्र, 5. 31

ādheyaśaktiyoga iti pañchaśikhaḥ, Sāṁkhyasūtra, 5. 31

[Meaning] Vyāpti (the state of pervasion) may also be defined as the relationship of the locus (adhāra) and located (ādheya).

For example, powerful is locus and power is located. Therefore, power (located) can also act as the means to know powerful (locus). Similarly, when mahāna originates from Prakṛti, Prakṛti becomes locus (pervader) and mahān located Pervaded).

The above criteria must be followed in learning or teaching process, or else the students will ever remain aloof of truth. Before including a text into the curriculum, its contents must be verified following the above criteria. Whatever is tested to be true, should be prescribed for teaching, otherwise not. It is said:

लक्षणप्रमाणाभ्यां वस्तुसिद्धिः ।

lakṣaṇapramāṇābhyāṁ vastusiddhiḥ.

[Meaning] The facts may be verified and validated based on definitions (prescribed norms) and various means of cognition.

अथ पठनपाठनविधिः

Atha paṭhanapāṭhanavidhiḥ

Teaching and Leaning Scheme

(Now we begin to explain learning and teaching scheme)

Vedāṅgas: Vedāṅgas need to be studied in the following order:

I. Phonetics (Śikṣā): First of all, phonetics should be taught to students. There is an authentic text on phonetics by Pāṇini called 'Pāṇinīya Śikṣā'. It is composed of sūtras (succinct aphorisms) and contains instructions about the mode of articulation of various sounds, places of their articulation and articulators. For example, 'p' sound has 'lips' as a place of articulation, tongue as articulator and articulated in spṛṣṭa (full contact) mode. In the same manner, the parents and teachers can teach the pronunciation of all other sounds to their children and students.

II. Grammar (Vyākaraṇa): Study of phonetics should be followed by the study of grammar. The complete range of study of Pāṇinian Sanskrit grammar involves following steps:

1. The first step involves the reading of 4000 sūtras (succinct aphorisms) like वृद्धिरादैच (1.1.1) of Aṣṭādhyāyī (8 chaptered work) by Pāṇini.

2. The second step involves splitting of words contained in sūtras (succinct aphorisms) of Pāṇini Aṣṭādhyāyī. For example,

वृद्धिरादैच् will be splitted as: वृद्धिः आदैच् वा आत्+ ऐच्

The third step is decomposition of compounded words, like आच्च+ ऐच्च + आदैच्

which is followed by the meaning of aphorisms, like वृद्धिरादैच् means आ, ऐ, औ are technically termed as vṛddhi (long vowels). Lastly, the applications of the aphorisms with regard to the derivation of various words are to be taught. This may be illustrated as under:

भाग is derived from root भज्+घञ् suffix. घ्, and ञ् of घञ् is elided as per grammatical rules and the remaining will be भज् अण् Vowel अ followed by भ is prolonged and ज् changes into ग् as per rules, thus transforming भज् into भाग.

Also in case of अध्याय (अधि+इङ्+घञ्), इ of इङ् is prolonged into ऐ and ऐ changes into आय making the segment as अध्याय.

Similar rules hold true in the case of the following:

a). नायक (नीञ्+ण्वुल्), where 'नी' is prolonged into नै+अक=नायक।

b). स्तावक (ण्वुल्+स्तु), where स्तु is prolonged into स्तौ +अक =स्तावक।

c). कारक= ण्वुल+कृञ्, where क is prolonged into कार्+अक = कारक।

While deriving the various words, all the applicable aphorisms of Pāṇini should be quoted along with their intended meaning. A student must be made to practice all the derivations on the slate or wooden board in detail systematically. For instance,

भज् + घञ् + सु
भज् + अ (घ् and ञ् are elided[170]) + सु
भाज् (अ followed by भ is prolonged[171]) + अ + सु

---

[170] हलन्त्यम्- (पा0 1.3.3); लशक्वतद्धिते-पा0 1.3.8; तस्य लोपः-(पा0 1.3.9)

[171] टचो ञ्णिति- पा0 7.2.115

भाग् (ज् changes into ग [172]) + अ + सु
भाग (अ merges into ग due to sandhi) + सु
भाग स् (m of सु is elided[173])
भागरु (स changes into रु [174])
भागर् (उ of रु is elided [175])
भागः (र् changes into विसर्ग (अः) [176]

Here students must be made to learn all the applicable aphorisms as cited in the footnotes. This will help them understand the basic process of grammar involved in the formation of various words.

III. Index of verbal roots (Dhatupāṭha): Having taught Aṣṭādhyāyī following the above-cited pattern, the students must be taught Index of verbal root called Dhātupāṭha composed by Pāṇini containing 2014 verbal roots. They should learn conjugation of various verbal roots in all the ten lakāras (verbal endings) along with the conjugational procedure involved including all applicable rules of exceptional as well as general nature. To illustrate it, as general rule would have it, the av.k~ ending is carried by all the verbal roots if they are preceded by an accusative noun, e.g.

कुम्भं + कृ + अण् = कुम्भकारः (potter)
नगरं + कृ + अण् = नगरकारः (city architect)

However, the same general rule doesn't hold good if the verbal root ends in आ (ā), as per the application of

---

172 चजोः कु घिण्ण्यतोः-पा0 7.3.52; स्थानेऽन्तरतमः- पा0 1.1.49

173 उपदेशेऽजनुनासिक इत् - पा0 1.3.2; तस्य लोपः-(पा0 1.3.9)

174 ससजुषो रु-पा0 8.2.66

175 उपदेशेऽजनुनासिक इत् - पा0 1.3.2; तस्य लोपः-(पा0 1.3.9)

176 विरामोऽवसानम्- पा0 1.4.109; खरवसानयोर्विसर्जनीयः - पा0 8.3.15

exceptional rule[177]. Examples are:

कम्बलं + दा + अण् = कम्बलदः (blanket giver)
अंगुलिं + त्रा + अण् = अंगुलित्रम् (glove)

In this connection, the students must also be taught that exceptional rules prevail over the general rules, but general rules cannot prevail over the exceptional rules. Just as the universal emperor prevails over all the kings and rulers of principalities, but rulers of principalities and kings cannot prevail over the universal emperor. Pāṇini has encapsulated all the rules governing the entire vocabulary of Sanskrit language along with meaning and relation between them (vocables and their meanings) within the 1000 couplets or verses or 4000 aphorisms (4 aphorisms make one couplet or verse).

IV. **Lexicon of appellative nouns (Uṇādigaṇa):** The course in Dhātupāṭha should be followed by the course in Uṇādigaṇa. Before taking the course in Uṇādigaṇa, a student must master or qualify the topic of nominal declensions as occurred in Pāṇini's Aṣṭādhyāyī. Afterwards, the second revision of Aṣṭādhyāyī focusing on clarifications of doubts, vārttikas (supplementary aphorisms by Katyāyana and Iṣṭikāras), paribhāṣās (definitions) should be carried out. (Recommended text is Kāśikā).

V. Commentary on Aṣṭādhyāyī (Mahābhāṣya): Lastly, a course in Mahābhāṣya must be offered. Sharp minded, intelligent, hardworking, and dedicated students can perfectly master the course in Aṣṭādhyāyī and Mahābhāṣya within three years and become eligible to learn and teach other Śāstras. The hard work as is required for learning grammar is not required for other

---

177 आतोऽनुपसर्गे कः- पा0 3.2.3

Śāstras. Whatever one can learn within three years due to mastery over the grammatical texts cited above cannot be learnt even in 50 years if we master the grammatical texts like Sārasvata Candrikā, Kaumudī, Manoramā etc. The reason is that the great sages of this country presented the most abstruse knowledge in a very simple and lucid manner, whereas the petty scholars are not capable of doing so.

The aim of great seers was to present knowledge, as far as possible, in a manner that it becomes easily comprehensible even to non-professionals in the shortest possible period. However, the petty scholars with mean mentality try to make their presentations as complex as possible, so that the learners gain little inspiration of hard work involving a lot of precious time. These books work on the theory of maximum input and minimum output. On the other hand, books written by sages gives us maximum output with minimal input.

VI. Etymology (Nirukta): After doing extremely well with grammar, one is required to study Nighanṭu and Nirukta composed by Yāska. They may devote six to eight months' time to excel the above texts. One may avoid unnecessary wastage of time in the study of Amarkoṣa, etc.

Note: Nighaṇṭu is Vedic lexicon and Nirukta is an etymological commentary on it. Etymology means to investigate the cultural, historical or scientific background behind the origin and development of words and phrases of a particular language.

VI. Metre (Chhanda): Students should now be taught Sanskrit metre. Chhandaśāstra composed by Piṅgala is the appropriate book for learning Vedic and Classical Sanskrit metres and to learn the composition of ślokas (poetry). This book can be mastered within four months only. It will be useless to spare time for the study of the books like 'Vṛttaratnākara' composed by lay scholars.

Post-Vedic literature: Further the study of Manusmṛti, Rāmāyaṇa, Mahābhārata till Udyogaparva and Vidurnīti etc. can be undertaken, so that one may get rid of evil tendencies and inculcate moral and ethical values. These texts may be taught along with metres, alaṅkāras, word-combinations, anvaya (sequence of words as per meaning), attributive epithets, nouns and the moral values involved therein. The study of the above texts may be completed within one year.

Philosophical texts (Six Systems of Indian Philosophy and Upaniṣad: Afterwards one can devote his precious time to the study of six systems of Indian philosophy like Pūrvamimānsā (or Mimānsā), Vaiśeṣika, Nyāya, Yoga, Sāṁkhya and Vedānta. For the study of these texts, commentaries of seers/sages or authentic scholars may be referred to. Here it is significant to note that prior to the study of Vedānta, a student is required to go through the following 10 Upaniṣads: Īśa, Kena, Kaṭha, Praśna, Muṇḍaka, Māṇḍukya, Aitareya, Śatapatha, Taittirīya, Chhāndogya and Bṛhadāraṇyaka. Two years are enough to complete the study of above philosophical texts.

Vedic Texts: After having studied philosophical texts, students should devote six years to study four Vedas and their Brāhmaṇas, i.e.

The *Aitareya Brāhmaṇa* of the *Ṛgveda*,

The *Śatapatha Brāhmaṇa* of the *Yajurveda*,

The *Sāma Brāhmaṇa* of the *Sāmaveda* and

The *Gopatha Brāhmaṇa* of the *Atharvaveda* along with accent, words, meanings, their relationship and verbal forms involved therein. The *Nirukta* (1.18) says:

स्थाणुरयं भारहारः किलाभू दधीत्य वेदं न विजानाति योऽर्थम्।
योऽर्थज्ञ इत्सकलं भद्रमश्नुते नाकमेति ज्ञानविधूतपाप्मा ।।

sthāṇurayaṁ bhārahāraḥ kilābhū dadhītya vedaṁ na vijānāti yo'rtham,
yo'rthajña itsakalaṁ bhadramaśnute nākameti jñānavidhūtapāpmā

[Meaning] One who recites Veda with an accent, but remains oblivious to its meaning, is like a pillar carrying the weight of a building. (He carries the weight like that of a tree carrying the weight of branches, leaves, fruits and flower or like that of an animal carrying burden on its back). On the other hand, one who knows the meaning of the Veda is blessed with all types of well-being, prosperity in life and attains emancipation hereafter having purged him of all evils by the knowledge of Veda.

The *Ṛgveda* (10.71.4) also states:

उत त्वः पश्यन्न ददर्श वाचमुत त्वः श्रृण्वन्न श्रृणोत्येनाम् ।
उतो त्वस्मै तन्वं१ वि सस्रे जायेव पत्य उशती सुवासाः ।।

uta tvaḥ paśyanna dadarśa vāchamuta tvaḥ śṛṇvanna śṛṇotyenām,
uto tvasmai tanvaṁ1 vi sasre jāyeva patya uśatī suvāsāḥ

[Meaning] A layman even while seeing the Veda documented in the form of creation cannot see (understand) it actually, even while listening it in the written form, cannot hear (understand) its meaning. On the other hand, the Veda expose its meaning to a deserving scholar, as if a well-dressed woman aspiring to join her husband exposes herself to him.

Further, the *Ṛgveda* (1.164.39) states:

ऋचो अक्षरे परमे व्योमन्यस्मिन्देवा अधि विश्वे निषेदुः ।
यस्तन्न वेद किमृचा करिष्यति य इत्तद्विदुस्त इमे समासते।

ṛcho akṣare parame vyomanyasmindevā adhi viśve niṣeduḥ,
yastanna veda kimṛchā kariṣyati ya ittadvidusta ime samāsate

[Meaning] The entire luminous universe resides in Almighty God, the Vedas containing knowledge of nitya padārthas speak of Him only. What will he, who knows not Brahman, do with the Vedas. One who doesn't know Brahman, what will Vedas do to him. Nevertheless, they who do know Him through Vedas, attains supreme bliss (are emancipated).

Hence, it is advisable that the study of Vedas without knowing their intended meaning is meaningless.

Upavedas: Thus having studied Vedas, one should resort to the study of Upavedas.

Ayurveda: The principles of Ayurveda consist in the books of Medical science like Charaka, Suṣruta, etc. composed by great seers and sages. One should learn within a period of 4 years theory and practice, instruments, surgery, therapeutics, materia medica, pathology, medicine, dietetics, anatomy, and characteristics of all things according to time and space.

Dhanurveda: Dhanurveda is the Science of Governance. It is divided into two parts - Official Administration and Public Administration. Official Administration consists of all Chiefs of Army, Navy and Airforce, arms and ammunition, military drills. Public Administration consists in protection and prosperity of civil life and property, an efficient judicial system for punishing the culprits and law-enforcing agency for maintaining law and order in society ensuring safety and security of common and noble men. One can learn the Science of Governance within two years.

Gāndharvaveda: Afterwards one can switch over to the study of Gādharvaveda, which is popularly known as science, and art of music and dance. One should learn properly, notes, tones, modes, modifications, time, harmony, measure, scale, tune, vocal and instrumental music and dance. Prominence may be given to chanting of Sāmagānas accompanying music. Books like Nārada Saṅhitā may be referred to, but one must avoid vulgar songs and pop music.

Arthaveda: Arthaveda is also known as what we call today as 'Science and Technology'. Properties and characterizes of various substances, technological know-how, developing various types of technology, comprehension of the laws of the matter right from the creation of the earth to celestial space and developing eco-friendly technology is the subject matter of Arthaveda.

Astronomy and Mathematics: Thereafter, one should thoroughly study the books on astronomy like Sūryasiddhānta, which includes arithmetic, algebra, geometry, geography and geology. It may take two years.

They should have a practical training in these sciences. They should also learn the proper handling and use of various machines and instruments. Here it may be advised that all books pertaining to astrological predictions based on planets and stars are false and fictitious. They should not form the part of the curriculum. There should be an effort on the part of teachers that the entire education is completed within 20 to 21 years so that students can thrive in their future life having acquired quality education. Here it may be borne in mind that the amount of knowledge that can be acquired within 20-21 years following the aforementioned scheme, cannot, otherwise, be acquired even within 100 years. The books composed by seers and sages have been recommended here because they were honest, generous, righteous and profound scholars who excelled in the field of their respective study. The scholars other than seers and sages have various limitations of time and space. They are more often than not narrow-minded and prejudicial to knowledge, as such their books are also not faultless and free from biases and prejudices. As such, following books are recommended.

Pūrvamimānsā with the commentary of Vyāsa Muni

Vaiśeṣika with a commentary of Gotam Muni

Nyāya Sūtras with a commentary of Vātsyāyana Muni

Yoga Sūtras with the commentary of Vyāsa Muni

Sāṅkhya Sūtra with the commentary of Kapil Muni

Vedānta Sūtra with the commentary of Vātsyāyana Muni or Baudhāyana Muni.

These Sūtra texts may be counted as the parts of Kalpa Sūtras.

Four Vedas- Ṛgveda, Yajurveda, Sāmaveda and Atharvaveda are the books of knowledge. Knowledge is the attribute of God. He is all knowing. As such, the authorship of knowledge can be assigned only to God. So authorship of Vedas is assigned to God.

Four Brāhmaṇas-Aitareya, Śatapatha, Sāma and Gopatha

Six Vedaṅgas- Śikṣā (Phonetics), Kalpa (Sūtra Literature like Dharma Sūtras, Gṛhya Sūtras, Śrauta Sūtras, Śulva Sūtras), Vyākaraṇa (Grammar), Nighanṭu (Vedic Lexicon), Nirukta (Etymology), Chhanda (Metre) and Jyotiṣa (Astronomy)

Six systems of Indian philosophy known as Upāṅgas

Upvedas-Arthaveda, Dhanurveda, Gāndharvaveda and Āyurveda

All the above-mentioned books except Vedas are authored by seers and sages. Therefore, their authority is acceptable in-so-far-as they conform to the Vedas. If they contain anything contrary to Vedas, that should be discarded. Since Vedas (pure knowledge) are authored by God, they are homo-mensura. Rest of the texts is dependent on Veda for their authority. Vedas have specifically been dealt with in Ṛgvedādibhāṣyabhūmikā. You may refer to it for the same. Rest will be delineated in this book.

Now you can keep track of the books, which are of spurious nature and so worth to be discarded. These books are:

Grammar: Kātantra, Sārsvata, Chandrikā, Mugdhabodha, Kaumudī, Śekhara, Manoramā, etc.

Lexicons: the Amarkoṣa

Metre: the Vṛttaratnākara

Phonetics: Books commencing with 'Now I explain phonetics of Pāṇini'

Astronomy: Śighrabodha, Muhurtta-cintāmaṇi, etc.

Poetry: Nāyikābheda, Kuvalayānanda, Raghuvañśa, Meghadūtam, Kirātārjunīyam, etc.

Mīmānsā: Dharmasindhu, Vratārkā, etc.

Vaiśeṣika: Tarkasaṅgraha, etc.

Nyāya: Jāgadīśī, etc.

Yoga: Haṭha-yoga-pradīpikā, etc.

Sāṅkhya: Sāṅkhya-tattva-kumudī, etc.

Vedānta: Yogavāsiṣṭha, Pañcadaśī etc.

Medicine: Śāraṅgadhara, etc.

Smṛtis: All Smṛtis and interpolated sections of Manusmṛti

All Tantra Texts

All Purāṇas

All sub-Purāṇas

Rāmacaritmānas of Tulsidāsa

Rukmaṇi-maṅgala, etc.

Question: Do you mean to say that there is no truth in these books?

Answer: There is some truth, but the amount of untruth is far greater. Like poisoned food, they are worthy to be discarded.

Question: Don't you accept the Purāṇa and Itihāsa?

Answer: Yes, I do, but only the valid texts and not the forged ones.

Question: How do you distinguish between valid and forged ones?

Answer: The Gṛhya Sūtra (Āśvalāyana Gṛhya Sūtra, 3.3.1) quotes:

ब्राह्मणानीतिहासान् पुराणानि कल्पान् गाथा नाराशंसीरिति ।

brāhmaṇānītihāsān purāṇāni kalpān gāthā nārāśaṁsīriti

[Meaning] Brāhmaṇa, Itihāsa, Purāṇas, Kalpas, Gāthā, Nārāśansī, etc.

This statement implies that Itihāsa, Purāṇa, Kalpa, Gāthā and Nārāśansī form the parts of Brāhmaṇa texts only. Śrimad Bhāgvad, etc. cannot be called Purāṇas.

Question: Why don't we accept truth found even in the spurious books?

Answer: Whatever truth they contain has actually come from authentic Śāstras like the Vedas. On the other hand, whatever is false is fabricated by their concerned authors. Accepting true Śāstras like Vedas means accepting the whole truth. If one strives to garner truth from the bundle of lies, he cannot claim to have immunity from untruth. So the truth of a book complemented by untruth needs to be abandoned as if pure food adulterated with poison has to be set aside.

Question: What is your opinion?

Answer: We comply with whatever is ordained in the Vedas. Since Vedas are acceptable to us, so our opinion is based on Vedas. All human beings, especially Aryans, should follow this view and express their unity.

Question: Even the Śāstras composed by seers and sages contain an element of both truth and untruth and have contradictions like other books composed by lay scholars. For example, six systems of Indian philosophy contradict each other on the question of creation.

According to Mīmānsā, karma is the cause of creation.

As per Vaiśeṣika darśana, time is the cause of creation.

Nyāya identifies atom as the cause of creation.

Yoga considers penance or energy (tapaḥ) as the prime cause of creation.

Saṅkhya finds primordial matter as the cause of creation.

Vedānta holds Brahman as the cause of creation.

Is this not contradiction?

Answer: First of all, you should bear in mind that none of the six systems, except Sāṅkhya and Vedānta, deals with the subject of creation. Secondly, there is no contradiction in their statements. The problem is that you have no concept of contradiction and conformity. Let me ask you, whether contradiction involves one subject or different subjects.

Question: Contradiction involves different statements made on the same subject. In this case, also we have one subject, that of creation.

Answer: Is there only one knowledge or many? If knowledge is one, then why do we have different disciplines, like grammar, medicine, astronomy, etc. For example, one knowledge may have many branches that are treated separately from each other. Similarly, the subject of creation has six different branches to be treated in six different Śāstras. It cannot be called a contradiction.

Let's take the case of an earthen pot. Six different causes take part in the making of an earthen pot. They are action, (karma), time, clay (material), desire, energy (tapaḥ) required for mixing and unmixing of different materials, properties of matter and Potter. Similarly in case of creation,

Mīmānsā deals with the subject of action required for creation.

Vaiśeṣika concentrates on the subject of time factors involved in creation.

Nyāya takes up the study of the subject of material cause.

Yoga studies the subject of penance or energy (tapaḥ)

Saṅkhya deals with properties of matter and its

evolution.

Vedānta takes up into consideration the subject of Brahman as efficient cause and His desire to give birth to creation[178].

There is least contradiction. You can also take for example the medical science. In it, the disciplines of pathology, therapeutics, administration of medicine and dietetics are separately discussed, but their aim is same, i.e. curing the disease. Similarly, there are six factors involved in creation. Each factor is treated by each author of six systems of Indian philosophy. Therefore, there is no basic contradiction between them. This subject will be explained in detail in the chapter dealing with 'Creation'.

Now we shall discuss impediments in teaching and learning process. They are to be avoided at any cost. For example, bad company, drinking, prostitution, child marriage (that is say, marriage before marriageable age - 25 years for male and 16 years for female), lack of complete celibacy, lack of political will-power and public

---

[178] There are many references in Brāhmaṇas which hold Brahman and His desire as the efficient cause of creation, e.g.

so' kāmayat bahusyām prajāyeyeti.

'He, for the sake of creation, desired to produce himself in many.'

tadaikṣat bahusyām prajāyeyeti.

'He thought to manifest Himself in many.'

'sa īkṣat lokānnusṛjā iti. sa imāñllokānusṛjata.

'He thought to create the universe. He created the universe.'

interest in promoting Vedic education, excessive eating and waking, observance of lethargy in teaching and learning and commission of unfair means during exams, not making education number one priority, lack of political will in boosting physical power, intellectual activities, courage, health, and economic prosperity, wasting unnecessary time in visiting temples, mosques, churches in place of meditating upon one Almighty Power, showing disrespect to parents, peripatetic monks, teachers and scholars, having neglected the professional duties (Varṇa) and social obligations (Aśrama), getting involved in superstitious ritual practices like observance of particular religious dress code and wearing other religious symbols, etc., blind faith in pilgrimages, gods and goddesses, escaping from education on being taken in by the oily tongues of the hypocrites and quacks, seeking possibilities of salvation through hearing and reading the stories of Purāṇas, instead of following proper means of knowledge acquisition, yoga and meditation, greed for money but lack of concern for spiritual education, killing time in unnecessary wanderings. Thus having involved in the above-cited useless activities, people deprive themselves of the benefit to be gained through knowledge acquisition and push themselves to various afflictions and acts of foolishness.

Present day communal minded Brahmins obsessed with stakes distract the mind of innocent people from real education and set a trap for them to exploit them mentally, physically and financially. For the fear of being exposed they never want people from other Varṇas to be educated. Thus, the state and the society should use every resource available to have these impediments removed so that youngsters can easy access to quality education.

Question: Should women and Śudras be educated in Vedas? Should they be educated, then what we will do? Moreover, there is no authority that endorses their education. They are prohibited from being educated. For instance,

स्त्रीशूद्रौ नाधीयातामिति श्रुतेः ।

strīśūdrau nādhīyātāmiti śruteḥ.

[Meaning] Women and Śudras must not be taught as per Vedic ordination.

Answer: Everybody irrespective of gender and Varṇa (professional class) has the right to education. You and your authority go to hell. This is not an actual authority but a satanic verse. The right to education for all has been clearly sanctioned in the Yajurveda (26.2) as under:

यथेमां वाचं कल्याणीमावदानि जनेभ्यः ।
ब्रह्मराजन्याभ्या शूद्राय चार्याय च स्वाय चारणाय ।।

yathemāṁ vāchaṁ kalyāṇīmāvadāni janebhyaḥ,
brahmarājanyābhyā śūdrāya chāryāya cha svāya chāraṇāya.

[Meaning] Just as God reveal this auspicious Vedic wisdom to the humanity at large, so you do irrespective of consideration of Brāhmaṇa, Kṣatrīya, Vaiśya, Śudras and women or servants.

Question: Here one may raise a query that in the above mantra the term 'jana' doesn't stand for humanity at large, rather it signifies twice born (Brahmaṇa, Kṣatrīya, Vaiśya) alone as the Smṛtis permit right to education only to Brahmaṇas, Kṣatrīyas and Vaiśyas and not to women and Śudras.

Answer: See, it is ordained by Veda itself, that Brahmaṇa, Rajanya (Kṣatrīya), Śudra, Arya (Vaiśya), Sva (women) and Araṇa (servants) all are entitled to be educated in Vedas. The meaning thereby is that each and everybody having excelled himself/herself in the Vedic education, practised virtue, shunned vice and consequently been freed from all sorrow and pain should lead a happy life. Now let us know, should we believe you or God (Veda)? Of course, God will be given preference. Even if you hold on to your flawed view, you will be no better than an atheist will, because an atheist is a non-believer in the Veda[179]. Do you mean, God doesn't want to protect the interest of ʃudras. Do you mean, God is so biased or prejudiced that He would permit twice born to study Veda and deny that privilege to ʃudras. Had God intended ʃudras not to study Veda or hear it read, He would not have endowed them with the ability to speak and hear. Just as God created cosmic bounties for the benefit of all, He also inspired Vedic wisdom for everyone to use. Where a prohibition is for a person who is unable to learn formally in an academic setting and not because of his social status. When you deny women the right to an education that is because of your foolishness, selfishness and lack of understanding. Let me quote an authority from *Atharvaveda* (11.5.18) endorsing the right to education for women.

ब्रह्मचर्य्येण कन्या युवानं विन्दते पतिम् ।

brahmacharyyeṇa kanyā yuvānaṁ vindate patim.

[Meaning] Having been educated, let a young woman choose her spouse in a similar manner as a young man chooses his spouse after having lived a student life.

Thus, the women are also entitled to education and leading a student life.

Question: Are women entitled to chant the Veda-

---

179 नास्तिको वेदनिन्दकः ।

mantras?

Answer: Yes, of course. Listen to what the Śrauta Sūtra says:

इमं मन्त्रं पत्नी पठेत्।

imaṁ mantraṁ patnī paṭhet.

[Meaning] Let this mantra be chanted by the wife.

If women is uneducated, how can she pronounce mantras with proper accent and speak Sanskrit sentences in Yajñas? There is a clear-cut evidence of Śatapatha Brāhmaṇa (14.6.6) that Gārgī and other women who are considered to be jewels among women of India, attained the highest education in the Vedic field.

If either of the spouses is illiterate, they will never be able to execute their functions satisfactorily and the result will be constant friction. Similarly, if women remain illiterate, who would teach in Girls' Schools and who would substitute them while executing delicate functions related to women in Government and Judiciary? Even the delineated household duties cannot be carried out satisfactorily for want of proper education.

There are proofs that women of ruling class in India were well versed in Dhanurveda and military science. Had this not been the case, how would Kaikeyī have accompanied her husband, Daśaratha in the battlefield and fought the war? So, a lady coming from family of Brāhmaṇa professionals must learn all sciences, a lady coming from the family of Kṣatrīya professionals must also take course in all sciences in addition to military science and administration, a lady coming from the family of Vaiśya professionals (marketing or merchant class) must go for business management and business administration and a lady coming from the family of Śudra professionals (agriculturist, art and craft viz.

technology, engineering and architecture) must at the least take a course in home science and food technology.

A Man should, at the least, attend a course in grammar, law (dharma) and a profession of his choice. Similarly, a woman is required to take a course, at the least, in grammar, law (dharma), medicine, arithmetic, arts and craft. Without these skills, a woman would not be able to deliver properly while dealing with (1) the question of right and wrong, (2) her spouse, (3) while being in family way, (4) bringing up and educating children, (5) managing affairs of home, (6) preparing or supervising preparation of nutritious meals following the rules of medical science, so that everyone at home can live hale and hearty.

For want of initiation into arts and craft, a woman would not be able to supervise the construction of a house and order designs of outfits and jeweller. For want of knowledge of arithmetic, she would not be able to maintain family budget and accounts properly. Lack of the knowledge of Vedas and other Śāstras will bar her from understanding the real nature of God and ignorance of the law (dharma) may lead her to commit unlawful acts.

Therefore, blessed are those parents and worthy to be hailed, who have done their best to make their children eligible to observe celibacy, acquire quality education and knowledge and gather physical and spiritual power. Such youngsters would be able to establish a cordial relationship within family and society. The knowledge is an inexhaustible treasure. The more you give of it, the more it grows. All other treasures are subject to exhaust on being spent. They are also sometimes shared by the inheritors. The treasure of knowledge cannot have any inheritor, nor can it be stolen by thieves. Knowledge is the subject of both state and society. It grows if funded and protected by state and society together. Manu (7.152) says-

कन्यानां सम्प्रदानं च कुमाराणां च रक्षणम्।

kanyānāṁ sampradānaṁ cha kumārāṇāṁ cha rakṣaṇam.

[Meaning] It is duty of state to enact a law to impart quality education to all eligible male and female students at a proper time.

If any parent disobeys this rule, they are liable to be prosecuted. As per rule, no boy or girl should be allowed to stay back home after the age group of eight, instead, they should be sent to schools under the care of their respective teachers. In addition, no student should be allowed to undergo nuptial bond before graduation. Stressing upon the importance of education, Manu (4.233) says:

सर्वेषामेव दानानां ब्रह्मदानं विशिष्यते।
वार्यन्नगोमहीवासस्तिलकाञ्चनसर्पिषाम्।

sarveṣāmeva dānānāṁ brahmadānaṁ viśiṣyate.
vāryannagomahīvāsastilakāñchanasarpiṣām

[Meaning] The gift of knowledge/education is far superior to gifts of water, food, cows, land, clothes, sesame, and gold and clarified butter.

Therefore, everyone must try his/her best to help disseminate knowledge of physical aid, moral support and financial assistance.

That country alone prospers where chastity is practised, moral values are promoted, quality education is imparted, knowledge is keenly sought after and Vedic laws are followed.

In the foregoing pages, we have offered a brief discourse on the education pertaining to Brahmacaryāśrama (student life). In the next chapter, we shall focus on Graduation, Marriage and Gṛhāśrama (family life).

इति श्रीमद्दयानन्दसरस्वतीस्वामिकृते सत्यार्थप्रकाशे सुभाषाविभूषिते शिक्षाविषये तृतीयः समुल्लासः सम्पूर्णः ।।३।।

iti śrīmaddayānandasarasvatīsvāmikṛte satyārthaprakāśe subhāṣāvibhūṣite śikṣāviṣaye tṛtīyaḥ samullāsaḥ sampūrṇaḥ.

Thus, herein, ends Third Chapter titled as 'Formal Education in Brahmacarya Āśrama'of Satyarth Prakash of Maharshi Dayanand Saraswati.

The world is fettered by the chain forged by superstition and ignorance. I have come to snap asunder that chain and to set slaves at liberty. It is contrary to my mission to have people deprived of their freedom.

Swami Dayanand Saraswati

CHAPTER 4

अथ समावर्त्तनविवाहगृहाश्रमविधिं वक्ष्यामः ।

atha samāvarttanavivāhagṛhāśramavidhiṁ vakṣayāmaḥ

Now we begin to explain school leaving, marriage and family life.

Brahmacharya or Student life

वेदानधीत्य वेदौ वा वेदं वाऽपि यथाक्रमम् ।
अविप्लुतब्रह्मचर्यो गृहस्थाश्रममावसेत् ॥ मनु. 3.2 ॥

vedānadhītya vedau vā vedaṁ vā'pi yathākramam,
aviplutabrahmacharyo gṛhasthāśramamāvaset.

Manu. 3.2 .

[Meaning] A student who has conducted himself/herself duly according to the advice of his/her Āchārya/Āchāryā and has studied in due order all the four Vedas or three, or two, or even one only, without breaking the (rules of Brahmacharya (studentship), shall enter the Gṛhāśrama (married life).

तं प्रतीतं स्वधर्मेण ब्रह्मदायहरं पितुः ।
स्रग्विणं तल्प आसीनमर्हयेत् प्रथमं गवा ॥ मनु. 3.3 ॥

taṁ pratītaṁ svadharmeṇa brahmadāyaharaṁ pituḥ,
sragviṇaṁ talpa āsīnamarhayet prathamaṁ gavā.

Manu. 3.3.

[Meaning] He/she who has successfully discharged his/her duties towards his/her Āchārya/Āchāryā and has received his/her education from his/her spiritual father (teacher), shall first honour his/her Āchārya/Āchāryā sitting on a couch and adorned with a garland, with (the present of) a cow. The student also deserves the similar gift of a cow from his/her father in law.

गुरुणानुमतः स्नात्वा समावृत्तो यथाविधि ।
उद्वहेत द्विजो भार्यां सवर्णां लक्षणान्विताम् ॥ मनु. 3.4 ॥

guruṇānumataḥ snātvā samāvṛtto yathāvidhi,
udvaheta dvijo bhāryāṁ savarṇāṁ lakṣaṇānvitām.

Manu. 3.4.

[Meaning] Having undergone the convocation ceremony with the permission of his Guru (teacher), and performed Samāvartana Sanskāra (the rite of Home returning), a dvija (a student who has completed his formal and professional education) shall marry an educated and talented spouse of his own Varṇa (equal to him in qualifications, profession and temperament).

असपिण्डा च या मातुरसगोत्रा च या पितुः ।
सा प्रशस्ता द्विजातीनां दारकर्मणि मैथुने ॥ मनु. 3.5 ॥

asapiṇḍā cha yā māturasagotrā cha yā pituḥ,
sā praśastā dvijātīnāṁ dārakarmaṇi maithune.

Manu. 3.5.

[Meaning] A girl who is neither a Sapiṇḍa on the mother's side (who does not belong to the gotra of six generations of boy's mother's side i.e.

mother gotra

mother's mother gotra

mother's mother's mother gotra

mother's mother's mother's mother gotra

mother's mother's mother's mother's mother gotra

mother's mother's mother's mother's mother's

mother gotra

nor belongs to the gotra of his father, is eligible for wedlock and conjugal union.

The purpose behind this type of marriage is explained in Śatpatha Brāhmaṇa which states:

परोक्षप्रिया इव हि देवाः प्रत्यक्षद्विषः ।
parokṣapriyā iva hi devāḥ pratyakṣadviṣaḥ.

[Meaning] Scholars have an attraction for the unknown, rather than known.

It is also a fact that love for the unknown is more intense as compared to known. For instance, a person who has heard about the characteristics of Miśri (a kind of sugar candy), but never tasted it, he would always think about it; or when we hear a praise of a person, who is not known to us, we are tempted to meet him. Similarly, a man should marry a girl, who comes from a distant family and is not a near relative either of his paternal family or maternal family. The advantages and disadvantages of distant and near marriages

The advantages and disadvantages of distant and near marriages are as under:

The children who have lived together, since their infancy, sporting, quarrelling, loving each other, knowing each other's temperament, virtues and vices of daily life and who have seen each other even in nude form cannot attract each other after their marriage.

The marriage between the parties belonging to the same paternal gotra (clan) or maternal gotra does not improve the race for want of interchange of dhatus (ingredients) of the body, as a mixture of two types waters doesn't make a specific difference.

As the addition of sugar and such medicines as ginger

improves the taste and quality of milk, so does the marriage of people belonging to different paternal or maternal gotras, improve the race.

Just as the change of climate improves the health of a sick person, so does the change of gotra of marrying parties improves the race.

The matrimonial alliance between the close relatives may unnecessary involve them even into their minor problems, setting a stage for a tense relationship. This is not possible in a matrimonial alliance between distant families. Moreover, distant matrimonial alliances often extend the sphere of friendship.

The distant matrimonial alliances give one an opportunity to understand distant cultures and to have an access to distant objects and places, which is not possible in a matrimonial alliance between close relatives. Perhaps, that is why, a daughter, in Sanskrit, is called

दुहिता दुर्हिता दूरे हिता भवतीति | निरु०|

duhitā durhitā dūre hitā bhavatīti. Nirukta

[Meaning] A girl is called *duhitā,* because her marriage to a distant gotra or place is beneficial.

The parental family of the bride may have to spend a lot of money by way of gifts given by them to their daughter for her repeated quick visits. If they are not rich enough, this may adversely affect their economic condition.

The matrimonial alliance between parties settled nearby may cause altercations quickly even on the non-significant trivial issue. On a slight misunderstanding, the wife may immediately desert her husband and repair to her parent's house, as women are generally short-tempered and sensitive. Due to the above reasons, it is not advisable to enter into a nuptial knot should the bride belongs either to the gotra of bridegroom's father or the gotras of sex generations of bridegroom's mother's side or the families of both live close by.

महान्त्यपि समृद्धानि गोऽजाविधनधान्यतः ।
स्त्रीसम्बन्धे दशैतानि कुलानि परिवर्जयेत् ॥ मनु.3.6

mahāntyapi samṛddhāni go'jāvidhanadhānyataḥ,
strīsambandhe daśaitāni kulāni parivarjayet.

Manu, 3.6

[Meaning] While going for the conjugal alliance, following ten families be avoided, be they ever so great in political power or rank, or ever so blessed with riches, cattle, property, gold or grain.

हीनक्रियं निश्पुरुषं निश्छन्दो रोमशार्शसम् ।
क्षयामयाव्य्ऽपस्मारिश्वित्रिकुष्ठिकुलानि च ॥ मनु. **3.7** ॥

hīnakriyaṁ niśpuruṣaṁ niśchhando romaśārśasam,
kṣayāmayāvy'pasmāriśvitrikuṣṭhikulāni cha.

Manu, 3.7.

[Meaning] The families are:
The family which performs no righteous act.

The family which is devoid of men of character

The family which has neglected the study of Veda

The Family whose family members have long and thick hair on the body

The family whose family members are suffering from such diseases as piles, tuberculosis, asthma, bronchitis, dyspepsia, epilepsy, leprosy, and advance leprosy; because all these diseases are transmitted genetically to the offspring.

नोद्वहेत् कपिलां कन्यां नाधिकाङ्गीं न रोगिणीम् ।
नालोमिकां नातिलोमां न वाचाटां न पिङ्गलाम् ॥ मनु. 3.8

nodvahet kapilāṁ kanyāṁ nādhikāṅgīṁ na rogiṇīm,
nālomikāṁ nātilomāṁ na vāchāṭāṁ na piṅgalām.

Manu, 3.8

[Meaning] Let a man never marry one who is pale and anaemic, nor one who is hexadactyly (having one extra sixth finger or toe), nor one who is sick, nor one who is with hair either too little or too much, nor one who is immoderately talkative, nor one with brown or inflamed eyes.

नर्क्षवृक्षनदीनाम्नीं नान्त्यपर्वतनामिकाम् ।
न पक्ष्यहिप्रेष्यनाम्नीं न च भीषणनामिकाम् ॥ मनु. 3.9

narkṣavṛkṣanadīnāmnīṁ nāntyaparvatanāmikām,

na pakṣayahipreṣyanāmnīṁ na cha bhīṣaṇanāmikām. manu. 3.9

[Meaning] 1. Let a man never marry one with the name of constellations like Bharani, Rohini, Ashwini, Revati bai, Chittari etc.

2. One with the name of a tree, like Tulsi, Gendā, Champā, Chameli

3. One with the name of a river, like Gaṅgā, Yamunā etc.

4. One with the name of a mountain, like Vindhya, Himalaya, Pārvati

5. One bearing a name of aliens, incorporated into Indian society very late, like Fiza, Cleopatra, etc.

6. One named after a bird, like Kokil, Menā, etc.

7. One named after a snake, like Nāgī, Bhujaṅgā, Ahimāyā etc.

8. One with the name ending in words denoting a slave, like Mādhodāsī, Mīrādāsī, etc.

9. One with a dreadful or horrible name, like Chaṇḍikā, Kālī, Bhimkunvari, etc.These names are dreadful and belong to other things as well.

अव्यङ्गाङ्गीं सौम्यनाम्नीं हंसवारणगामिनीम् ।
तनुलोमकेशदशनां मृद्वङ्गीमुद्वहेत् स्त्रियम् ॥ मनु. 3.10 ॥

avyaṅgāṅgīṁ saumyanāmnīṁ haṁsavāraṇagāminīm,
tanulomakeśadaśanāṁ mṛdvaṅgīmudvahet striyam.

Manu, 3.10

[Meaning] Let him choose for his wife, a girl who has a graceful figure without any deformity, who has a pretty name, who walks gracefully like a swan or an elephant, who has fine hair and lovely teeth, and whose body is exquisitely soft."

Age for marriage

Question: What is the best age for marriage and what kind of marriage is deemed best?

Answer: The best age for marriage of a girl is from the sixteenth to the twenty-fourth year and for a man, from the twenty-fifth to the forty-eighth year. The marriage of a girl of sixteen to a man of twenty-five years is called Inferior marriage. Of a girl of eighteen to twenty with a man of thirty-five to forty is called medium marriage. Of a girl of twenty-four with a man of forty-eight is called superior marriage.

The best kind of marriage is that by choice (Swayaṁvara), after the education of the contracting parties is finished and their Brahmacharya for the aforesaid period completed. Happy is the country wherein the people devote themselves to the pursuit of knowledge, live chaste lives, and adopt the aforesaid form of marriage. Down into the depths of misery sinks that country wherein the people do not practice

Brahmacharya, nor acquire knowledge, where early marriage and marriage between the unsuitable, are prevalent, for, marriage preceded by the practice of Brahmacharya and perfection of knowledge is the basis of all true reform and the source of all true happiness; the reverse of it brings absolute ruin of people who follow it.

Question:

अष्टवर्षा भवेद् गौरी नववर्षा च रोहिणी।
दशवर्षा भवेत्कन्या तत ऊर्ध्वं रजस्वलाम् ||१||
aṣṭavarṣā bhaved gaurī navavarṣā cha rohiṇī,
daśavarṣā bhavetkanyā tata ūrdhva rajasvalām

माता चैव पिता तस्या ज्येष्ठो भ्राता तथैव च |
त्रायस्ते नरकं यान्ति दृष्ट्वा कन्यां रजस्वलाम्भ्||२||

mātā chaiva pitā tasyā jyeṣṭho bhrātā tathaiva cha dya,
trāyaste narakaṁ yānti dṛṣṭvā kanyāṁ rajasvalāmbh

The above verses are from the text of Parāśara and Śīghrabodha. The very meaning is:

[Meaning] A girl at the age of eight is called Gaurī, at nine, Rohiṇī, at ten, Kanyā and thereafter she reaches the stage of puberty. If she is not married before she reaches puberty, her father, mother and elder brother are destined to go to hell.

Answer:

एकक्षणा भवेद् गौरी द्विक्षणेयन्तु रोहिणी।
त्रिक्षणा सा भवेत्कन्या ह्यत ऊर्ध्वं रजस्वला ||१||

ēkakṣaṇā bhaved gaurī dvikṣaṇeyantu rohiṇī।
trikṣaṇā sā bhavetkanyā hyata ūdhrvaṁ rajasvalā

माता पिता तथा भ्राता मातुलो भगिनी स्वका |
सर्वे ते नरकं यान्ति दृष्ट्वा कन्यां रजस्वलाम्भ ||२||
mātā pitā tathā bhrātā mātulo bhaginī svakā,
sarve te narakaṁ yānti dṛṣṭvā kanyāṁ rajasvalāmbha.

These verses belong to Brahma Purāṇa (just composed by us) which say:

[Meaning] In one second after birth, a girl is called Gaurī, in two seconds she becomes Rohiṇī, in three, Kanyā, and thereafter reaches puberty. If she be not married till she reaches puberty, her father, mother, brother, sister and maternal uncle, all are cursed with hell.

Question: The verses, you have quoted, are not authentic.

Answer: Why are they not authentic? If Brahmā's verses are not authentic how could yours be?

Question: Well! Well! Do you not hold even Parāśara and Kāśīnātha as authorities?

Answer: Do you not hold Brahmā an authority? Is Brahma not greater than Parāśara and Kāśīnātha? If you have no faith in Brahmā, why do we have in your Parāśara and Kāśīnātha.

Question: Your verse cannot be held authentic, as it talks about something which is practically impossible. Thousands of seconds are taken in child's birth alone, how could a girl, then, be married when she is only one, two or three seconds old; nor the very purpose of marriage can be served at that stage.

Answer: If our verses talk something which is practically impossible, so do yours; because a marriage even at the age of eight, nine, or ten years is useless, for it is only at the age of twenty-five year, that a man's body is matured and achieves reproductive capabilities; and it is at the age of sixteen, that a woman's body also matures into an adult body with all her reproductive organs fully developed.

All support systems necessary to permit a child to fully develop are not in place in a girl of eight years. (The modern researches have also proved that girls who become pregnant before the age of 16 have a 40-times greater risk of dying during childbirth. They are also more likely to give birth to premature babies). Besides naming girls, as, Gaurī (fair), and Rohiṇī (red) is simply absurd, because a girl may be dark as well as fair. Again Gaurī was the wife of Mahādeva and Rohiṇī of Vasudeva, whom Paurāṇika Hindus regard as mothers. If you name a girl child as Gaurī and Rohiṇī, how could it be possible and justified to marry them?

It follows, therefore, that both your verses and ours are interpolations. Just as we interpolated few verses and ascribed them to Brahmā, so also other people interpolated them in the name of Parāśara and other sages. It is, therefore, advisable to reject all these so-called authorities and go by the authority of the Veda alone in all matters.

Let me quote Manu (9.90):

त्रीणि वर्षाण्युदीक्षेत कुमार्यृतुमती सती।
ऊर्ध्वं तु कालादेतस्माद्विन्देत सदृशं पतिम्।।

trīṇi varṣāṇyudīkṣeta kumāryṛtumatī satī,
ūrdhvaṁ tu kālādetasmādvindeta sadṛśaṁ patim.

[Meaning] Let a girl having reached the age of puberty wait for at least another three years for marriage to a person who is a suitable match for her in terms of qualification, profession and temperament.

As menstruation cycle takes place every month, thus having attained 36 menstruation cycles in 3 years, a girl becomes marriageable but not before that.

काममामरणात्तिष्ठेद् गृहे कन्यर्तुमत्यपि।
न चैवैनां प्रयच्छेत्तु गुणहीनाय कर्हिचित्।। मनु० 9.89

kāmamāmaraṇāttiṣṭhed gṛhe kanyartumatyapi,
na chaivaināṁ prayachchhettu guṇahīnāya karhichit.

Manu, 9.89

[Meaning] It is better for a girl or a boy though being marriageable to remain unmarried life long, than to marry a spouse who is a mismatch for them,i.e. destitute of equal qualification, profession and temperament.

All this goes to prove that it is not proper that marriages before aforesaid period, or of unsuitable, should ever take place.

Question: Should marriage be under the control of parents or the spouses?

Answer: It is advisable that marriage should take place with the mutual consent of spouses. If parents ever think of match-making, it should be with the approval of the spouses. When people are free to choose their life partners themselves, there is less likelihood of dissention and the children born of such unions are of superior quality.

The dissention is the cause of distress. Marriage serves the purpose of wife and husband and not that of their parents. If they (wife and husband) are happy with their marriage, they enjoy, nor suffer.

सन्तुष्टो भार्यया भर्त्ता भर्त्रा भार्य्या तथैव च।
यस्मिन्नेव कुले नित्यं कल्याणं तत्र वै ध्रुवम्।। मनु० 3.60

santuṣṭo bhāryayā bharttā bhartra bhāryyā tathaiva cha
yasminneva kule nityaṁ kalyāṇaṁ tatra vai dhruvam.

Manu, 3.60

[Meaning] That family is permanently blessed with fortune, festivities and prosperity, where a husband and wife are well pleased with each other. (Otherwise it is cursed with poverty and misery).

So the tradition of Swayaṁvara (marriage by self-choice) as is prevalent in Āryāvartta, is the best form of marriage. Before two people are locked in wedding, there should be a compatibility analysis in terms of their qualifications, conduct, character, figure, age, health, family and physique. Until and unless there is a compatibility with regard to above-cited factors, the marriage doesn't end in happiness, nor can a child marriage do so.

युवा सुवासाः परिवीत आगात्स उ श्रेयान्भवति जायमानः ।
तं धीरासः कवय उन्नयन्ति स्वाध्यो मनसा दवे यन्तः ।। ऋ. 3.8.4

yuvā suvāsāḥ parivīta āgātsa u śreyānbhavati jāyamānaḥ,
taṁ dhīrāsaḥ kavaya unnayanti svādhyo manasā dave yantaḥ. *RV. 3.8.4*

[Meaning] (yuvā) A young man/woman (āgāt) who enters Gṛhastha Āśrama (married life) (parivīta) having initiated into all-round knowledge and (suvāsā) well clad. (sa bhavati) He/she is (śreyān) honoured and blessed with fortune (jāyamānaḥ) in his/her married life. (dhirāsaḥ kavayaḥ) Steadfast scholars (tama devayantaḥ) wishing his/her well-being (unnayanti) guide him/her to the path of social and spiritual progress.

He/she who marries without committing himself/herself to proper Brahmacharya, knowledge and education, or who do so at an early age, is absolutely ruined, nor are they ever respected by the wise and the learned.

आ धेनवों धुनयन्तामशिश्वीः सबर्दुघाः शशया अप्रदुग्धाः ।
नव्यांनव्या युवतयो भवंन्तीर्महद्देवानांमसुरत्वमेकंम् ॥ ऋ. 3.55.16
ā dhenavo dhunayantāmaśiśvīḥ sabardughāḥ śaśayā apradugdhāḥ,
navyānavyā yuvatayo bhavantīrmahaddevānāmasura-

tvamekam.

[Meaning] (yuvatayaḥ) Let girls, (apradugdhāḥ dhenavaḥ) who are virgins, resembling cows that have never been milked before, (aśiśvī) who have crossed the age of childhood and (śaśayāḥ) have reached the age of matured adult, who are (navyā-navyā bhavanti) in their full bloom of youth, (sabardughāḥ) who are capable to bear all the responsibilities of married life, and who, by the practice of Brahmacharya, have attained (ekam, mahat, asuratvam) a state of excellence (devānām) which is attained only by high profile scholars, should marry husbands of mature age and (adhunyantām) bear children.

Never should they think of contacting men even in their dreams in their childhood. This alone can give them happiness here and hereafter. Early marriage is even more harmful to a woman than to a man.

पूर्वीरहं शरदः शश्रमाणा दोषावस्तो रुषसो जरयन्तीः ।
मिनाति श्रियं जरिमा तनूनामप्यू नु पत्नीर्वृषाणो जगम्युः ।। ऋ० 1.171.1

pūrvīrahaṁ śaradaḥ śaśramāṇā doṣāvasto ruṣaso jarayantīḥ,
mināti śriyaṁ jarimā tanūnāmapyū nu patnīrvṛṣāṇo jagamyuḥ. *RV. 1.171.1*

[Meaning] Man and woman (vṛṣaṇaḥ) having attained maturity in reproductive capabilities, (jagamyuḥ) and having married to each other in their matured adulthood should act in such a way as to complete 100 years of their life blessed with children and grandchildren. Just as (śaradaḥ) seasons, (uṣasaḥ) mornings and evenings, (doṣāvastoḥ) days and nights, all tend to (mināti) take away (jarimā) the age and (śriyam) the beauty (tanūnām) of the bodies in due course of time, so should (aham) I, man and a woman, (api) determine to marry in due course of time after acquiring (u) proper knowledge and physical strength by observing Brahmacharya.

Violation of this rule is a violation of Vedic teaching, and such a marriage can never bring happiness and joy in life.

As long as the sages, seers, emperors, kings and other people of this country led a celibate life to acquire knowledge and opted for Svayaṁvara (self-choice) system of marriage, it progressed and prospered continuously. Since the time the people neglected Brahmacharya and the pursuit of knowledge, and took to child-marriage under the patronage of their parents, this country, Āryāvartta, steadily declined. So, it behoves to all gentleman to do away with this faulty system and follow previous Svayaṁvara system. Marriages should be performed in accordance with Varṇa system and Varṇa system should be based on the (Guṇa) qualifications, (Karma) profession and (Svabhāva) temperament of human beings.

Question: Is a son of parents coming from Brāhmaṇa profession called Brāhmaṇa? Can a son of parents who is not coming from a Brāhmaṇa profession also become professionally Brāhmaṇa.

Answer: Yes, many from parents coming from a non-Brāhmaṇa profession, in the past, have become professionally Brāhmaṇa, many in the present do and many in future will. For instance, we are informed from the Chhāndogya Upaniṣad that the sage Jābālal from an unknown family became a Brāhmaṇa; in the Mahābhārata period too, Viśvāmitra from Kṣatriya parents became a Brāhmaṇa, so did the sage Mātaṅga from a Chāṇḍāla family. Even at the present day, a high profile scholar possessing good character deserves to be a Brāhmaṇa and an idiot is treated as Śudra (uneducated).

So will it be in the future?

Question: How can the body constitution of a Brāhmaṇa sperm and ovum change into some other type of sperm and ovum?

Answer: Varṇa (profession) of a person is not decided genetically. However,

स्वाध्यायेन जपैर्होमैस्त्रैविद्येनेज्यया सुतैः ।
महायज्ञैश्च यज्ञैश्च ब्राह्मीयं क्रियते तनुः ।। मनु० 2.28

svādhyāyena japairhomaistraividyenejyayā sutaiḥ,
mahāyajñaiścha yajñaiścha brāhmīyaṁ kriyate tanuḥ.

Manu, 2.28

[Meaning] Svādhyaya (the study of the Vedas), Vrata (vow or practice of austerity), Yajñas, Traividyā (threefold sciences: Ādhyātmika, Ādhidaivika, and Ādhibhautika), Ijyā (performing various iṣṭis like Paurṇamāsa-iṣṭī etc.), Suta (procreation), Mahāyajñas [5 great yajñas like Brahmayajña (acquisition of knowledge), Devayajña (Agnihotra for purifying the atmosphere), Pitṛyajña (providing care to elders), Atithiyajña (hosting peripatetic monks and scholars) Balivaiśvadevayajña (feeding of animals and birds in your vicinity] and other Śrauta yajñas (allegorical Vedic yajñas explaining the process of creation) are meant to transform the human body into a Brāhmaṇa body.

Don't you believe in this verse?

Yes, I do.

If so, then why do you want to determine Varṇa (profession) on the basis of genetic (sperm and ovum)? It's not me alone, but there are many who have the custom to determine Varṇa (profession) by birth.

Question: Do you disapprove of the most ancient customs?

Answer: No! But we don't accept your wrong interpretation, so we do.

Question: Do you have any proof that your interpretation is right and ours is wrong?

Answer: It's very simple. You call only six or seven generations old custom as the eternal (most ancient) custom, whilst we call that custom eternal which has been in vogue from the time of the origin of the Veda and that of creation. Don't you see that sometimes good parents beget bad children, and sometimes good children are born to bad parents, sometimes both are good or bad? Similarly, Brahmaṇa (learned) parents may have children of Śudra nature (who are unwilling to gain knowledge) and Śudra (uneducated/illiterate) parents may have children of Brāhmaṇa nature (who are knowledge thirsty). You people are confused. Let us see here the opinion of Manu (4.178):

येनास्य पितरो याता येन याता पितामहाः ।
तेन यायात्सतां मार्गं तेन गच्छन्न रिष्यते ।। मनु० 1.178

yenāsya pitaro yātā yena yātā pitāmahāḥ,
tena yāyātsatāṁ mārgaṁ tena gachchhanna riṣyate.

Manu, 1.178

[Meaning] Let children walk in the footsteps of their forefathers, had they been good, and not otherwise; since by treading the path of good persons, no one ever suffers.

Do you believe this?

Yes, I do.

Moreover, be assured that only God's creation is eternal and because the same is expressed in the Veda, so whatever is said in the Veda is also eternal and contrary to it can never be eternal. Should all people accept it or not?

Certainly, they should.

If someone refuses to accept it, he should be asked, "Should a rich person discard his wealth, simply because his father was poor? Should a blind father's son have no right to see through his eyes? Should the son of a wicked father not involve into good acts? No, never. It is essential for all to pursue virtue and discard vice.

He who believes that Varṇa (profession) is determined by birth, not by his/her own qualification, nature of profession and personality traits, should be asked why do a person of Brāhmaṇa origin who has converted into Antyajas (Christianity, or Islam), not continue to be a Brāhmaṇa? The only answer is, because he has left the karmas/profession to be performed by a Brāhmaṇa, so he no longer continues to be a Brāhmaṇa. The other way round, this argument proves our contention that a person is called Brāhmaṇa because of his qualifications, profession and temperament becoming of a status of a Brāhmaṇa. Similarly, a person born to parents coming from some other Varṇa (profession) if endowed with Guṇa (qualifications), karmas (profession) and temperament suitable to Brāhmaṇa profession, he should enjoy the status of Brāhmaṇa. On the other hand a person of Brāhmaṇa parentage if induges into the functions of other Varṇas (professions), he/she cannot be inducted into a profession of Brāhmaṇa, rather would be inducted into Varṇa whose functions he/she performs.

Question: There is a mantra in the *Yajurveda* (31.11) which reads as follows:

ब्राह्मणोऽस्य मुखमासीद् बाहू राजन्यः कृतः ।
ऊरू तदस्य यद्वैश्यः पद्भ्या शूद्रो अजायत ।।

brāhmaṇo'sya mukhamāsīd bāhū rājanyaḥ kṛtaḥ,

ūrū tadasya yadvaiśyaḥ padbhyā śūdro ajāyata.

[Meaning] A human being is born Brāhmaṇa by his mouth, Kṣatriya by his arms, Vaiśya by his stomach, and śudra by his legs.

The above-cited mantra says "Brāhmaṇas were born of God's mouth, Kṣatriyas, out of His arms, Vaiśyas, out of His thighs, and Śūdras, out of His feet." Now just as the mouth can never become an arm, nor can an arm become the mouth, so can never a Brāhmaṇa become a Kṣatriya, and vice versa.

Answer: Your interpretation of the aforesaid mantra is wrong. Here the Primal man (Formless Omnipresent God) is intended by the term Puruṣa. Being Formless, He cannot have such organs as the mouth, etc. Should He be possessed of these organs, He could never be Omnipresent, nor therefore Omnipotent, nor could He then be Creator, Upholder and Decreator of this universe, Dispenser of justice according to pāpa (moral and ethical acts) and puṇya (immoral and unethical acts) karmas of human beings, Omniscient, Unborn, Immortal and the like.

The true meaning, therefore, of this mantra is that Brāhmaṇa, Rājanya (Kṣatriya), Vaiśya and Sūdra form the head, the arms, the thighs, and the feet of the formless Universal Puruṣa (Brahmāṇḍa Puruṣa) at the macro level by way of personification. Similarly, at micro level, they form the head, the arms, the thighs, and the feet of the Individual Puruṣa (human). As such, each human being internalises aspects of all the varṇas. Each human is Brāhmaṇa by his head, Kṣatriya by his arms, Vaiśya by his thighs and Śudra by his feet. On the basis of the same, four functional groups are formed in society, named as Brāhmaṇa, Rājanya (Kṣatriya), Vaiśya and Sūdra. If the function of an individual involves mainly his/her mind/head, he/she is called a Brāhmaṇa, if arms a Kṣatriya, if thighs a Vaiśya and if feet (never applies his mind being uneducated or illiterate) a Śudra.

Śatapatha Brāhmaṇa also explains this mantra in a similar way. For example,

यस्मादेते मुख्यास्तस्मान्मुखतो ह्यसृज्यन्त।

yasmādete mukhyāstasmānmukhato hyasṛjyanta

[Menaing] Because of applying their heads (intellectual power) mainly, they were made head dominant.

Just as the head is the main organ in the body, so is a visionary person (Brāhmaṇa) in society who is endowed with perfect vision, qualifications, functions and nature. Just as personified formless God cannot have body parts, so it is impossible to take birth from such body parts as head etc. This appears like a tale of the marriage of the son of a barren woman. So, your interpretation of the aforementioned mantra is misleading. Manu (10.65) holds the similar view.

शूद्रो ब्राह्मणतामेति ब्राह्मणश्चैति शूद्रताम्।
क्षत्रियाज्जातमेवन्तु विद्याद्वैश्यात्तथैव च।। मनु०10.65

śūdro brāhmaṇatāmeti brāhmaṇaśchaiti śūdratām,
kṣatriyājjātamevantu vidyādvaiśyāttathaiva cha.

Manu, 10.65

[Meaning] A person coming from an endogamous Śudra birth-descent groups may enter into Brāhmaṇa, Kṣatriya or Vaiśya groups respectively as per his guṇa (qualifications), karma (profession), and svabhāva (temperament). The same holds true of persons coming from Brāhmaṇa, Kṣatriya or Vaiśya groups. They may also enter into Varṇa groupings conforming to their guṇa (qualifications), karma (profession), and svabhāva (temperament) irrespective of the Varṇa groupings of their birth-descent.

Āpastambha Sūtra also lays down a similar rule.

धर्मचर्य्यया जघन्यो वर्णः पूर्वं
पूर्वं वर्णमापद्यते जातिपरिवृत्तौ ।

dharmacharyyayā jaghanyo varṇaḥ pūrvaṁ
pūrvaṁ varṇamāpadyate jātiparivṛttau,

अधर्मचर्य्यया पूर्वो वर्णो जघन्यं
जघन्यं वर्णमापद्यते जातिपरिवृत्तौ ।

adharmacharyyayā pūrvo varṇo jaghanyaṁ
jaghanyaṁ varṇamāpadyate jātiparivṛttau.

[Meaning] A person coming from the higher functional Varṇa groupings (professions) in order of Brāhmaṇa, Kṣatriya, Vaiśya and Sūdra (may relegate to the lower ones due to their work and conduct. Similarly, a person coming from the lower functional Varṇa groupings (professions) may elevate to the higher ones due to their work and conduct.

The same rule applies to women in determining their Varṇa groupings (professions). Due to this, the people in lower Varṇa groupings will try to elevate themselves to the higher Varṇa groupings and people from higher Varṇa groupings will try to maintain their status in order to avoid relegation into lower Varṇa groupings. This will also prevent intermixing of various Varṇa groupings.

Question: Suppose a family of a particular Varṇa group has only one child and that enters into a different Varṇa group as per his/her qualifications, profession and temperament, who will care for the old parents? Besides, the family line will break. How would you manage in such conditions?

Answer: Neither old parents will go uncared for nor

will the family line break because their children will be eligible to choose their spouse from a compatible Varṇa group. So there is no possibility of mismanagement.

Here it may be noted that the females should be assessed for their Varṇa group at their marriageable age of 16 and males at their marriageable age of 24. They should accordingly marry a person of the compatible Varṇa group. This is how they would be able to lead a happy married life and perform duties of their respective Varṇas efficiently.

Qualifications and duties of the four Varṇas

अध्यापनमध्ययनं यजनं याजनं तथा ।
दानं प्रतिग्रहं चैव ब्राह्मणानामकल्पयत् ॥ मनु. 1.88

adhyāpanamadhyayanaṁ yajanaṁ yājanaṁ tathā,
dānaṁ pratigrahaṁ chaiva brāhmaṇānāmakalpayat.

Manu. 1.88

[Meaning] The duty of teaching and studying, performing yajña for one's own benefit and for others, work of charity, and making approvals are assigned to a Brahmaṇa.

But it should be borne in mind that taking gifts is a mean thing.

शमो दमस्तपः शौचं क्षान्तिरार्जवमेव च।
ज्ञानं विज्ञानमास्तिक्यं ब्रह्मकर्मस्वभावजम्।।

śamo damastapaḥ śauchaṁ kṣāntirārjavameva cha,
jñānaṁ vijñānamāstikyaṁ brahmakarmasvabhāvajam.

[Meaning] The following are the qualifications of a true Brāhmaṇa.

1. (Śama) Restraining the mind from entertaining evil thoughts and indulging into adharma (immoral and unethical acts).

2. (Dama) Restraining senses from the pursuit of acts of injustice and directing them, instead, to the path of dharma (moral and ethical acts).

3. (Tapaḥ) Observing dharma (moral and ethical values) while practising Brahmacharya and control of senses.

4. (Śaucha) Purity of mind and body.

Regarding purity, it is stated in Manusmṛti (5.109)

अद्भिर्गात्राणि शुध्यन्ति मनः सत्येन शुध्यति ।
विद्यातपोभ्यां भूतात्मा बुद्धिर्ज्ञानेन शुध्यति ॥

adbhirgātrāṇi śudhyanti manaḥ satyena śudhyati,
vidyātapobhyāṁ bhūtātmā buddhirjñānena śudhyati.

[Meaning] Water washes off the impurities of the body, the practice of truth exalts the mind, education and observance of austerity elevate the soul and right information (knowledge) refines the Buddhi (intellect).

One should purify him/herself by removing the internal and external impurities as well as by adoration of truth and abhorrence of falsehood.

5. (Kṣānti) Forbearance, that is complete adherence to dharma, unmindful of criticism or admiration, pleasure or pain, cold or hot, hunger or thirst, profit or loss, honour or disgrace, and sorrow or joy.

6. (Ārjava) Tender-heartedness, humility, straightforwardness and maintaining simplicity and to give up crookedness and other sinister designs.

7. (Jñānam) Ability to go through the Vedas and other Śāstras along with their ancillary texts, to decide the things as they are and to distinguish truth from falsehood.

8. (Vijñāna) To develop basic knowledge about

nature and natural objects and to use the same for the development of necessary technology and techniques.

9. (Āstikya) Having unflinching faith in God, salvation, past and future lives of the soul, dharma, education, company of the good and the learned persons and care of elderly mother, father, teacher and other learned visitors often engaged in social service and never a show of disrespect to any of the above.

The duties and functions of a true Brāhmaṇa have thus cited above.

प्रजानां रक्षणं दानमिज्याऽध्ययनमेव च ।
विषयेष्वप्रसक्तिश्च क्षत्रियस्य समासतः ॥ मनु. 1.89

prajānāṁ rakṣaṇaṁ dānamijyā'dhyayanameva cha,
viṣayeṣvaprasaktiścha kṣatriyasya samāsataḥ.manu. 1.89

[Meaning] Providing protection to the people without favour or fear, doing charity for promotion of education, dharma, financial aid to the needy and deserving, conducting yajñas, study, and abstaining from sensual pleasures are the functions assigned to a Kṣatriya.

शौर्यं तेजो धृतिर्दाक्ष्यं युद्धे चाप्यपलायनम् ।
दानमीश्वरभावश्च क्षात्रं कर्म स्वभावजम् ।। गीता

śauryaṁ tejo dhṛtirdākṣayaṁ yuddhe chāpyapalāyanam,
dānamīśvarabhāvaścha kṣātraṁ karma svabhāvajam. Gītā

[Meaning] (Śaurya) To be fearless even while fighting single handed with thousands of enemies put together. (Tejaḥ) To be bold, and firm. (Dhṛti) To be resolute and cool under all circumstances. (Dākṣya) To be expert in discharging Government and public duties and to excel in the study of all Śāstras. (Yuddhe aplāyanam) Never to retreat or withdraw from the war. To ensure victory and safety even if one has to pretend to retreat or recede. (Dāna) To make charities. (Īśvarabhāva) To conduct impartially and to keep one's words at all cost.

These eleven are the duties and qualifications of a Kṣatrīya.

पशूनां रक्षणं दानमिज्याऽध्ययनमेव च ।
वणिक्पथं कुसीदं च वैश्यस्य कृषिमेव च ॥ मनु. 1.90

paśūnāṁ rakṣaṇaṁ dānamijyā'dhyayanameva cha,
vaṇikpathaṁ kusīdaṁ cha vaiśyasya kṛṣimeva cha.
Manu, 1.90

[Meaning] The function of domestication of animals, charity for the promotion of education and dharma, the performance of Yajña, the study of Vedas and Śāstras, trading and manufacturing of goods, money lending/banking and agriculture are assigned to Vaiśya. The rate of interest while lending money may range from .25%, .35%, .5%, .75%, 1% or 1.25% per annum. It should never cross the limit of 200% even after 100 years.

एकमेव तु शूद्रस्य प्रभुः कर्म समादिशत् ।
एतेषामेव वर्णानां शुश्रूषामनसूयया ॥ मनु. 1.91

ēkameva tu śūdrasya prabhuḥ karma samādiśat,
ēteṣāmeva varṇānāṁ śuśrūṣāmanasūyayā. Manu, 1.91

[Meaning] Duty of a Śudra (uneducated or illiterate persons) is to provide various services without jealousy, blame, and conceit to people coming from other Varṇa groups (professions).

The guṇas (qualifications) and karmas (profession) of all the four Varṇa groups have briefly been described. All individuals should be placed in different Varṇa groups they are entitled to as per their qualifications and profession. This system will ensure advancement and progress of all in society. The people placed in higher Varṇa groups would try to maintain their status for the fear of being demoted to the lower Varṇa groups and the people from lower Varṇa groups would be encouraged and put their concerted efforts for promotion to higher Varṇa groups.

The responsibility of promotion of the education and legal institutions be given to the people belonging to Brāhmaṇa Varṇa groups. They will be able to discharge their duties efficiently because of their excellence in education and law. If the affairs of a state are being entrusted to the people of Kṣatriya profession, a state will never suffer from lawlessness or anarchy. The duty of domestication of animals be assigned to people of Vaiśya profession because they have expertise in this field. The people from Śudra profession be engaged in the service sector, because of lack of proper education they can handle the works involving physical labour. Thus it is the duty of the ruler and civilised society to ensure that people from all Varṇa groups are enjoying the right to work.

Types of Marriage

ब्राह्मो दैवस्तथैवार्षः प्राजापत्यस्तथाऽऽसुरः ।
गान्धर्वो राक्षसश्चैव पैशाचश्चाष्टमोऽधमः ।। मनु० 3.12

brāhmo daivastathaivārṣaḥ prājāpatyastathā''suraḥ,
gāndharvo rākṣasaśchaiva paiśāchaśchāṣṭamo'dhamaḥ.

Manu, 3.12

[Meaning] There are eight types of marriage. They are Brāhma, Daiva, Ārṣa, Prājāpatya, Āsura, Gāndharva, Rākṣasa and Paiśācha. They are defined as under:

Brāhma: The marriage of two persons (male and female) who are well behaved, endowed with moral and ethical values and have acquired scholarship after a due practice of Brahmacharya upon their mutual consent is called Brāhma marriage.

Daiva: Daiva marriage is one in which the bride decked in gay attire and ornaments is given to bridegroom who is officiating as priest in the marriage sacrament.

Ārṣa: Ārṣa marriage is solemnized in lieu of consideration received from the bridegroom.

Prājāpatya: The marriage of a couple done to promote the interest of married life is called the Prājāpatya.

Āsura: Āsura marriage is solemnized in lieu of consideration of a gift from either side.

Gāndharva: The Gāndharva marriage or love marriage is solemnised between a man and woman based on the mutual attraction with no rituals, witnesses or family participation.

Rākṣasa: Rākṣasa marriage is the forcible or fraudulent abduction of a maiden from her home.

Paiśācha: Paiśāca marriage is outraging the modesty of a lady under sleep or impression of drink or unconscious or lunar struck.

Of all these 8 types of marriages, Brāhma is the best, Daiva and Prājāpatya are of a medium type, Ārṣa, Āsura and Ghāndharva of inferior type, Rākṣasa is base, whilst Paiśācha is the lowest and most wicked. So, it is advisable that the man and woman should not be allowed to meet each other secretly before marriage, since, such a meeting of young people may lead to corruption. When the marriageable age of boys and girls is approaching near or say when 6 to 12 months are left in the completion of Brahmacharya Aśrama and their education, let the photographs or pictures of boys be sent to the Girls' schools, and those of girls, to the Boys' schools for matching. If the photographs are matched, the school record of the concerned students be examined. Upon the match of guṇa (qualifications), karma (profession) and svabhāva (temperament), the compatibility of the marriage be ascertained and the prospective couples be allowed to inspect each others' photo and life history to take a final decision with regard to their marriage. Should they give their consent, their convocation ceremony be performed simultaneously.

The marriage ceremony can be performed in the witness of their teachers in Gurukula or parents at the house of the bride. They may be allowed to converse with each other and hold discussions, if they so desire, in the presence of their teachers, parents and other respectable people. They are free to exchange their views on confidential issues in writing in the presence of the relatives and teachers assembled over there.

As soon as they confirm their marriage, let it be ensured that they are provided with a healthy diet, so that their lean and thin body due to observing penances due to studies in Brahmacharya Āśrama may tone up like the waxing moon.

Best Time of Marriage

As soon as the monthly course of a girl is over, a small function accompanied by a havan be held to honour learned men and women. When the day of Ṛtudāna (consummation of marriage) is fixed, the marriage ceremony be performed by 10 pm or 12 pm as per the procedure laid down in 'Sanskāra Vidhi' and thereafter newlyweds couple should retire in seclusion. Let the husband and wife follow the proper method of insemination. They should take care that the sperm and ovum preserved with austerity should not go waste, so as to ensure the birth of a unique and superior kind of child. When the semen is ejaculated within the reproductive tract of the mother during sexual intercourse, man and woman should both be still, their bodies being straight, overlapping each other nose to nose and eyes to eyes in an orgasmic state. The man should relax his body at the time of the ejection, and the woman should contract her reproductive organs and pull up the semen discharged into her reproductive tract so that it is finally planted in the uterus. Thereafter, let them both take bath with fresh water.

A wise woman becomes aware of conception at the very moment it takes place. In any case, non-occurrence of periods at the end of the month will make it clear to all. Let them take boiled cooled milk mixed with ginger, saffron, asgandh (myrrh), cardamom and sālam miśrī (ayurvedic herb) and go to sleep. The same procedure needs to be followed each and every time the conception is intended.

When the pregnancy is confirmed, husband and wife should refrain from sexual indulgence for one year, as it may help conceive a superior quality of child and others to follow are also as good as the first one, otherwise semen is wasted causing reduction in longevity of the life span of the husband and the wife and infliction of several diseases upon them. Nevertheless, both of them should be affectionate towards each other and conduct in the matter of diet and dress in such a manner that the husband may not lose his semen in nocturnal emissions, while the foetus is well nourished to grow into an extraordinary baby in terms of beauty, health, energy and valour and is delivered within 10th sidereal month of pregnancy (one sidereal month consists of 27 days).

Speical care is needed in the 4th month of pregnancy when baby's skeleton starts to harden from rubbery cartilage to bone and 8th month when his layers of fat are filling him out, making him rounder, and his lungs are well developed. The pregnant lady should avoid intake of purgatives, intoxicants and other substances that are prejudicial to the growth of intellect and physical strength. On the other hand, cow ghee, cow milk, good quality rice, wheat, lentils and other pulses should form the part of her regular diet.

There are two Sanskārs to be conducted during pregnancy, viz. Punsvana (foetus protection) in the 4th month and another Simantonayana (parting of pregnant woman's hair) in the 8th month. After delivery, the mother and baby need to be given special care. Śuṇṭhi-pāka (decoction of ginger) or Saubhāgya-śuṇṭhi-pāka (a preparation made of dry ginger) to serve to the mother should be prepared in advance. After delivery umbilical cord be severed by means of a soft thread tied about 2 inches from the navel cord, thereafter, it should be tied in such a manner that not a single drop of blood escapes from the child's body. The mother and newly born baby should then be given a bath with warm and scented water. The room should be well cleansed and havan be performed with ghee and fragrant substances. The father should, then, utter osnksṪlhfr "thy name is Veda" in the right ear of the child and write the syllable ओ३म् 'Om' with a golden bar dipped in a mixture of honey and ghee (taken in unequal proportion) on its tongue, and also allow the baby to lick it and then the baby be left to the care of its mother. If baby so desires, the mother may feed it on her breast. For want of lactation or other health, let the baby be nursed by some wet nurse who has undergone a health and compatibility test[180].

---

[180] A wet nurse can help when a baby's natural mother is unable or chooses not to feed the infant. There are many reasons why a mother is unable to lactate or to produce sufficient breast milk. Reasons include the serious or chronic illness of the mother and her treatment which creates a temporary difficulty to nursing. Additionally, a mother's taking drugs (prescription or recreational) may necessitate a wet nurse if a drug in any way changes the content of the mother's milk. Some women choose not to breastfeed for social reasons. Wet nurses have also been used when a mother cannot produce sufficient breast milk, i.e., the mother feels incapable of adequately nursing her child, especially following multiple births. Wet nurses tend to be more common in places where maternal mortality is high.

The practice of using wet nurses is ancient and common to many cultures. It has been linked to social class, where monarchies, the aristocracy, nobility or upper classes had their children wet-nursed in the hope of becoming pregnant again quickly. Lactation inhibits ovulation in some women, thus the practice has a rational basis. Poor women, especially those who suffered the stigma of giving birth to an illegitimate child, sometimes had to give their baby up, temporarily or permanently, to a wet-nurse.

A woman can only act as a wet-nurse if she is lactating. It is not necessary that a wet-nurse must have recently undergone childbirth. Regular breast suckling can elicit lactation via a neural reflex of prolactin production and secretion. Some adoptive mothers have been able to establish lactation using a breast pump so that they could feed an adopted infant. As such wetnurse can be both, a woman who had undergone child birth or a professional.

The mother and the child should then be shifted to another clean, and well-ventilated room wherein Homa is performed with ghee and fragrant herbs daily, morning and evening. Let the child be fed on its mother's breast for the first six days who should, in turn, be fed on nourishing food for her health and healing.

On the sixth day, if the mother is unable or chooses not to feed the infant or want to become pregnant soon, a wet nurse be engaged for baby care and nursing. The wet nurse should also be given a staple diet. She nurses the baby on her milk. The mother should keep a close vigil on her child so that it is not neglected or mistreated in any way. Let her also apply some plaster over the nipple of her breasts so as check the secretion of milk. She should also continue to take a staple diet.

Let the parents of the child perform the Naming and other SanskÈras in due course of time as per *SanskÈra Vidhi*[181]. Upon taking a hygiene bath after a monthly course, wife may under insemination again if next baby is planned

Manu (3.45) observes in this regard as follows:

ऋतुकालाभिगामी स्यात्स्वदारनिरतः सदा।
ब्रह्मचार्य्येव भवति यत्र तत्राश्रमे वसन्।। मनु० 3.45।।

ṛtukālābhigāmī syātsvadāraniratah̤ sadā,
brahmachāryyeva bhavati yatra tatraśrame vasan.

Manu, 3.45.

[Meaning] A married man who is contented with his own wife and approaches her in her monthly course is as better as a BrahmachÈrÏ.

---

[181] A book written by Swami Dayanand Saraswati on 16 Sanskāras.

सन्तुष्टो भार्यया भर्ता भर्त्रा भार्या तथैव च ।
यस्मिन्नेव कुले नित्यं कल्याणं तत्र वै ध्रुवम् ॥ मनु० 3.60 ॥
santuṣṭo bhāryayā bhartā bhartrā bhāryā tathaiva cha,
yasminneva kule nityaṁ kalyāṇaṁ tatra vai dhruvam.

Manu, 3.60

[Meaning] Wherever the husband is contented with his wife, and the wife with her husband, in that family alone all prosperity, fortune and happiness perpetually dwell. And wherever they clash, poverty, ill-fortune and misery rules the roost.

यदि हि स्त्री न रोचेत पुमांसं न प्रमोदयेत् ।
अप्रमोदात् पुनः पुंसः प्रजनं न प्रवर्तते ॥ मनु० 3.61 ॥
yadi hi strī na rocheta pumāṁsaṁ na pramodayet,
apramodāt punaḥ puṁsaḥ prajanaṁ na pravartate.

Manu, 3.61

[Meaning] If the wife does not love and please her husband, he will remain displeased, and, consequently no offspring will be produced.

स्त्रियां तु रोचमानायां सर्वं तद् रोचते कुलम् ।
तस्यां त्वरोचमानायां सर्वमेव न रोचते ॥ मनु० 3.62 ॥

striyāṁ tu rochamānāyāṁ sarvaṁ tad rochate kulam,
tasyāṁ tvarochamānāyāṁ sarvameva na rochate.

Manu, 3.62

[Meaning] When a woman is happy, the whole family is happy. But, if she is unhappy, the whole family is unhappy and miserable.

पितृभिर्भ्रातृभिश्चैताः पतिभिर्देवरैस्तथा ।
पूज्या भूषयितव्याश्च बहुकल्याणमीप्सुभिः ॥ मनु० 3.55 ॥
pitṛbhirbhrātṛbhiśchaitāḥ patibhirdevaraistathā,
pūjyā bhūṣayitavyāścha bahukalyāṇamīpsubhiḥ.

Manu, 3.55

[Meaning] Women must be honoured and adorned

by their fathers, brothers, husbands and brothers-in-law, who desire (their own) welfare.

यत्र नार्यस्तु पूज्यन्ते रमन्ते तत्र देवताः ।
यत्रैतास्तु न पूज्यन्ते सर्वास्तत्राफलाः क्रियाः ॥ मनु० 3.56 ॥

yatra nāryastu pūjyante ramante tatra devatāḥ,
yatraitāstu na pūjyante sarvāstatrāphalāḥ kriyāḥ.

Manu, 3.56

[Menaing] Where women are honoured, their householders are divinely inspired and great men are born; but where they are not honoured, no act yields reward.

शोचन्ति जामयो यत्र विनश्यत्याशु तत् कुलम् ।
न शोचन्ति तु यत्रैता वर्धते तद् हि सर्वदा ॥ मनु० 3.57 ॥

śochanti jāmayo yatra vinaśyatyāśu tat kulam,
na śochanti tu yatraitā vardhate tad hi sarvadā.

Manu, 3.57

[Meaning] Where the female folk live in grief, the family soon perishes; but that family where they don't suffer ever prospers.

तस्मादेताः सदा पूज्या भूषणाच्छादनाशनैः ।
भूतिकामैर्नरैर्नित्यं सत्कारेषूत्सवेषु च । मनु० 3.59

tasmādetāḥ sadā pūjyā bhūṣaṇāchchhādanāśanaiḥ,
bhūtikāmairnarairnityaṁ satkāreṣūtsaveṣu cha.

Manu, 3.59

[Meaning] Hence people seeking (their own) welfare and progress, should always honour and treat women kindly on hospitable moments and festivals with gifts of ornaments, clothes, and taking them for dinners and lunches.

It may be reminded that the word Pujā here is intended for respectful treatment and not for worship.

They (wife and husband) should use the term 'Namaste' to exchange pleasantries with each other.

सदा प्रहृष्टया भाव्यं गृहकार्येषु दक्षया।
सुसंस्कृतोपस्करया व्यये चामुक्तहस्तया।। मनु० 5.150।।

sadā prahṛṣṭayā bhāvyaṁ gṛhakāryeṣu dakṣayā,
susaṁskṛtopaskarayā vyaye chāmuktahastayā.

Manu, 5.150

[Meaning] A woman must always be cheerful, dexterous in (the management of her) household affairs, careful in the cleanliness of her house and utensils, and economical in expenditure.

She should cook nutritious food cleanly and hygienically, so that it may build up our immune system. She should keep proper account of expenses and bring it to the notice of her husband. She should take work from the servants of the house as per their capacity and capability and see that nothing goes wrong in the house.

स्त्रियो रत्नान्यथो विद्या सत्यं शौचं सुभाषितम्।
विविधानि च शिल्पानि समादेयानि सर्वतः।। मनु०2.240।।

striyo ratnānyatho vidyā satyaṁ śauchaṁ subhāṣitam,
vividhāni cha śilpāni samādeyāni sarvataḥ.

Manu, 2.240

[Meaning] Good women, all sorts of gems, knowledge, truth, cleanliness, excellent speech, and all sorts of technology may be received from anyone and from any country.

सत्यं ब्रूयात्प्रियं ब्रूयान्न ब्रूयात् सत्यमप्रियम्।
प्रियं च नानृतं ब्रूयादेष धर्मः सनातनः।। मनु० 4.138।।

satyaṁ brūyātpriyaṁ brūyānna brūyāt satyamapriyam,
priyaṁ cha nānṛtaṁ brūyādeṣa dharmaḥ sanātanaḥ.

Manu, 4.138

[Meaning] Let a man always speak what is true and pleasing. Let him not speak a truth which is not pleasing or irritating (e.g. never call a one-eyed man as 'one-eyed'). Let one also never tell lie to please others.

भद्रं भद्रमिति ब्रूयाद्भद्रमित्येव वा वदेत्।
शुष्कवैरं विवादं च न कुर्यात् केनचित्सह।। मनु० 4.139।।

bhadraṁ bhadramiti brūyādbhadramityeva vā vadet,
śuṣkavairaṁ vivādaṁ cha na kuryāt kenachitsaha.

Manu, 4.139

[Meaning] Let a man always speak what is good for others. He should not enter into unwarranted and uninvited enmity, i.e. he should not oppose anybody or quarrel with anybody without his fault.

If something is beneficial, one must bring it to the notice of the concerned person even if it appears unpleasant to him/her.

पुरुषा बहवो राजन् सततं प्रियवादिनः।
अप्रियस्य तु पथ्यस्य वक्ता श्रोता च दुर्लभः।। विदुरनीति।।

puruṣā bahavo rājan satataṁ priyavādinaḥ.
apriyasya tu pathyasya vaktā śrotā cha durlabhaḥ.

Viduranīti

[Meaning] There are many who constantly speak pleasing words in praise of others, but scarce are those who speak harsh truth beneficial to the listener.

It is becoming of a noble-man to make others aware of their faults in their presence and to listen to their own faults patiently, but to talk of merits in absence. On the other hand, it is customary on the part of a wicked person to praise a person in his/her presence and find fault with him/her in his/her absence. So long as persons become accustomed to hear their own faults from others and to make others aware of their faults, nobody can become immune of faults and inculcate good qualities.

Never speak ill of others. Speaking ill means to read merit in demerits and demerit in merits. On the other hand, praise means to read merit in merit and demerit in a demerit. Another way round, it can be maintained that falsehood involves ill-speak and truthfulness involves praise.

बुद्धिवृद्धिकराण्याशु धन्यानि च हितानि च।
नित्यं शास्त्रण्यवेक्षेत निगमांश्चैव वैदिकान्।। मनु० 4.20।।

buddhivṛddhikarāṇyāśu dhanyāni cha hitāni cha,
nityaṁ śāstraṇyavekṣeta nigamāṁśchaiva vaidikān.

Manu, 4.20

[Meaning] Let them hear and read regularly the Vedas and other ƒÈstras that quickly promote wisdom, wealth and welfare.

Let all men and women carefully revise and pass on to others all that they had studied in their Brahmacharya Āśrama (student life).

यथा यथा हि पुरुषः शास्त्रं समधिगच्छति।
तथा तथा विजानाति विज्ञानं चास्य रोचते।। मनु० 4.20।।

yathā yathā hi puruṣaḥ śāstraṁ samadhigachchhati,
tathā tathā vijānāti vijñānaṁ chāsya rochate.

Manu, 4.20

[Meaning] The more a man thoroughly understands the Śāstras, the more increases his grasping power and the greater his love for scientific inquiries.

ऋषियज्ञं देवयज्ञं भूतयज्ञं च सर्वदा।
नृयज्ञं पितृयज्ञं च यथाशक्ति न हापयेत्।। मनु०4.21।।

ṛṣiyajñaṁ devayajñaṁ bhūtayajñaṁ cha sarvadā,
nṛyajñaṁ pitṛyajñaṁ cha yathāśakti na hāpayet.

Manu, 4.21

अध्यापनं ब्रह्मयज्ञः पितृयज्ञश्च तर्प्पणम्।
होमो दैवो बलिर्भौतो नृयज्ञोऽतिथिपूजनम्।। मनु०3.70।।

adhyāpanaṁ brahmayajñaḥ pitṛyajñaścha tarppaṇam,
homo daivo balirbhauto nṛyajño'tithipūjanam.

Manu, 3.70

स्वाध्यायेनार्चयेतर्षीन् होमैर्देवान् यथाविधि।
पितृन् श्राद्धैश्च नृनन्नैर्भूतानि बलिकर्मणा।। मनु० 3.81।।

svādhyāyenārchayetarṣīn homairdevān yathāvidhi,
pitṛn śrāddhaiścha nṛnannairbhūtāni balikarmaṇā.

Manu, 3.81.

[Meaning] Let a person never neglect five great yajñas to be performed daily. Ṛṣiyajña (Brahmayajña), Devayajña (Agnihotra), Bhūtayajña (Balivaiśvadevayajña), Pitṛyajña (care of elderly persons at home) and Nṛyajña (Atithiyajña) to the best of his/her capacity and capability.

Teaching work is Brahma yajña, care of elders is Pitṛ yajña, Agnihotra is Deva yajña, feeding the birds and animals in surrounding area is Bhūta yajña and hosting a learned Saṁnyāsī is Nṛ yajña (Human Yajñja).

Ṛṣis Should be honoured by taking recourse to studies, natural forces should be augmented by Agnihotra performed duly, elderly persons honoured by proper care, learned Saṁnyāsī-s by good treatments and birds and animals by the gift of eatables.

Out of these five Yajñas, two have already been described under the subject of Brahmacharya in the third chapter. The first one is Brahmayajña, i.e. study and teaching of Vedas and Śāstras, Sandhyā and Upāsanā (prayer) and practice of Yoga. The second one is Nṛ Yajña, i.e. respectfully hosting learned Saṁnyāsī-s and other scholars in society, purity, inculcation of good qualities, charity and promotion of knowledge. Both of these yajñas should be performed daily in morning and evening. It is maintained in the Atharva Veda (19.73;19.7.4),

सायंसायं गृहपतिर्नो अग्निः प्रातः सौमनसस्य दाता ।। अथर्व. 19.7.3

sāyaṁsāyaṁ gṛhapatirno agniḥ prātaḥ saumanasasya dātā

प्रातर्गृहपतिर्नो अग्निः सायंसायं प्रातः सौमनसस्य दाता ।। अथर्व.19.7.4

prātargṛhapatirno agniḥ sāyaṁsāyaṁ prātaḥ saumanasasya dātā

[Meaning] The Havan performed in the evening sandhyā (dusk) continues its beneficial effect of purifying environment till next morning. And the Havan performed in the morning sandhyā (dawn) continues its beneficial effect of purifying environment till evening.

तस्मादहोरात्रस्य संयोगे ब्राह्मणः सन्ध्यामुपासीत ।
उद्यन्तमस्तं यान्तम् आदित्यम् अभिध्यायन् ।। षडविंश ब्राह्मण, 4.5

tasmādahorātrasya saṁyoge brāhmaṇaḥ sandhyāmupāsīta,
udyantamastaṁ yāntam ādityam abhidhyāyan.

Ṣaḍaviṁśa Brāhmaṇa, 4.5

[Meaning] Therefore, sandhyā should be performed by a person of Brāhmaṇa profession at the twilight hours, both at sunrise and sunset.

न तिष्ठति तु यः पूर्वां नोपासते यस्तु पश्चिमाम् ।
स साधुभिर्बहिष्कार्यः सर्वस्माद्द्विजकर्मणः ।। मनु.2.30

na tiṣṭhati tu yaḥ pūrvāṁ nopāsate yastu paśchimām,
sa sādhubhirbahiṣkāryaḥ sarvasmāddvijakarmaṇaḥ.

Manu. 2.30

[Meaning] A person from educated classes who does not perform morning and evening sandhyās should, therefore, be ousted from educated classes and be considered in uneducated class.

NB: There was emphasis on work and conduct instead of mere qualifications.

Question: Why should not Sandhyā be performed three times a day?

Answer: Day and night do not meet three times a day. Light and darkness meet but twice in 24 hours, i.e., in the morning and in the evening. Should a man refuse to accept this argument and persist on third midday sandhyā, he should also perform midnight sandhyā. Should he be willing to do so, let him do so at the junction of every praharas (period of 3 hours), every ghaṭī (24 minutes make one ghaṭī), every pala (24 seconds make one pala) and every kṣaṇa (second) which is not possible. Besides, there is no provision of midday Sandhyā in any Śāstra. So, it is advisable to perform Sandhyā and Agnihotra at twilight hours. There are three divisions of time viz, present, past and future and not that of Sandhyā.

3. Pitṛyajña

Third Pañcha Mahāyajña named Pitṛyajña consists in providing care to learned men, seers and teachers, parents, elders, the wise and great yogis. The Pitṛyajña is of two types. First one is Śrāddha and second one is Tarpaṇa. Śrāddha is derived from the word śrat meaning truth.

श्रत्सत्यं दधाति यया क्रियया सा श्रद्धा श्रद्धया यत्क्रियते तच्छ्राद्धम्।

śratsatyaṁ dadhāti yayā kriyayā sā śraddhā śraddhayā yatkriyate tachchhrāddham.

[Meaning] Śraddhā is that action whereby truth is accepted and Śrāddha is that action which is done with śraddhā.

Tarpaṇa is defined as

तृप्यन्ति तर्पयन्ति येन पितृन् तत्तर्पणम्।

tṛpyanti tarpayanti yena pitṛn tattarpaṇam.

[Meaning] Tarpaṇa is that action whereby living parents and elders are pleased by giving good care.

Note: Tarpaṇa is performed for a living and not for the dead.

Tarpaṇa is further divided into three classes:

3.1. Deva Tarpaṇa (Honouring of Learned Men)

ब्रह्मादयो देवास्तृप्यन्ताम्। ब्रह्मादिदेवपत्न्यस्तृप्यन्ताम्।
ब्रह्मादिदेवसुतास्तृप्यन्ताम्। ब्रह्मादिदेवगणास्तृप्यन्ताम्।

brahmādayo devāstṛpyantām, brahmādidevapatnyas-tṛpyantām,

brahmādidevasutāstṛpyantām, brahmādidevagaṇāstṛp-yantām.

[Meaning] Learned men like Brahmā be honoured. Learned ladies like the wife of Brahmā and those of others be honoured. Learned children (sons, daughters and disciples) of Brahmā and others be honoured. The learned attendants of learned men like Brahmā be honoured.

There is a statement in The Śatapatha Brāhmaṇa which reads as follows:

विद्वांसो हि देवाः।

vidvāṁso hi devāḥ

Only learned men are called Devas. Who are well versed in four Vedas and their ancillary sciences are called Brahmā. The persons inferior to Brahmā in knowledge are called Devas or learned men. Ladies who are equally learned are called Devīs or Brāhmaṇīs. The sons, daughters, disciples or attendants also equally learned are known as Devas/Devīs. Śrāddha or Tarpaṇa is nothing else but giving due honour to all of them.

3.2. Ṛṣi Tarpaṇa (Honourable treatment to the Teachers and Researchers):

अथ ऋषितर्पणम्।

Atha ṛṣitarpaṇam

ओं मरीच्यादय ऋषयस्तृप्यन्ताम्। मरीच्याद्यृषिप.त्न्यस्तृप्यन्ताम्। मरीच्याद्यृषिसुतास्तृप्यन्ताम्। मरीच्याद्यृषिगणास्तृप्यन्ताम्॥ इति ऋषितर्पणम्॥

ōṁ marīchyādaya ṛṣayastṛpyantām, marīchyādyṛṣipa-tnyastṛpyantām, marīchyādyṛṣisutāstṛpyantām, marīchyādyṛṣi- gaṇāstṛpyantām. iti ṛṣitarpaṇam

[Meaning] Let Marichi etc. Ṛṣis be given care with due honour. Let wives of Marichi etc. Ṛṣis given care with due honour. Let sons of Marichi etc. Ṛṣis be given care with due honour. Let attendants of Marichi etc. Ṛṣis given care with due honour.

Ṛṣi Tarpaṇa is giving care with due honour to learned men and women who are as good (in knowledge) as seers like Marichi, the great grandson of Brahmā, their wives, sons, daughters, disciples and attendants who are engaged in teaching and research.

3.3. Pitṛ Tarpaṇa (Care of Elderly Persons)

अथपितृतर्पणम्

Athapitṛtarpaṇam

ओं सोमसदः पितरस्तृप्यन्ताम्। अग्निष्वात्ताः पितरस्तृप्यन्ताम्। बर्हिषदः पितरस्तृप्यन्ताम्। सोमपाः पितरस्तृप्यन्ताम्। हविर्भुजः पितरस्तृप्यन्ताम्। आज्यपाः पितरस्तृप्यन्ताम्। यमादिभ्यो नमः यमादींस्तर्पयामि। पित्रे स्वधा नमः पितरं तर्पयामि। पितामहाय स्वधा नमः पितामहं तर्पयामि। मात्रे स्वधा नमो मातरं तर्पयामि। पितामह्यै स्वधा नमः पितामहीं तर्पयामि। स्वपत्न्यै स्वधा नमः स्वपत्नीं तर्पयामि। सम्बन्धिभ्यः स्वधा नमः सम्बन्धींस्तर्पयामि। सगोत्रेभ्यः स्वधा नमः

सगोत्रंस्तर्पयामि।। इति पितृतर्पणम्।।

ōṁ somasadaḥ pitarastṛpyantām, agniṣvāttāḥ pitarastṛpyantām, barhiṣadaḥ pitarastṛpyantām, somapāḥ pitarastṛpyantām, havirbhujaḥ pitarastṛpyantām, ājyapāḥ pitarastṛpyantām, yamādibhyo namaḥ yamādīṁstarpayāmi, pitre svadhā namaḥ pitaraṁ tarpayāmi, pitāmahāya svadhā namaḥ pitāmahaṁ tarpayāmi, mātre svadhā namo mātaraṁ tarpayāmi, pitāmahyai svadhā namaḥ pitāmahīṁ tarpayāmi, svapatnyai svadhā namaḥ svapatnīṁ tarpayāmi, sambandhibhyaḥ svadhā namaḥ sambandhīṁstarpayāmi, sagotrebhyaḥ svadhā namaḥ sagotraṁstarpayāmi. iti pitṛtarpaṇam.

[Meaning] Let the elderly persons who are well versed in spiritual knowledge be taken care of. Let the elderly persons who had been scientists and technocrats be taken care of. Let the elderly persons who were an authority on law and code of conduct be given proper care. Let the elderly persons who were engaged in health profession be given care. Let elderly persons who used to supply pure and unadulterated food and drinks be given proper care. Let the elderly persons who were engaged in protection and storage of food and other necessary items be given a care in their old age. Let the elderly persons who spent their time in socially useful activities be taken care of. Let the elderly persons who used to punish the evildoers and protect the good persons by administering justice without any favour or fervour be respected and given care. Let father be provided with all necessaries of life respected and cared in his old age. Let the grandfather be respected and cared. Let the mother be respected and cared. Let the grand-mother be treated with respect and cared. Let wife be treated well and given proper care. Let the relatives be treated respectfully and cared. Let brothers, sisters and other kinsmen be treated properly and cared well.

Pitṛ Tarpaṇa is elder care. Elders be treated respectfully and cared up to their full satisfaction by providing them with all necessaries of life in their old age. Pitṛ Tarpaṇa also includes respectful treatment to wife, sisters, relatives and other elders who are helpless in your vicinity.

4. Vaiśvadeva-yajña

(Feeding of Surrounding Birds and Animals)

Vaiśvadeva-yajña is the fourth Pañchmahāyajña to be performed daily. A portion of the cooked food (leaving sour, salty and acidic dishes) should be offered to the fire in the form of āhuti taken out of the fireplace meant for cooking food and the part of offering be escaped for feeding the birds and animals that live in our vicinity. In this regard, Manu (3.84) observes:

वैश्वदेवस्य सिद्धस्य गृह्येऽग्नौ विधिपूर्वकम् ।
आभ्यः कुर्य्याद्देवताभ्यो ब्राह्मणो होममन्वहम् ।। मनु० ।।

vaiśvadevasya siddhasya gṛhye'gnau vidhipūrvakam,
ābhyaḥ kuryyāddevatābhyo brāhmaṇo homamanvaham. Manu

[Meaning] A learned man should offer in the Gṛhyāgni (household fire) a portion of the cooked food meant for the Vaiśvadevas (various creatures that surround us). Āhutis may be offered to the following deities:

ओम् अग्नये स्वाहा। सोमाय स्वाहा। अग्नीषोमाभ्यां स्वाहा। विश्वेभ्यो देवेभ्यः स्वाहा। धन्वन्तरये स्वाहा। कुह्वै स्वाहा। अनुमत्यै स्वाहा। प्रजापतये स्वाहा। सह द्यावापृथिवीभ्यां स्वाहा। स्विष्टकृते स्वाहा।

ōm agnaye svāhā, somāya svāhā, agnīṣomābhyāṁ svāhā, viśvebhyo devebhyaḥ svāhā, dhanvantaraye svāhā, kuhvai svāhā, anumatyai svāhā, prajāpataye svāhā, saha dyāvāpṛthivībhyāṁ svāhā, sviṣṭakṛte svāhā,

[Meaning] First āhuti to Agni (energy), next to Soma (matter), then to both conjointly, further to all the devas (natural powers), and (then) to Dhanvantarī, further to Kuhu (new-moon day), to Anumati (full-moon day), to Prajāpati (Galaxy), to light space and observer space conjointly, and finally to Agni Sviṣṭakṛt (energy, the material cause of creation).

Thus having been duly offered ahutis (oblations) in the burning fire to the Devas mentioned above, let Bali (share) be offered in a plate or on a leaf placed on the ground in all directions beginning with the east accompanied by the recitation of the following mantras:

ओं सानुगायेन्द्राय नमः। सानुगाय यमाय नमः। सानुगाय वरुणाय नमः। सानुगाय सोमाय नमः। मरुद्भ्यो नमः। अद्भ्यो नमः। वनस्पतिभ्यो नमः। श्रियै नमः। भद्रकाल्यै नमः। ब्रह्मपतये नमः। वास्तुपतये नमः। विश्वेभ्यो देवेभ्यो नमः। दिवाचरेभ्यो भूतेभ्यो नमः। नक्तञ्चारिभ्यो भूतेभ्यो नमः। सर्वात्मभूतये नमः।।

ōṁ sānugāyendrāya namaḥ, sānugāya yamāya namaḥ, sānugāya varuṇāya namaḥ, sānugāya somāya namaḥ, marudbhyo namaḥ, adbhyo namaḥ / vanaspatibhyo namaḥ, śriyai namaḥ, bhadrakālyai namaḥ, brahmapataye namaḥ, vāstupataye namaḥ, viśvebhyo devebhyo namaḥ, divācharebhyo bhūtebhyo namaḥ, naktañchāribhyo bhūtebhyo namaḥ, sarvātmabhūtaye namaḥ.

[Meaning] Let this bali (share) be for Indra direction (east), let this be for Yama direction (south), let this be Varuṇa direction (west), let this be Soma direction (north), let this be for our doorsteps, let this be for waters, let this be for plants, let this be for our fortune, let this be for our good or wellbeing, let this be for the protection of our intellectual power, let this be for the wellbeing of the owner of house, let this be for all devas (natural forces), let this be for creatures living in lighted places, let this be for creatures living in dark places (where there is no sunlight), let this be for self-elevation.

These balis (portions taken out of cooked food) should either be offered to an Atithi (peripatetic monk/mendicant) or offered to the fire of Yajña. Thereafter six portions from the cooked food should be gently placed on the ground in the names of dogs, of those engaged in pāpakarmas (immoral and unethical acts), of dog-keepers, of those afflicted with diseases caused due to immoral acts done in past lives, crows, and insects by reciting the following:

श्वभ्यो नमः। पतितेभ्यो नमः। श्वपग्भ्यो नमः। पापरोगिभ्यो
नमः। वायसेभ्यो नमः। कृमिभ्यो नमः।।

śvabhyo namaḥ, patitebhyo namaḥ, śvapagbhyo namaḥ, pāparogibhyo
namaḥ, vāyasebhyo namaḥ, kṛmibhyo namaḥ.

Thereafter this portion of food may be distributed among needy persons or offered to dogs, crows or other animals. In this regard, Manu (3.92) says:

शुनां च पतितानां च श्वपचां पापरोगिणाम्।
वायसानां कृमीणां च शनकेर्नि शनकैर्निर्वपेद् भुवि।। मनु० 3.92।।

śunāṁ cha patitānāṁ cha śvapachāṁ pāparogiṇām,
vāyasānāṁ kṛmīṇāṁ cha śanakerni śanakairnirvaped

bhuvi. *Manu, 3.92*

[Meaning] Separate portions of the cooked food should be gently escaped on the ground in the name of dogs, of those engaged in pāpakarmas (immoral and unethical acts), of dog-keepers, of those afflicted with diseases caused due to immoral acts done in past lives, crows, and insects.

Here the term 'namaḥ' applies to the offering of food

to the ants, birds, animals or hungry person, etc.

Havan in this connection is done in order to keep the air of kitchen clean whilst that of offering food is to make up for the damage done by us through violence exercised inadvertently to the unknown microorganism.

5. Atithi Yajña

An Atithi is one who has no date fixed for his arrival. Whenever a Saṁnyāsī (peripatetic monk), who is well up in spirituality, preacher of truth, travels for the public good, perfect in knowledge, a Yogī of the highest order, happens to visit a house-holder uninformed, he should be given a warm welcome by offering water to wash his feet, face, and to sip. Thereafter, he should be offered a seat and be treated well with meals, etc. Then a patient hearing be given to his discourses on science and spirituality to redeem the goal of dharma (acquisition of knowledge), artha (attaining material means), kāma (fulfilment of worldly desires) and mokṣa (emancipation) in life. Also, follow their teachings in your day to day life. On some particular occasions, even a house-holder and a royal dignitary deserve to be treated as atithi. However, Manu (4.30) says

पाषण्डिनो विकर्मस्थान् वैडालवृत्तिकान् शठान्।
हैतुकान् वकवृत्तींश्च वाङ्मात्रेणापि नार्चयेत्।।

pāṣaṇḍino vikarmasthān vaiḍālavṛttikān śaṭhān,
haitukān vakavṛttīṁścha vāṅmātreṇāpi nārchayet.

[Meaning] Let him not honour, even by a greeting who is heretics, men who perform actions forbidden by Veda (e.g. telling lie), men who act like cats, i.e serve their interests at the cost of others, rogues who know nothing and listen to none, giving ill-logical arguments like modern day Vedantists who argues that they are God and the world is false, and those who live like a heron. (Just as a heron stands quietly on one leg as if in deep meditation but lookout for a prey of fish to satiate his hunger, so do the Vairāgī-s (so-called world renouncers) and Khākis (ash-besmeared mendicants)) and other mendicants of today who are very stubborn, obstinate and anti-Veda.

If due credence is given to such persons, they will emerge in the majority and push the whole world towards adharma (immorality). Not only they themselves do such works as degrade them, but cause their attendants and followers too to delve deep into the ocean of ignorance and misery.

Advantage of Pañcha-mahāyajña

1. Brahmayajña fosters the noble Sanskāras of knowledge, education, dharma, culture and civilisation.

2. Agnihotra renders air, rain and water pollution free. Pollution free rain is the cause of prosperity of the world. Pollution free air is healthy for the respiratory system. Pure meals and drinks are healthy for body and mind. They act as energy boosters enabling one to redeem dharma, artha, kāma and mokṣa. That is why it called as Deva-yajña.

3. Pitṛ-yajña or care of mother, father, learned men, saints and sages boost up the knowledge of caregiver which in turn helps a man to decide between truth and falsehood and so he can follow truth and abandon falsehood to make his life happy and comfortable. It also creates a sense of gratitude. One feels obliged to repay to his/her elderly parents and teachers for what he/she has received from them during his/her young age.

4. The advantages of Balivaiśvadeva Yajña have already been explained above.

5. So long as high profile Atithis are not available in the world, no progress is possible, as they go about in all countries of the world, teaching and preaching the truth, no hypocritical and fraudulent practices can flourish. The house-holders can also easily attain true spiritual knowledge in all places. Same values will prevail among all men. Unless there are Atithis, doubts cannot be dispelled, and without the removal of doubts, there can be no firm faith and there can be no happiness without firm faith?

ब्राह्मे मुहूर्ते बुध्येत धर्मार्थौ चानुचिन्तयेत् ।
कायक्लेशांश्च तन्मूलान् वेदतत्त्वार्थमेव च ॥ मनु० 4.92 ॥

brāhme muhūrte budhyeta dharmārthau chānuchintayet,
kāyakleśāṁścha tanmūlān vedatattvārthameva cha.

Manu, 4.92.

[Meaning] One should wake up early in the morning (the Brāhma muhūrta i.e. 4 am). Having performed daily duties, he should think upon means of dharma (moral and ethical values and duties), artha (material gains), the root cause of his physical ailments, and meditate upon God.

He should never indulge into immoral and unethical acts because

नाधर्मश्चरितो लोके सद्यः फलति गौरिव ।
शनैरावर्त्यमानस्तु कर्तुर्मूलानि कृन्तति ॥ मनु० 4.172 ॥

nādharmaścharito loke sadyaḥ phalati gauriva ।
śanairāvartyamānastu karturmūlāni kṛntati.

Manu, 4.172.

[Meaning] Adharma (immoral and unethical acts) committed in this world never go unpunished. However, when it (adharma) is committed, it immediately produces no result, so an ignorant does not have a fear of it. But be assured that the practice of adharma slowly cuts off the very root of your happiness.

In the same context, following verses are noteworthy.

अधर्मेणैधते तावत् ततो भद्राणि पश्यति ।
ततः सपत्नान् जयति समूलस्तु विनश्यति ॥ मनु० 4.174 ॥

adharmeṇaidhate tāvat tato bhadrāṇi paśyati,
tataḥ sapatnān jayati samūlastu vinaśyati.

Manu, 4.174.

[Meaning] The commission of adhrama (foul means, cheating, hypocrisy, deceit and condemnation of Vedas) may help one flourish and achieve high status in society for a moment like that of unbounded waters of tank. It may also help him to defeat enemies for a while, but ultimately it causes a speedy ruin like that of a rootless tree.

सत्यधर्मार्यवृत्तेषु शौचे चैवारमेत् सदा ।
शिष्यांश्च शिष्याद् धर्मेण वागबाहूदरसंयतः ॥ मनु० 4.175 ॥

satyadharmāryavṛtteṣu śauche chaivāramet sadā,
śiṣyāṁścha śiṣyād dharmeṇa vāgabāhūdarasaṁyataḥ.

Manu, 4.175.

[Meaning] Let a learned man always practice truth, ethical and moral values, purity and conduct himself in a noble and civilised manner. He should exercise restraint in the matter of speech, hands, and stomach. He should impart instructions to his disciples into moral and ethical values.

ऋत्विक्पुरोहिताचार्यैर्मातुलातिथिसंश्रितैः ।
बालवृद्धातुरैर्वैद्यैर्ज्ञातिसम्बन्धिबान्धवैः ॥ मनु० 4.179 ॥

ṛtvikpurohitāchāryairmātulātithisaṁśritaiḥ,
bālavṛddhāturairvaidyairjñātisambandhibāndhavaiḥ.

Manu, 4.179

मातापितृभ्यां जामीभिर्भ्रात्रा पुत्रेण भार्यया ।
दुहित्रा दासवर्गेण विवादं न समाचरेत् ॥ मनु० 4.180 ॥

mātāpitṛbhyāṁ jāmībhirbhrātrā putreṇa bhāryayā,
duhitrā dāsavargeṇa vivādaṁ na samācharet.

Manu, 4.180

[Meaning] Let him never be at loggerhead with a Ṛtvik (one who officiates at a Yajña), a Purohita (priest), a teacher or a preceptor, a maternal uncle, an atithi (a visiting scholar or a peripatetic monk), a dependent, children, aged people, sick men, doctors or physicians, one's kinsmen, relatives, friends, parents, sisters, brothers, son, wife, daughter and servants.

अतपास्त्वनधीयानः प्रतिग्रहरुचिर्द्विजः ।
अम्भस्यश्मप्लवेनैव सह तेनैव मज्जति ॥ मनु० 4.190 ॥

atapāstvanadhīyānaḥ pratigraharuchirdvijaḥ,
ambhasyaśmaplavenaiva saha tenaiva majjati.

Manu, 4.190

[Meaning] A person devoid of the practice of Brahmacharya (celibacy) and truthfulness, one who does not study, one who is fond of accepting gifts; these three swim on a stone made boat to make themselves sink into the ocean of miseries.

त्रिष्वप्येतेषु दत्तं हि विधिनाऽप्यर्जितं धनम् ।
दातुर्भवत्यनर्थाय परत्रादातुरेव च ॥ मनु० 4.193 ॥

triṣvapyeteṣu dattaṁ hi vidhinā'pyarjitaṁ dhanam,
dāturbhavatyanarthāya paratrādātureva cha.

Manu, 4.193

[Meaning] Any legitimately earned money given in charity to the above mentioned three, ruins the donor here itself and the donee hereafter.

यथा प्लवेनोपलेन निमज्जत्युदके तरन् ।
तथा निमज्जतोऽधस्तादज्ञौ दातृप्रतीच्छकौ ॥ मनु० 4.194 ॥

yathā plavenopalena nimajjatyudake taran,
tathā nimajjato'dhastādajñau dātṛpratīchchhakau.

Manu, 4.194

[Meaning] As a person swimming with a stone made boat is destined to sink, even so an ignorant donor and an ignorant donee sink to lower species. Means they will not be born as human beings in the next life.

Characteristices of hypocrites

Hypocrites should neither be trusted nor respected. They are of the following 11 types:-

धर्मध्वजी सदा लुब्धश्छाद्मिको लोकदम्भकः ॥
बैडालव्रतिको ज्ञेयो हिंस्रः सर्वाभिसन्धकः ॥ मनु० 4.195 ॥

dharmadhvajī sadā lubdhaśchhādmiko lokadambhakaḥ.
baiḍālavratiko jñeyo hiṁsraḥ sarvābhisandhakaḥ.

Manu, 4.195

[Meaning] Dharmadhvajī (one who cheats people in the name of religion), ever greedy, fraudulent, one who boasts of his greatness, one who prey on others, one who keeps all good and bad elements in good humour. The above six ought to be regarded cunning like a cat (cat nature).

अधोदृष्टिर्नैष्कृतिकः स्वार्थसाधनतत्परः ।
शठो मिथ्याविनीतश्च बकव्रतचरो द्विजः ॥ मनु० 4.196 ॥

adhodṛṣṭirnaiṣkṛtikaḥ svārthasādhanatatparaḥ,
śaṭho mithyāvinītaścha bakavratacharo dvijaḥ.

Manu, 4.196

[Meaning] One who looks down in order to gain reputation, who is revengeful, self centred, rascal, humble looking but not really so - the above five should be regarded stork natured.

धर्मं शनैः सञ्चिनुयाद् वल्मीकमिव पुत्तिकाः ।
परलोकसहायार्थं सर्वभूतान्यपीडयन् ॥ मनु० 4.238 ॥

dharmaṁ śanaiḥ sañchinuyād valmīkamiva puttikāḥ,
paralokasahāyārthaṁ sarvabhūtānyapīḍayan.

Manu, 4.238

[Meaning] One should slowly and steadily accumulate virtuous Sanskāras to support the life hereafter (next life) without inflicting pain on any living being, just as white ant gradually make its hill.

नामुत्र हि सहायार्थं पिता माता च तिष्ठतः ।
न पुत्रदारं न ज्ञातिर्धर्मस्तिष्ठति केवलः ॥ मनु० 4.239 ॥

nāmutra hi sahāyārthaṁ pitā mātā cha tiṣṭhataḥ,
na putradāraṁ na jñātirdharmastiṣṭhati kevalaḥ.

Manu, 4.239

[Meaning] For parents, wife, son or daughter are not going to help you hereafter. Sanskāras alone are helpful shaping the next life.

NB: According to Vedanta philosopher, Sanskāras act as a seed for attaining next life. संस्कारबीजात् सृष्टिः ।

एकः प्रजायते जन्तुरेक एव प्रलीयते ।
एकोऽनुभुङ्क्ते सुकृतमेक एव च दुष्कृतम् ॥ मनु० 4.240 ॥

ekaḥ prajāyate jantureka eva pralīyate,
eko'nubhuṅkte sukṛtameka eva cha duṣkṛtam.

Manu, 4.240

[Meaning] An individual is born and dies alone. He/she alone enjoys awards of his/her virtues or suffers pain for his/her vices.

एकः पापानि कुरुते फलं भुंक्ते महाजनः ।
भोक्तारो विप्रमुच्यन्ते कर्त्ता दोषेण लिप्यते ।।

महाभारत, उद्योगपर्व, (अध्याय 32)

ēkaḥ pāpāni kurute phalaṁ bhuṁkte mahājana,

bhoktāro vipramuchyante katratā doṣeṇa lipyate.

Mahābhārata, Udyogaparva, adhyāya 32

[Meaning] If a bread earner earns money by unlawful means and the whole dependant family enjoys it. Only the bread earner will be held guilty not the whole dependant family.

मृतं शरीरमुत्सृज्य काष्ठलोष्टसमं क्षितौ ।
विमुखा बान्धवा यान्ति धर्मस्तमनुगच्छति ॥ मनु० 5.241 ॥

mṛtaṁ śarīramutsṛjya kāṣṭhaloṣṭasamaṁ kṣitau,
vimukhā bāndhavā yānti dharmastamanugachchhati.

Manu, 5.241

[Meaning] When a man dies, his relations leave his corpse like a log or a lump of clay on the ground, and retire home with averted faces. No one accompanies him. It is his virtuous Sanskāras (dharma) alone that bears his company (in the next life).

तस्माद् धर्मं सहायार्थं नित्यं सञ्चिनुयात्शनैः ।
धर्मेण हि सहायेन तमस्तरति दुस्तरम् ॥ मनु० 4.242 ॥

tasmād dharmaṁ sahāyārthaṁ nityaṁ sañchinuyātśanaiḥ,
dharmeṇa hi sahāyena tamastarati dustaram.

Manu, 4.242

[Meaning] Let a man, therefore, slowly and steadily accumulate good Sanskāras (dharma) for the welfare of next life, since it is through the help of virtuous Sanskāras alone that a person can traverse successfully the most untraversable dark species (lower species of insects, animals and plants devoid of light of knowledge and wrapped in ignorance of darkness).

NB: According to Vedic philosophical thought, it is difficult to regain the human life. Generally, a person undergoes 84 lakh lower species due to his bad karmic sanskāras before regaining human life. So slow and steady accumulation of dharma (good karmic Sanskāras) has been suggested to cross over the lives of miseries (lower species wrapped in darkness).

धर्मप्रधानं पुरुषं तपसा हतकिल्बिषम् ।
परलोकं नयत्याशु भास्वन्तं खशरीरिणम् ॥ मनु० 4.243 ॥

dharmapradhānaṁ puruṣaṁ tapasā hatakilbiṣam,
paralokaṁ nayatyāśu bhāsvantaṁ khaśarīriṇam.

Manu, 4.243

[Meaning] A man who holds virtuous Sanskāras (dharma) supreme, and whose bad Sanskāras have been washed away due to the observance of austerity and penances, quickly attains mokṣa, i.e. merging with the shining and space like All-pervading Brahman.

दृढकारी मृदुर्दान्तः क्रूराचारैरसंवसन् ।
अहिंस्रो दमदानाभ्यां जयेत् स्वर्गं तथाव्रतः ॥ मनु० 4.246 ॥

dṛḍhakārī mṛdurdāntaḥ krūrāchārairasaṁvasan,
ahiṁsro damadānābhyāṁ jayet svargaṁ tathāvrataḥ.

Manu, 4.246

[Meaning] He who is firm in action, soft in disposition, subjugates passions, shuns the company of cruel and wicked men and injures none can attain divinity (a stage of life where a person becomes ready to attain mokṣa) by subjugating his mind (desires) and disseminating knowledge and selfless service to others.

NB: If a person is unable to subjugate his mind (desires) he attains species developed at Manomaya Kośa (mind dominating species), like animals etc.

But it should also be borne in mind that

वाच्यर्था नियताः सर्वे वाङ्मूला वाग्विनिःसृताः ।
तांस्तु यः स्तेनयेद् वाचं स सर्वस्तेयकृन्नरः ॥ मनु० 4.256 ॥

vāchyarthā niyatāḥ sarve vāṅmūlā vāgviniḥsṛtāḥ,
tāṁstu yaḥ stenayed vāchaṁ sa sarvasteyakṛnnaraḥ.

Manu, 4.256

[Meaning] All expressable behaviour of a human being has a speech at its base and expressed by speech. Should a person fail to speak the truth, he is deemed to commit theft of all types.

Let a person, therefore, avoid acts of misconduct like telling lie and resort to acts of good conduct like Brahmacharya and self-control

आचाराद्लभते ह्यायुराचारादीप्सिताः प्रजाः ।
आचाराद् धनमक्षय्यमाचारो हन्त्यलक्षणम् ॥ मनु०4.156 ॥

āchārādlabhate hyāyurāchārādīpsitāḥ prajāḥ,
āchārād dhanamakṣayyamāchāro hantyalakṣaṇam.

Manu, 4.156

[Meaning] Through good conduct a person he obtains long life, good offspring, imperishable wealth and becomes devoid of bad tendencies.

One should always follow the persons of good conduct.

दुराचारो हि पुरुषो लोके भवति निन्दितः ।
दुःखभागी च सततं व्याधितोऽल्पायुरेव च ॥ मनु० 4.157 ॥

durāchāro hi puruṣo loke bhavati ninditaḥ,
duḥkhabhāgī cha satataṁ vyādhito'lpāyureva cha.

Manu, 4.157

[Meaning] For a man of bad conduct is disgraced in society. He is afflicted with misery, constantly suffers from diseases and becomes short-lived.

यद् यत् परवशं कर्म तत् तद् यत्नेन वर्जयेत् ॥
यद् यदात्मवशं तु स्यात् तत् तत् सेवेत यत्नतः । मनु० 4.159

yad yat paravaśaṁ karma tat tad yatnena varjayet,

yad yadātmavaśaṁ tu syāt tat tat seveta yatnataḥ.

Manu, 4.159

[Meaning] A person should give up all those actions which can be pursued depending on others. On the other hand, he should diligently pursue those actions which he can do independent of others.

सर्वं परवशं दुःखं सर्वमात्मवशं सुखम् ।
एतद् विद्यात् समासेन लक्षणं सुखदुःखयोः ॥ मनु० 4.160 ॥

sarvaṁ paravaśaṁ duḥkhaṁ sarvamātmavaśaṁ sukham,
ētad vidyāt samāsena lakṣaṇaṁ sukhaduḥkhayoḥ.

Manu, 4.160

[Meaning] Dependence is painful, whilst independence is pleasurable. This should be briefly known as definition of pleasure and pain..

But the work of interdependent nature should be accomplished interdependently. For instance, matrimonial duties are to be carried out by wife and husband together without any opposition whatsoever. Wife and husband can look after domestic and external affairs respectively preventing each other from being trapped into vices and temptations.

At the time of marriage, husband and wife are tied together to share each others' emotions, expressions and reproductive elements. Let them never do anything against each other's wish. Adultery and extramarital relations are among the most prominent factors that adversely affect their happy married life. Let them avoid these. Let the husband always remain contented with his wife, and the wife with her husband.

If a couple belongs to Brāhmaṇa profession, let the husband teach boys, and his well-educated wife teach girls. Let them transform them into good scholars through good education and lectures. Let the husband be respectable and worshipable God for the wife and the wife be a respectable and worshipable goddess for the husband.

As long as boys and girls remain in their respective Gurukulas, let them look upon their teachers and preceptors as their parents, whilst the teachers should consider their pupils as their children.

Qualifications of male and female teachers

आत्मज्ञानं समारम्भस्तितिक्षा धर्मनित्यता।
यमर्थानापकर्षन्ति स वै पण्डित उच्यते।।

(महाभारत, उद्योगपर्व, विदुरप्रजागर, 33.20)

ātmajñānaṁ samārambhastitikṣā dharmanityatā,
yamarthānāpakarṣanti sa vai paṇḍita uchyate.

Mahābhārata, Udyogaparva, Viduraprajāgara, 33.20

[Meaning] He is worthy to be known as the wise man who knows himself; properly, who is never idle; who is affected by pleasure or pain, profit or loss, honour or dishonour, praise or condemnation; who always maintains virtuous Sanskāras (dharma); and who is never swayed by temptations.

निषेवते प्रशस्तानि निन्दितानि न सेवते।
अनास्तिकः श्रद्दधान एतत्पण्डितलक्षणम्।।

(महाभारत, उद्योगपर्व, विदुरप्रजागर, 33.20)

niṣevate praśastāni ninditāni na sevate,
anāstikaḥ śraddadhāna ētatpaṇḍitalakṣaṇam.

Mahābhārata, Udyogaparva, Viduraprajāgara, 33.20

[Meaning] A wise man practices what is commendable and not what is condemnable. He believes in God and His knowledge, the Veda. He firmly reposes his faith and trust in God.

क्षिप्रं विजानाति चिरं श्रृणोति, विज्ञाय चार्थं भजते न कामात्।

नासम्पृष्टो ह्युपयुङ्क्ते परार्थे, तत्प्रज्ञानं प्रथमं पण्डितस्य।।
(महाभारत, उद्योगपर्व, विदुरप्रजागर, 33.27)

kṣipraṁ vijānāti chiraṁ śṛṇoti, vijñāya chārthaṁ bhajate na kāmāt,
nāsampṛṣṭo hyupayuṅkte parārthe, tatprajñānaṁ prathamaṁ paṇḍitasya.
Mahābhārata, Udyogaparva, Viduraprajāgara, 33.27

[Meaning] The first qualification of a wise man is that he should be able to grasp the most abstruse subject in a very short time, should devote years of his life to the study of the Śāstras and apply his knowledge for the altruistic welfare and never for his selfish gain. He never gives his opinion uninvited or on unsuitable occasions and times.

नाप्राप्यमभिवाञ्छन्ति नष्टं नेच्छन्ति शोचितुम्।
आपत्सु च न मुह्यन्ति नराः पण्डितबुद्धयः।।
(महाभारत, उद्योगपर्व, विदुरप्रजागर, 33.28)

nāprāpyamabhivāñchhanti naṣṭaṁ nechchhanti śochitu,
āpatsu cha na muhyanti narāḥ paṇḍitabuddhayaḥ.
Mahābhārata, Udyogaparva, Viduraprajāgara, 33.28

[Meaning] Such people are endowed with real wisdom as do not aspire for what is not worth to aspire, or desire for what they don't deserve, nor lament for losses nor lose their presence of mind when there is some emergency.

प्रवृत्तवाक् चित्रकथ ऊहवान् प्रतिभानवान्।
आशु ग्रन्थस्य वक्ता च यः स पण्डित उच्यते।।
(महाभारत, उद्योगपर्व, विदुरप्रजागर, 33.33)

pravṛttavāk chitrakatha ūhavān pratibhānavān,
āśu granthasya vaktā cha yaḥ sa paṇḍita uchyate.
Mahābhārata, Udyogaparva, Viduraprajāgara, 33.33

[Meaning] He should be known as wise who is capable to deliberate upon all subjects; who is prolific speaker of multi-disciplines; who is blessed with unparalleled reasoning and logic; who has sharp memory; and who quickly explains and elucidate the intended sense of Śāstras.

श्रुतं प्रज्ञानुगं यस्य प्रज्ञा चैव श्रुतानुगा।
असम्भिन्नार्यमर्यादः पण्डिताख्यां लभेत सः।।

(महाभारत, उद्योगपर्व, विदुरप्रजागर, 33.34)

śrutaṁ prajñānugaṁ yasya prajñā chaiva śrutānugā,
asambhinnāryamaryādaḥ paṇḍitākhyāṁ labheta saḥ.

Mahābhārata, Udyogaparva, Viduraprajāgara, 33.34

[Meaning] The man is entitled to be called as wise who is intellectually capable of learning Śāstras; who is capable of transforming himself as per the teachings of Śāstras; who never transgresses the boundaries set by men of piety.

Where there are such teachers at the helm of education, there spread happiness and prosperity and the knowledge, moral and ethical values and righteous conduct is promoted.

Sign of undeserving teacher and fool

अश्रुतश्च समुन्नद्धो दरिद्रश्च महामनाः।
अर्थांश्चाऽकर्मणा प्रेप्सुर्मूढ इत्युच्यते बुधैः।।

(महाभारत, उद्योगपर्व, विदुरप्रजागर, 33.35)

aśrutaścha samunnaddho daridraścha mahāmanāḥ,
arthāṁśchā'karmaṇā prepsurmūḍha ityuchyate budhaiḥ.

Mahābhārata, Udyogaparva, Viduraprajāgara, 33.35

[Meaning] He who has neither read a Śāstra, nor heard it read; who is extremely haughty; who thinks of big projects without any means; who desires to obtain things without putting any effort for it; is called a fool by the wise.

अनाहूतः प्रविशति ह्यपृष्टो बहु भाषते।
अविश्वस्ते विश्वसिति मूढचेता नराधमः।।
(महाभारत, उद्योगपर्व, विदुरप्रजागर, 33.41)

anāhūtaḥ praviśati hyapṛṣṭo bahu bhāṣate,
aviśvaste viśvasiti mūḍhachetā narādhamaḥ.
Mahābhārata, Udyogaparva, Viduraprajāgara, 33.41

[Meaning] That man is mean and foolish who goes to a meeting or anybody's house uninvited; (who would like to occupy a position he/she doesn't deserve); who speaks in meeting without permission; who trusts the untrustworthy or unreliable.

Where there are respect and recognition for above type of teachers, preachers, and preceptors, there prevails ignorance, unrighteousness, vulgarity, quarrel, opposition, and animosities multiplying miseries.

Qualifications of a student

आलस्यं मदमोहौ च चापल्यं गोष्ठिरेव च।
स्तब्धता चाभिमानित्वं तथाऽत्यागित्वमेव च।
एते वै सप्त दोषाः स्युः सदा विद्यार्थिनां मताः।।
(महाभारत, उद्योगपर्व, विदुरप्रजागर, 40.05)

ālasyaṁ madamohau cha chāpalyaṁ goṣṭhireva cha,
stabdhatā chābhimānitvaṁ tathā'tyāgitvameva cha,
ēte vai sapta doṣāḥ syuḥ sadā vidyārthināṁ matāḥ.
Mahābhārata, Udyogaparva, Viduraprajāgara, 40.05

[Meaning] Lethargy in body and mind, use of intoxicants, infatuation, fickleness, idle gossip, break in studies, haughtiness, lack of renunciation - students suffering from above cited seven vices can never acquire knowledge.

सुखार्थिनः कुतो विद्या कुतो विद्यार्थिनः सुखम्।
सुखार्थी वा त्यजेद्विद्यां विद्यार्थी वा त्यजेत्सुखम्।।
(महाभारत, उद्योगपर्व, विदुरप्रजागर, 40.06)

sukhārthinaḥ kuto vidyā kuto vidyārthinaḥ sukham,
sukhārthī vā tyajedvidyāṁ vidyārthī vā tyajetsukham.
Mahābhārata, Udyogaparva, Viduraprajāgara, 40.06

[Meaning] How can a pleasure-seeker seek knowledge and how can a student (knowledge seeker) seek pleasure? A pleasure-seeker should give up the idea of learning and a student (seeker of knowledge) should give up the idea of pleasure, (since both things cannot go together).

Following students attain education

सत्ये रतानां सततं दान्तानामूर्ध्वरेतसाम्।
ब्रह्मचर्यं दहेद्राजन् सर्वपापान्युपासितम्।। (महाभारत, भीष्मपर्व)

satye ratānāṁ satataṁ dāntānāmūrdhvaretasām,
brahmacharyaṁ dahedrājan sarvapāpānyupāsitam.
Mahābhārata, Bhīṣmaparva

[Meaning] They alone have a true Brahmacharya life (student life) and become learned who always lead a life of good conduct, have control over their senses and observe celibacy and stay away from all pāpa karmas (wicked acts).

Therefore, the teachers and students should possess good qualities.

The teachers should take care that their students are true to their words, thoughts and actions. They are civilized, have control over their senses, gentle, physically and spiritually strong and well-versed in the Vedas and Śāstras. It is the duty of teachers to make their students get rid of evil habits and impart knowledge to them. On the other hand, students are required to cultivate self-control, mental stability, love for their teachers, thoughtfulness and habits of diligence. They should try their best to acquire perfect knowledge, perfect Dharma and full age (100 years), so as to make all their four ends (dharma, artha, kāma and mokṣa) of life meet diligently. These are duties suitable to a person from Brāhmaṇa profession. Duties of Kṣatriya professional will be described in the sixth chapter dealing with Government and Administration.

Those who want to chose the profession of Vaiśyas as per their guṇa (qualifications/merit), karma (profession) and svabhāva (temperament), they should first learn Vedas with a vow of chastity followed by their marriage. Afterwards, they can learn languages of various countries, get training in different trade skills, practical training in export import. They should keep themselves updated with exchange rates of major world currencies, rates of various commodities in the world market and should be ready to undertake foreign travels for the purposes of trade, etc. They can engage in profitable business, promote cattle rearing, agriculture and help to strengthen the economy of the nation, so that expenditure on education (both moral and professional) can be augmented. All persons engaged in Vaiśya profession should be truthful and honest in dealings. There should be a proper storage facility for all types of goods, so that everything is well preserved and protected and nothing go waste.

Śudras (uneducated skilled and unskilled labours) should be well trained in all services and cooking art, so that they may earn handsome amount to sustain themselves and their families.

The people from all the four Varṇas (three educated and one uneducated professional class) should work harmoniously with the sense of helping each other. They should have affection for each other and should be ready to share each other's pleasure and pain, profit and loss. They should unitedly contribute to the progress and development of the country with body, mind and all material resources at their command.

The spouses (husband and the wife) should never live separately, because-

पानं दुर्जनसंसर्गः पत्या च विरहोऽटनम |
स्वप्नोऽन्यगेहवासश्च नारीसन्दूषणानि षट् || मनु० 9.13||

pānaṁ durjanasaṁsargaḥ patyā cha virahoaiṭanama dya
svapnoainyagehavāsaścha nārīsandūṣaṇāni ṣaṭ dyadya
Manu, 9.13

[Meaning] The following six vices spoil women: (1) use of liquor or other intoxicants, (2) association with the wicked persons, (3) separation from the husband, (4) wandering about aimlessly, (5,6) sleeping and dwelling in another person's house

These very vices spoil men too. The separation between the husband and the wife may take place on two accounts; firstly, on account of business or service spouses may be separated, secondly, on account of death the surviving spouse may suffer separation. Separation of the first kind can be managed if the wife and husband are posted at one place or near to each other's place of posting, or if the husband takes his wife along with him whenever he goes abroad or distant postings, so that the spouses are not allowed to live separately for s long period.

Question: Is polygamy or polyandry allowed?

Answer: No

Question: Is re-marriage allowed?

Answer: Yes. For instance, according to Manu (9.179):

स चेद् अक्षतयोनिः स्याद् गतप्रत्यागतापि वा।
पौनर्भवेन भत्र्रा सा पुनः संस्कारमर्हति।।

sa ched akṣatayoniḥ syād gatapratyāgatāpi vā,
paunarbhavena bhatrarā sā punaḥ saṁskāramarhati.

[Meaning] If a woman is virgin after marriage or she has returned to her parental house after death of her husband, she is entitled to re-marry.

But re-marriage should be absolutely prohibited at least among educated people, when the first marriage has consummated, although there may be a provision of some relaxation in case of uneducated people.

Question: What are disadvantages in re-marriage?

Answer: 1. Decrease in love between husband and wife, since either of them can desert the other at their sweet will and marry another person.

2. On the death of one spouse, the surviving will take away the property of his or her deceased spouse when he or she marries again. This will give rise to family disputes.

3. Family line of several noble families will break and their property destroyed (by constant alienation).

4. Re-marriage will promote a breach of loyalty to husband and wife and promote divorces.

It is for these reasons that re-marriage of those whose first marriage has consummated, as well as polygamy and polyandry, should be prohibited at least among educated people.

Question: In absence of issue due to the premature death of one of the spouses, the family line will break.

Men and women may commit adultery and indulge into corrupt practices like abortions. Therefore, re-marriage is desirable.

Answer: No no. If the widows and widowers desire to practice Brahmacharya, there is no problem in allowing them to do so. For the family line to continue, a widow or widower may adopt a child from their close relations leaving no space for corruption. Those who want to have their own children can have recourse to Niyoga. Those who can control their passions can go for artificial insemination and those who cannot control their passions may go for natural insemination.

NB: Here it may be clarified that practice of Niyoga was sanctioned in Vedas and other Śāstras. Niyoga was the exercised by 1. Artificial stimulation of female ovum or male sperm for reproduction. 2. Artificial or natural insemination by a sperm or ovum donor. Artificial or natural insemination is the deliberate introduction of sperm into a female for sexual reproduction if a man or woman wishes to bear or beget a child in absence of his or her married partner or his or her partner is infertile. Natural insemination was performed by a sperm donor ejaculating within a fertile female's reproductive tract during sexual intercourse. Natural insemination is always a type of in vivo fertilisation. Artificial insemination, on the other hand, was performed by introduction of sperm of sperm donor into the reproductive tract of a fertile female by means other than sexual intercourse. This process is also a type of in vivo fertilisation. But if the female happened to be infertile or suffered from the genetic disorder, her mature eggs were collected and fertilised by the sperm of sperm donor outside the uterus, a technique called in vitro fertilisation. The embryos were also developed in vitro and baby used to born out of an urn (tube) and not from the womb of the mother. Here it may also be pointed out that only diseased or infertile partner's younger or elder brother often called as devara or his one of cousins from his six pedigrees was allowed to donate sperm for artificial or natural insemination.

Question: What is the differences between re-marriage and Niyoga (surrogacy through artificial or natural insemination by sperm donor)?

Answer:1. After remarriage, a widow leaves her parental house or her deceased husband's house and lives with her second husband, but in the case of Niyoga, she continues to live in her deceased husband's house or parental house as the case may be.

2. The progeny created by married partner belongs to him and inherit his property and surname, whereas, progeny created by niyukta partner (partner appointed to donate sperm in Niyoga i.e. natural or artificial insemination) neither belongs to him nor inherits his surname. The niyukta partner (sperm donor or surrogate father) has no right to them. Rather they are called children of the deceased husband of the widow and inherits his surname and property. They also live in the deceased house.

3. The married partners have legal liabilities to each other, while appointed partners (sperm donor surrogate father or ovum donor surrogate mother) have no legal liability to each other.

4. Married partners have a life long relation, while appointed (niyukta) partners keep no contact except on the appointed day for Niyoga (natural insemination).

5. The married partners discharge their household duties mutually, while niyukta (appointed) partners discharge the duties of their respective households of

their own.

Question: Are the rules of marriage and Niyoga (artificial or natural insemination by sperm donor) same or different?

Answer: They are little different. A few differences have already been enumerated, and here are some more to reckon with:

Married partners can produce children up to the limit of ten, while the niyukta (appointed) partners cannot produce more than two or four children. Here it may be reminded that marriage is allowed between bachelors and maids, whereas Niyoga (artificial or natural insemination) is permissible when one of the married partner is either dead or infertile. Married partners always live together but niyukta (appointed) partners cannot do so. They can contact each other on the appointed date only for natural insemination, but in the case of artificial insemination, they cannot establish any contact. If a woman wants to bear a child through sperm donor (surrogate father) when she does not have a male partner or her partner is infertile., she cannot contact the niyukta (appointed) partner (sperm donor) beyond the second conception in the case of natural insemination. Similarly if a man doesn't have a partner or his partner is infertile and wants to become father through natural insemination, he cannot contact his appointed partner (surrogate mother) beyond her second conception, although she is permitted to look after the child for two to three years before to surrender him to the father.

As such a widow can bear through Niyoga (surrogacy) two children for herself and two each for four widowers (surrogate fathers). Similarly, a widower can father two children for himself and two each for four widows by Niyoga (by way of surrogacy). Thus maximum ten children are permissible in the Veda, which reads as under:

इमां त्वमिन्द्र मीढ्वः सुपुत्रां सुभगां कृणु ।
दशास्यां पु त्रानाधेहि पतिमेकाद शं कृधि ।। ऋ० 10.85.45

imāṁ tvamindra mīḍhvaḥ suputrāṁ subhagāṁ kṛṇu,
daśāsyāṁ pu trānādhehi patimekāda śaṁ kṛdhi.
RV. 10.85.45

[Meaning] Let you O potent husband raise upon your wife good children bestowing upon them good fortune. Beget up to ten children by your wife making her as the 11th member of the family. Same is applicable to a widower. He can also beget up to 10 children by different widows under a contract of Niyoga (surrogacy) with him.

O woman! let ten children be borne by you from your husband making him the 11th member of the family. Same is applicable to a widow. She can also bear 10 children for different widowers who signed a contract of Niyoga (surrogacy) with her.

The above Vedic injunction requires at least educated persons to produce not more than ten children, least the offsprings are physically and intellectually weak and short-lived. Even parents indulging in the procreation of excessive progeny may become weak, short-lived, afflicted with the disease and suffer in old age.

Question: But Niyoga (surrogacy through natural insemination) looks like adultery.

Answer: Just as the extra marital affair is adultery, so is sexual affair without a contract of Niyoga (surrogacy) between widows and widowers is adultery. From this it follows that just as marriage recognised legally doesn't come in the purview of adultery, even so, Niyoga (surrogacy through natural insemination) when recognised legally cannot be termed adultery. For instance, sexual activities after the lawful marriage between a daughter of one family and son from another family are no longer viewed as adultery or shameful act, similarly, lawful Niyoga (surrogacy) will not be regarded as adulterous or shameful act.

Question: This is all right, but, still, it sounds like prostitution.

Answer: Certainly not. A prostitute sticks to no particular man, nor is there any specific rule to govern her sexual activities, while Niyoga (surrogacy through natural insemination) like marriage is governed by certain rules. Just as one does not feel ashamed of giving away his daughter in marriage to another person or having sexual relations with his/her married partner, in like manner there ought to be no shame in contracting Niyoga (surrogacy through artificial or natural insemination). Do you think, corrupt man and woman, avoid extramarital relations after marriage?

Question: We doubt about the constitutionality of Niyoga (surrogacy through natural insemination).

Answer: Should you think that Niyoga is unconstitutional practice, why don't you regard marriage also as unconstitutional? Unconstitutionality is in derecognizing Niyoga (surrogacy through natural insemination), for according to the laws of nature, the natural instinct of man and woman cannot be checked or modified, unless one is indifferent to worldly affairs or a profound scholar and a Yogi of the highest order. Don't you regard abortions (deliberate terminations of pregnancy) and the sufferings of widows and widowers a pāpa. For, so long as they are young, aspire for progeny and feel the sexual urge, they may form illegal alliances, if the law and society forbid them to do so. The only way to check adultery and corrupt practice is to let those, who can control their passions, do without Niyoga or even marriage, but those who do not possess so much self-restraint must be allowed to marry, or in case of emergency contract Niyoga (surrogacy through natural insemination), so that the chances of adultery may be greatly minimized, giving rise to addition of good children in society born out of love of legitimately united persons. This will also do away with the practice of feticide.

Marriage and Niyoga will do away with such wicked practices as the illicit relationship between a low profile man and a high profile woman or between an elite family man and a sex worker leading to defamation of noble families and breaking their family lines. This will also assuage the widows and widowers of their sufferings. So Niyoga is desirable.

Question: What should be the rules and regulations governing Niyoga?

Answer: Niyoga (surrogacy through artificial or natural insemination) should be solemnized publicly even as marriage is. As marriage requires the sanction of society and consent of couple, so does Niyoga. In other words, when a widow and widower have agreed to Niyoga, they should declare before their family members and relatives that they want to contract Niyoga for progeny. Once the very purpose of Niyoga is served, they will not have contact. Otherwise, they are liable to be punished by state or society as the case may be. They will have intercourse only for once during woman's monthly fertile period and will have no contact thereafter.

Question: Should Niyoga be allowed with a person of one's own Varṇa (profession) or with persons of different varṇa (professions)?

Answer: A woman should go for Niyoga with a person of her own varṇa (profession and personality type) or with the one who is better than her. Our object is to beget superior kind of children which is scientifically possible when the sperm is of equal or better quality than the egg. The sperm of Brāhmaṇa, Kṣatriya, Vaiśya and Śudras varṇas (professionals) are considered superior in order. The main objective of God creating man and woman is to create progeny based upon their marriage or Niyoga as enjoined in the Veda.

Question: What is need of Niyoga, when there is an option of remarriage?

Answer: We have already said that Vedas and other Śāstras allow educated persons to marry only once, never for a second time. Morality and Natural justice demand that a celibate man should marry a celibate woman. It is against the norms of natural justice and morality for a widower to marry a celibate woman, and for a widow to a celibate man. Just as a celibate man does not like to marry a widow, so does a celibate woman to a widower. If no virgin will marry a widower, and no celibate man will marry a widow, the need of Niyoga will arise. Moreover, morality demands, like must meet like.

Question: Is there any Vedic and Śāstric authority in favour of Niyoga, as there are in support of the marriage institution?

Answer: There are many authorities in this regard. See for example,

कुह स्विद्दो षा कुह वस्तोर श्विना कुहापिभिपि त्वं करतकुहोषतुः । :
को वां शयु त्रा विधवेवपिव दे वरं मर्य्यं न योषा कृणुते स धस्थ आ । ।

ऋ० 10.40.2

kuha sviddo ṣā kuha vastora śvinā kuhāpibhipi

tvaṁ karata: kuhoṣatuḥ,
ko vāṁ śayu trā vidhavevapiva de varaṁ maryya na yoṣā kṛṇute sa dhastha ā. RV. 10.40.2

[Meaning] O man and woman, just as a widow shares her bed with her husband's brother after signing a contract of Niyoga to beget a child and married woman shares her bed for the same purpose with her legally wedded husband, similarly let me know where both of you (man and woman) reside during day and night, where you get your desired things from, where you sleep, who you are and what your native place is?

The above verse indicates that husband and wife should always live together whether at home or abroad and that a widow may also beget children through Niyoga.

Question: Suppose the deceased husband of a widow has no younger brother, with whom should she sign Niyoga?

Answer: With her devara (secondary husband), but the word devara does not mean what you think. In this regard the Nirukta says:

देवरः कस्माद् द्वितीयो वर उच्यते। निरुक्त, 3.15
devaraḥ kasmād dvitīyo vara uchyate, nirukta, 3.15

[Meaning] Devara is so named because he acts as the secondary husband of a married woman when she gets widowed.

Anybody with whom Niyoga is signed by the widow may be called her Devara (secondary husband), whether he be the younger brother or elder brother or a cousin within six pedigrees of the deceased husband of the concerned widow or any other person from the same varṇa (profession) or the higher one.

उदीर्ष्व नार्यभिजीवलोकं गतासुमेतमुप शेष एहि ।
हस्तग्राभस्य दिधिषोस्तवेदं पत्युर्जनित्वमभि संवभृथ ।। ऋग्वेद, 10.18.8

udīrṣva nāryabhijīvalokaṁ gatāsumetamupa śeṣa ēhi, hastagrābhasya didhiṣostavedaṁ patyurjanitvamabhi saṁvabhṛtha. *RV. 10.18.8*

[Meaning] (नारि) O woman, (एतं गतासुम्) give up hope of the deceased one (शेषे अभि जीव लोकम् उपैहि) choose from the living ones for surrogacy. (उदीर्ष्व) But remember that if you sign Niyoga in favour of the surrogate father (widower) who grasped your hand for Niyoga, then the child born to you (जनित्वं) will relate to the widower (हस्तग्राभस्य दिधिषोः) Should you contract this Niyoga in favour of you, (तव इदं) the child will belong to you. (अभि संबभूथ) Let this be made clear.

The same rule applies to the widower who contracts Niyoga (surrogacy).

अदेवृघ्न्यपतिघ्नीहैधि शिवा पशुभ्यः सुयमा सुवर्चाः ।
प्रजावती वीरसूर्देवृकामा स्योनेममग्निं गार्हपत्यं सपर्य ।। अथर्ववेद, 14.2.18

adevṛghnyapatighnīhaidhi śivā paśubhyaḥ suyamā suvarchāḥ,
prajāvatī vīrasūrdevṛkāmā syonemamagniṁ gārhapatyaṁ saparya. *Atharvaveda, 14.2.18*

[Meaning] O non-violent woman to the husband or to the devara (secondary husband by Niyoga), in this Gṛhasthāśrama be benevolent to the cattle, be an abider of yama and niyama, be rich in knowledge and beauty, have children and grandchildren, give birth to brave sons, desire for devara (by Niyoga) in case of sudden demise of your husband, be soft and pleasant to your husband or devara and conduct household rites in household fire.

According to Manu (9.69):

यस्या म्रियेत कन्याया वाचा सत्ये कृते पतिः ।
तामनेन विधानेन निजो विन्देत देवरः ॥

yasyā mriyeta kanyāyā vāchā satye kṛte patiḥ,
tāmanena vidhānena nijo vindeta devaraḥ.

[Meaning] If the husband of a virgin dies after the engagement, her brother-in-law (younger brother of her deceased husband) can also marry her according to the injunction of Śāstras.

Question: How many times can a man or woman go for Niyoga? What names are to be given to the husband by marriage and to sperm donors appointed for Niyoga (surrogacy through natural insemination)?

Answer:

सोमः प्रथमो विविदे गन्धर्वो विविद उत्तरः ।
तृतीयो अग्निष्टे पतिस्तुरीयस्ते मनुष्यजाः ।। ऋग्वेद, 10.85.40

somaḥ prathamo vivide gandharvo vivida uttaraḥ,
tṛtīyo agniṣṭe patisturīyaste manuṣyajāḥ.

Ṛgveda, 10.85.40

[Meaning] O woman! your first married husband is named Soma because he was a chaste bachelor (before marriage). Your second-time sperm donor appointed for Niyoga (surrogacy through natural insemination) is called Gandharva, on account of his previous consummation with a woman. Your third time appointed sperm donor for Niyoga is named Agni, on account of his excessive passions. All other sperm donors appointed for Niyoga (surrogacy through natural insemination) from third time onward are called Manuṣyajas.

According to the above mantra, a woman may contract Niyoga with eleven sperm donors (one after another), similarly, a man may enter into Niyoga with eleven surrogate mothers (egg donors) (one after another).

Question: Why should not the word eleven be taken to refer to ten sons and the husband as the eleventh (member of the family)?

Answer: With this interpretation, you will not be able to explain phrases like vidhveva devaram (as a widow with sperm donor), devaraḥ kasmād dvitiyo vara uchyate (devara means secondary sperm donor), adevṛghni (not violent with sperm donor), gandharvo vivid uttaraḥ (the next sperm donor is called gandharva) and other Vedic phrases. Your interpretation doesn't allow even a secondary husband.

Manu (9, 59; 58) says:

देवराद्वा सपिण्डाद्वा स्त्रिया सम्यङ् नियुक्तया।
प्रजेप्सिताधिगन्तव्या सन्तानस्य परिक्षये।। 9.59

devarādvā sapiṇḍādvā striyā samyaṅ niyuktayā,
prajepsitādhigantavyā santānasya parikṣaye. 9.59

ज्येष्ठो यवीयसी भाग्र्या यवीयान्वाग्रजस्त्रियम् ।
पतितौ भवतो गत्वा नियुक्तावप्यनापदि।। 9.58

jyeṣṭho yavīyasī bhāyryā yavīyānvāgrajastriyam,
patitau bhavato gatvā niyuktāvapyanāpadi. 9.58

[Meaning] On failure of issue (by her deceased husband), a widow (desirous of bearing a child) may contract Niyoga with a widower, who may be her brother in law or other sapiṇḍa (a cousin within the six pedigrees) of her deceased husband. (59)

An elder brother, who approaches the widow of the younger to donate sperm, and a younger brother, who approaches the widow of the elder to donate sperm even when the necessity of getting children has ceased to operate, even though appointed for sperm donation, shall be punished with degradation to the lower position. (58)

In other words, the physical contact with sperm donor in case of natural insemination lasts only up to the conception of a second child. If the Niyoga was contracted in favour of both parties, the period of contact may be extended up to the conception of a fourth child (two for widow and two for a widower). Accordingly, ten children may be produced with the help of successive sperm donors.

If the period of physical contact with sperm donors is maintained beyond the limit of the conception of a 10th child, it amounts to be an illicit relationship and invites punishment. Even if married partners keep physical contact after the conception of a 10th child, they will also be considered amorous and held in great contempt, because marriage and Niyoga are meant for procreation and not for the gratification of passions like animals.

Question: Can a woman go for Niyoga (artificial or natural insemination by sperm donor) only after the death of her husband or even when he is alive?

Answer: She can contract Niyoga even when her husband is alive.

अन्यमिच्छस्व सुभगे पतिं मत्।। ऋग्वेद, 10.10.10

anyamichchhasva subhage patiṁ mat.

Ṛgveda, 10.10.10

[Meaning] When a husband is infertile or suffering from the genetic disorder, he should address his wife as follows: O fortune seeking wife, you seek another sperm donor to bear offspring, as I am no longer capable of raising offspring upon you. Upon this, the wife may contract Niyoga with a widower to donate sperm. She should, however, continue to serve her husband by marriage. Similarly, when a woman is infertile or suffers from a genetic disorder, let her also allow her husband to contract Niyoga with a widow who can bear a child for them.

There are some historical evidence to support Niyoga (artificial stimulation of female ovum or male sperm for reproduction, or artificial or natural insemination by donating sperm). For example, Kunti and Mādrī, wives of King Pāṇḍu had recourse to Niyoga i.e. artificial stimulation from various energies of their ovum for reproduction.

NB: This technique is still known as Parthenogenesis. Parthenogenesis is the corrupt form of Pṛthājanana, i.e. production by way of Pṛthā or Kuntī. Such experiments are done in modern science to produce young ones only in lower animals and not in human beings. However, ancient Indian scientists used this technique in the human beings. In the modern times, the technique of Parthenogenesis produced all the females from the female. However, the ancient Indian scientist went far advance to produce sons from Kuntī as well as Mādrī. Though this technique has been discovered in the 51st century of Kali era by the modern science, yet the experiments are in the premature state. The technique and experiments of modern medical science can be updated with the help of the techniques and experiments done in the past in Bhārata.

Vyāsa, on the death of his brothers, Chitrāṅgada and Vichitravīrya donated his sperm to their wives and their maid for artificial insemination, so that they may bear progeny. Consequently, Ambikā gave birth to Dhṛtarāṣṭra, Ambālikā to Pāṇḍu and their maid to Vidura.

Let us read Manu,

प्रोषितो धर्मकार्यार्थं प्रतीक्ष्योऽष्टौ नरः समाः ।
विद्यार्थं षड् यशोऽर्थं वा कामार्थं त्रीस्तु वत्सरान् ।। मनु० 9.76 ।।

proṣito dharmakāryārthaṁ pratīkṣayo'ṣṭau naraḥ samāḥ dya
vidyārthaṁ ṣaḍ yaśo'rthaṁ vā kāmārthaṁ trīstu vatsarān dyadya, Manu, 9.76

[Meaning] If a husband went abroad to undertake spiritual and moral pursuits, his wife must wait for eight years; if he went to acquire knowledge and name, for six years; if for material gains, for three years. If he does not turn up after the expiry of the prescribed periods, she may beget children through artificial or natural insemination by a sperm donor.

Upon arrival of married husband, the contract of Niyoga will automatically become infructuous. Similarly, there is rule for husband-

वन्ध्याष्टमेऽधिवेद्याब्दे दशमे तु मृतप्रजाः ।
एकादशे स्त्रीजननी सद्यस्त्वप्रियवादिनी ।। मनु० 9.81 ।।

vandhyāṣṭame'dhivedyābde daśame tu mṛtaprajāḥ
ēkādaśe strījananī sadyastvapriyavādinī. Manu, 9.81

[Meaning] If the wife is barren, the husband must wait for eight years; if her children die after birth, for 10 years; if she bears only daughters and no sons, for eleven years; but if she is quarrelsome, he should forsake her immediately, and enter into agreement of Niyoga with another lady and beget children upon her.

Likewise, if the husband is very cruel, let his wife forsake him and bear children through artificial insemination by a sperm donor, so that they may become heirs of the married husband's property.

All these authorities and arguments go to prove that each man and woman in society has a right to progeny to improve his/her family line, be it Swayaṁvara Vivaha - marriage by choice ṣ or Niyoga (artificial or natural insemination).

औरसः क्षेत्रजश्चैव दत्तः कृत्रिम एव च ।
गूढोत्पन्नोऽपविद्धश्च दायादा बान्धवाश्च षट्।। मनु .9.159।।

aurasaḥ kṣetrajaśchaiva dattaḥ kṛtrima ēva cha,
gūḍhotpanno'paviddhaścha dāyādā bāndhavāścha ṣaṭ.
Manu, 9.159.

[Meaning] Just as an Aurasa child, i.e. a child born of marriage alliance has the right of inheritance to the property of his father, so is a Kṣestraja child - a child born of Niyoga alliance, i.e. artificial or natural insemination by donation of a sperm or ovum, adopted child, artificially created child through the technique of Parthenogenesis by stimulating sperm or ovum alone, test tube baby without ovum and the child rejected by the natural parents, but adopted by the surrogate parents.

Men and women should always bear in mind that the (male or female) reproductive element is invaluable. Whosoever wastes this invaluable element in an illicit relationship with other people's wives, prostitutes, or lewd men, is the greatest fool because even a farmer or a gardener, ignorant though he is, does not sow the seed in a field or a garden that is not his own. When such precaution is taken even by a fool in the case of an ordinary seed, he is surely the most foolish who sows the seed of such an excellent tree as the body of human being in an improper field, as it will yield him no fruit thereof.

The Brāhmaṇa text says: vkRek oS tk;rs iq=% i.e. a son is born of his father's self. The Sāma Mantra Brāhmaṇa (1.5.18) also declares:

अङ्गादङ्गात्सम्भवसि हृदयादधि जायसे ।

आत्मासि पुत्र मा मृथा स जीव शरदः शतम्।। साम मन्त्र ब्राह्मण, 1.5.18

aṅgādaṅgātsambhavasi hṛdayādadhi jāyase,
ātmāsi putra mā mṛthā sa jīva śaradaḥ śatam.

Sāma Mantra Brāhmaṇa, 1.5.18

[Meaning] O son! you are born of my sperm which is drawn from all the bodily organs and from the heart. You are, therefore, my own self. May you never die before me. May you live a full course of a hundred years' life.

It is the biggest pāpa to sow the good seed of sperm, which caused the birth of great men in past, in a bad soil of prostitutes or to let a good soil be impregnated with a bad seed of sperm.

Question: What is need of marriage? It unnecessary binds a man and woman and makes them suffer and sacrifice. They can have live-in-relationship so long as they love each other and can break away when they are tired of each other.

Answer: This is the life-style of birds and animals and not those of human beings. If the institution of marriage is abolished from the society, there will be no charm in household life. Nobody will come forward to take care and help the needy. Adultery will be rampant, and people will die soon on account of various types of sexually transmitted diseases like HIV/AIDS etc. and lack of physical and mental strength, no one will fear another, nobody will take care of elderly persons in family or society. There will be a complete break-down of the family system. No one will have a title to succeed to another's property, nor will any person be able to retain possession of anything for long. Family institution is the only remedy for all these evils.

Question: Under the system of marital monogamy, an

individual is supposed to have only one life partner, what will an individual do if one of the partners is unable to have sexual intercourse due to some unavoidable circumstances like chronic disease or pregnancy when another partner is youthful and have a strong urge for sex?

Answer: This question has already been answered while dealing with the issue of Niyoga (surrogacy through artificial or natural insemination). First of all, an individual should try to keep restraint on his passions. If he/she fails to do so, the Niyoga (natural insemination) is the only remedy for it. They can go for Niyoga (surrogacy) and bear a child for the needy in their family, but adultery or commercial sex is nevertheless a solution.

There should a genuine effort on the part of individuals to achieve that which they don't have and to preserve carefully that which they have already achieved, and to multiply that which they have preserved carefully. They should spend the excess money in public or national interest. Let everybody perform duties in public interest due to him/her as per his/her merit, profession and personality type. They should diligently give care to their parents, in-laws in their old age when they need it and be sociable to their friends, neighbours, boss, learned persons, physicians and other gentlemen. They should not neglect or bear malice to wicked and evil-doers, instead, try to reform them. They should put maximum possible efforts in securing quality education to their children and transforming them into good scholars and great personalities. Let them also lead a virtuous life in order to attain salvation, so that they may enjoy eternal bliss. They should not pay heed to such verses as quoted below:

पतितोऽपि द्विजः श्रेष्ठो न च शूद्रो जितेन्द्रियः ।

निर्दुग्धा चापि गौः पूज्याः न च दुग्धवती खरी ।। 1 ।।

patito'pi dvijaḥ śreṣṭho na cha śūdro jitendriyaḥ, nirdugdhā chāpi gauḥ pūjyāḥ na cha dugdhavatī kharī.

अश्वालम्भं गवालम्भं संन्यासं पलपैत्रिकम् ।
देवराच्च सुतोत्पत्तिं कलौ पंच विवर्जयेत् ।। 2 ।।

aśvālambhaṁ gavālambhaṁ saṁnyāsaṁ palapaitrikam,
devarāchcha sutotpattiṁ kalau paṁcha vivarjayet.

नष्टे मृते प्रव्रजिते क्लीबे च पतिते पतौ ।
पंचस्वापत्सु नारीणां पतिरन्यो विधियते ।। 3 ।।

naṣṭe mṛte pravrajite klībe cha patite patau,
paṁchasvāpatsu nārīṇāṁ patiranyo vidhiyate.

[Meaning] Even a corrupt educated person is superior to the uneducated person who has restrained his passions. Likewise, a dry cow is sacred compared to a milch jenny.

Horse sacrifice, cow sacrifice, initiation into Saṁnyāsa, offering flesh in śrādha ceremony, producing a child through artificial or natural insemination when sperm is donated by a brother in law or a cousin within six pedigrees of a married partner, these five practices should be abandoned in Kaliyuga.

A woman may remarry in the following conditions if her husband is missing or untraceable; or he is dead; or he has taken Saṁnyāsa; or he is impotent; or he is corrupt.

The above verses are from a spurious book called Pārāśarī. What is greater bias, injustice, unethical than to regard a wicked educated person better than a virtuous uneducated person? A jenny is equally an object of care for the Potter, as a milch or dry cow to the milkman. Even the illustration is oddly placed since the educated and uneducated men belong to the human species whereas cow and Jenny belong to animal species. Should an illustration from the animal kingdom be partly applicable to human beings, this verse cannot be regarded as true by learned men, its intention being ridiculous.

Horse-sacrifice and cow-sacrifice are not sanctioned in the Vedas, so what is the purpose of imposing a prohibition on them in Kaliyuga. Moreover, their prohibition in Kaliyuga will inversely entail their currency in other Yugas like Tretā etc. If wicked act like animal sacrifice is not permitted even in Kaliyuga, how can they be permitted in other Yugas which are considered better than Kaliyuga? Initiation into the order of Saṁnyāsa finds sanction in the Vedas and other Śāstras, therefore it is baseless to forbid it in Kaliyuga. If meat is prohibited, it applies equally to all ages. When reproduction through devara (a brother in law or a cousin within six pedigrees of husband appointed for donating sperm for artificial or natural insemination) is sanctioned in Vedas, why the author is making unnecessary hue and cry.

If a woman remarries keeping in view of her missing husband without taking divorce, whose wife would she be called if her missing husband comes back? You may say 'of the former husband'. We may accept it, but this provision is not laid down in the Pārāśarī. Moreover, are there only five occasions of emergency for a wife? His husband may have a prolonged illness or both of them may not be in good terms, as such the occasions of emergency may be more than five. So never believe and follow such statements.

Question: Why don't you accept the authority of Parāś ara?

Answer: Any statement opposed to the Vedas is no acceptable. Besides, this is not the statement of Parāśara. People have forged books in the name of eminent scholars like Brahmā, Vasiṣṭha, Rāma, Śiva, Viṣṇu and Devī, so that their books may become popular and earn them a handsome amount of money. So, they compose books on controversial issues. Barring few interpolations, the Manusmṛti is only reliable book among Smṛtis that follow Vedas. The same test can be applied to verify other forged books.

Question: How would you value Gṛhastha Āśrama (household life) as compared to others?

Answer: Every Āśrama has its exclusive duties. In this regard, we may refer to Manu.

यथा नदीनदाः सर्वे सागरे यान्ति संस्थितिम् ।
तथैवाश्रमिणः सर्वे गृहस्थे यान्ति संस्थितिम् ॥ मनुस्मृति, 6-90 ॥

yathā nadīnadāḥ sarve sāgare yānti saṁsthitim,
tathaivāśramiṇaḥ sarve gṛhasthe yānti saṁsthitim.
Manusmṛti, 6-90.

[Meaning] As all rivers and rivulets find their resting place in the ocean, so do men of all Āśrams depend on men of Gṛhastha Āśrama.

यथा वायुं समाश्रित्य वर्तन्ते सर्वजन्तवः ।
तथा गृहस्थमाश्रित्य वर्तन्ते सर्व आश्रमाः ॥ मनुस्मृति, 3-77

yathā vāyuṁ samāśritya vartante sarvajantavaḥ,
tathā gṛhasthamāśritya vartante sarva āśramāḥ.
Manusmṛti, 3-77

[Meaning] As all living creatures subsist on support from the air, even so, do the men of all Āśramas subsist on support from the householders (men of Gṛhastha Āśrama).

यस्मात् त्रयोऽप्याश्रमिणो दानेनान्नेन चान्वहम् ।

...न्ते तस्माज् ज्येष्ठाश्रमो गृही ॥ मनुस्मृति, 3-78 ॥

...trayo'pyāśramiṇo dānenānnena chānvaham,
...henaiva dhāryante tasmāj jyeṣṭhāśramo gṛhī.
Manusmṛti, 3-78

...leaning] As men of the three Āśramas - ...umacharya, Vānaprastha and Saṁnyāsa - are daily ...pported by the house holders for their daily needs and ...equirements. That is why, Gṛhastha Āśrama is superior of all.

Gṛhastha Āśrama is the centre of all activities.

स सन्धार्यः प्रयत्नेन स्वर्गमक्षयमिच्छता ।
सुखं चेहेच्छताऽत्यन्तं योऽधार्यो दुर्बलेन्द्रियैः ॥ मनुस्मृति, 3-79 ॥

sa sandhāryaḥ prayatnena svargamakṣayamichchhatā,
sukhaṁ chehechchhatā'tyantaṁ yo'dhāryo durbalendriyaiḥ. Manusmṛti, 3-79

[Meaning] So a person desirous of eternal bliss hereafter and comforts of the mundane world here, should carefully opt for Gṛhastha Āśrama, as the duties of Gṛhastha Āśrama cannot be performed by weak and coward.

Gṛhastha Āśrama is the centre and at the base of all activities of the world. Had there been no Gṛhastha Āśrama, there would have been no future generations and all Āśramas would have ceased functioning. Appreciable is he who speaks highly of Gṛhastha Āśrama and who condemns it, is himself condemnable. But remember, only those couples have good experience of Gṛhastha Āśrama, who are happy with each other, well educated, industrious and well versed in worldly affairs. Moreover, Brahmacharya (celibacy) and Svayaṁvara (consent marriage) mainly add to the happiness of this Āśrama.

In this chapter marriage and family life has been briefly discussed. Now on we shall discuss retirement and renunciation.

इति श्रीमद् दयानन्दसरस्वतीस्वामिकृते सत्यार्थप्रकाशे सुभाषाविभूषिते समावत्र्तनविवाहगृहाश्रमविषये चतुर्थः समुल्लासः सम्पूर्णः ।।

iti śrīmad dayānandasarasvatīsvāmikṛte satyārthaprakāśe subhāṣāvibhūṣite samāvatratanavivāhagṛhāśramaviṣaye chaturthaḥ samullāsaḥ sampūrṇaḥ

Thus ends the fourth chapter on 'Marriage and Family Life' of Satyarth Prakash by Swami Dayanand Saraswati.

"The world is fettered by the chain forged by superstition and ignorance. I have come to snap asunder that chain to set slaves at liberty. It is contrary to my mission to have people deprived of their freedom.'

Swami Dayanand Saraswati

CHAPTER 5

Retirement and Renunciation

अथ वानप्रस्थसंन्यासविधिं वक्ष्यामः ।

Atha vānaprasthasaṁnyāsavidhiṁ vakṣayāmaḥ

Now we shall explain procedure and life of Vānaprastha (retirement) and Saṁnyāsa (renunciation).

Vānaprastha (Retirement)

ब्रह्मचर्याश्रमं समाप्य गृही भवेत् गृही भूत्वा वनी भवेद्वनी भूत्वा प्रव्रजेत् ।

शतपथ ब्राह्मण, 14

brahmacharyāśramaṁ samāpya gṛhī bhavet gṛhī bhūtvā vanī bhavedvanī bhūtvā pravrajet.

Śatapatha Brāhmaṇa, 14

Having completed his Brahmacharya, let a man enter Gṛhastha Āśrama (married life), and thereafter retire in the forest (Vānaprastha) and finally take Saṁnyāsa. This is the consecutive order of the different Āśramas.

एवं गृहाश्रमे स्थित्वा विधिवत् स्नातको द्विजः ।
वने वसेत् तु नियतो यथावद् विजितैन्द्रियः ॥ मनुस्मृति, 6-1 ॥

evaṁ gṛhāśrame sthitvā vidhivat snātako dvijaḥ,
vane vaset tu niyato yathāvad vijitaindriyaḥ.

Manusmṛti, 6-1.

[Meaning] Having lived in Gṛhastha Āśrama, let an

educated man, who had duly completed his studentship (Brahmacharya) life, retire in the forest with firm resolve and control over his senses.

गृहस्थस्तु यथा पश्येद् वलीपलितमात्मनः ।
अपत्यस्यैव चापत्यं तदाऽरण्यं समाश्रयेत् ॥ मनुस्मृति, 6-2 ॥

gṛhasthastu yathā paśyed valīpalitamātmanaḥ,
apatyasyaiva chāpatyaṁ tadā'raṇyaṁ samāśrayet.

Manusmṛti, 6-2.

[Meaning] When a man of Gṛhastha Āśrama perceives his wrinkled skin, grey hairs and grand-child, let him then repair to a forest.

सन्त्यज्य ग्राम्यमाहारं सर्वं चैव परिच्छदम् ।
पुत्रेषु भार्यां निक्षिप्य वनं गच्छेत् सहैव वा ॥ मनुस्मृति, 6-3 ॥

santyajya grāmyamāhāraṁ sarvaṁ chaiva parichchhadam,
putreṣu bhāryāṁ nikṣipya vanaṁ gachchhet sahaiva vā

Manusmṛti, 6-3

[Meaning] Let him renounce all good things of town such as tasty dishes, fine clothes, commit his wife to the care of his sons, or take her along with and repair to a forest.

अग्निहोत्रं समादाय गृह्यं चाग्निपरिच्छदम् ।
ग्रामादरण्यं निःसृत्य निवसेन्नियतेन्द्रियः ॥ मनुस्मृति, 6-4 ॥

agnihotraṁ samādāya gṛhyaṁ chāgniparichchhadam,
grāmādaraṇyaṁ niḥsṛtya nivasenniyatendriyaḥ.

Manusmṛti, 6-4

[Meaning] Let him take all luggage necessary for performing Agnihotra and dwelling in a forest and depart from the town to take a refuse in a lonely wood with his senses perfectly subjugated.

मुन्यन्नैर्विविधैर्मेध्यैः शाकमूलफलेन वा ।

एतानेव महायज्ञान्निर्वपेद् विधिपूर्वकम् ॥ मनुस्मृति, 6-5 ॥

munyannairvividhairmedhyaiḥ śākamūlaphalena vā,
ētāneva mahāyajñānnirvaped vidhipūrvakam.

Manusmṛti, 6-5

[Meaning] Let him perform five Pañcha Mahāyajñas (five great yajñas) duly with various kinds of fresh food (such as sāmā rice), leafy vegetables, roots, fruits used by Munis.

स्वाध्याये नित्ययुक्तः स्याद् दान्तो मैत्रः समाहितः ।
दाता नित्यमनादाता सर्वभूतानुकम्पकः ॥ मनुस्मृति, 6-8 ॥

svādhyāye nityayuktaḥ syād dānto maitraḥ samāhitaḥ,
dātā nityamanādātā sarvabhūtānukampakaḥ.

Manusmṛti, 6-8

[Meaning] He should always focus his mind in studies, exercise self-control, befriend to all, remain composed, always give knowledge to others, but never accept a gift from them. He should also be kind to all living beings.

अप्रयत्नः सुखार्थेषु ब्रह्मचारी धराशयः ।
शरणेष्वममश्चैव वृक्षमूलनिकेतनः ॥ मनुस्मृति, 6-26 ॥

aprayatnaḥ sukhārtheṣu brahmachārī dharāśayaḥ,
śaraṇeṣvamamaśchaiva vṛkṣamūlaniketanaḥ.

Manusmṛti, 6-26

[Meaning] Let him not seek physical comforts, let him be a Brahmachari (chaste), that is, abstain from physical contact even of his won wife, sleep on the ground, have no attachment to his dependents or to his belongings, and dwell under a tree.

तपः श्रद्धे ये ह्युपवसन्त्यरण्ये शान्ता विद्वांसो भैक्षचर्यां चरन्तः ।
सूर्यद्वारेण ते विरजाः प्रयान्ति यत्राऽमृतः स पुरुषो ह्यव्ययात्मा ।।

मुण्डक उप. 2.2

tapaḥ śraddhe ye hyupavasantyaraṇye śāntā vidvāṁso bhaikṣacharyāṁ charantaḥ,

sūryadvāreṇa te virajāḥ prayānti yatrā'mṛtaḥ sa puruṣo hyavyayātmā. *Muṇḍaka Up. 2.2*

[Meaning] Learned scholars with calm and composed minds, relying on austerities, truth and virtue alone, subsisting on alms for their life, having freed free from all impurities, leave their body at the time of death when the solar channel (right nostril) is active and merge with Unchangeable and Immortal Brahman, i.e. attain salvation.

A man desiring a life of Vānaprastha (forest dweller), should pray as under:

अभ्यादधामि समिधमग्ने व्रतपते त्वयि।
व्रतंच श्रद्धा चोपैमीन्धे त्वां दीक्षितो अहम्।। यजुर्वेद, 20.24

abhyādadhāmi samidhamagne vratapate tvayi,
vrataṁcha śraddhā chopaimīndhe tvāṁ dīkṣito aham.
Yajurveda, 20.24

[Meaning] O Agni, presiding deity of vow or resolution, I offer Samidhā-s (kindle-sticks) on you (for conducting Agnihotra), so that having been initiated into Vānaprastha Āśrama upon performing a Homa, I may keep my resolve and faith in Vānaprastha Āśrama intact.

Thus having initiated into Vānaprastha, he should attain knowledge and purity by means of austerity, a company of good persons and practice of Yoga. Thereafter, if he so desires, he can take Saṁnyāsa along with his wife or have sent her back home, if she doesn't want to take Saṁnyāsa.

This is a brief note on Retirement.

Saṁnyāsa (Renunciation)

वनेषु च विहृत्यैवं तृतीयं भागमायुषः ।
चतुर्थमायुषो भागं त्यक्त्वा सङ्गान् परिव्रजेत् ॥ मनुस्मृति, 6.33

vaneṣu cha vihṛtyaivaṁ tṛtīyaṁ bhāgamāyuṣaḥ,
chaturthamāyuṣo bhāgaṁ tyakvā saṅgān parivrajet.

Manusmṛti, 6.33

[Meaning] After spending the third stage of life (50-75 years) in forests, let a man in the fourth stage renounce all connections and become a Saṁnyāsī.

Question: Is it morally wrong to become a direct Saṁnyāsī without going through the intermediate stages of Gṛhastha and Vānaprastha?

Answer: It is both wrong as well as right.

Question: How is it?

Answer: It is wrong when one undertakes Saṁnyāsa impulsively direct from Brahmacharya, and afterwards attracted to immoral acts. Nevertheless, it it would be a right decision if he is able to maintain his status of a renunciate.

Jābāla Upaniṣad (4) observes:

यदहरेव विरजेत्तदहरेव प्रव्रजेद्वा गृहाद्व ब्रह्मचर्यादेव प्रव्रजेत् ।

yadahareva virajettadahareva pravrajedvā gṛhādva brahmacharyādeva pravrajet.

[Meaning] Let a man renunciate (become a Saṁnyāsī) on the very day he becomes indifferent to worldly affairs, no matter whether he is a Vānaprasthī, Gṛhasthī or even a Brahmachārī.

First of all, a normal course for taking Saṁnyāsa is described followed by alternative provisions in view of exceptional circumstances. Accordingly, one of the alternatives is to take Saṁnyāsa directly from Gṛhastha Āśrama without undergoing Vānaprastha stage. The second alternative is to embrace Saṁnyāsa immediately after Brahmacharya Āśrama jumping over the intervening two stages of Vānaprastha and Gṛhastha, provided one is a perfect scholar, subdued his passions and carnal desires, and imbued with the excessive desire of propakāra (public good).

This practice is also sanctioned in the Vedas. For instance, we may quote from Ṛgveda (8.6.18) which reads as under:

यतयः ब्राह्मणस्य विजानतः।

yatayaḥ brāhmaṇasya vijānataḥ.

[Meaning] Let a Brahman seeker become a Saṁnyāsī.

However,

नविरतो दुश्चरितान्नाशान्तो नासमाहितः।
नाशान्तमनसो वापि प्रज्ञानेनैनमाप्नुयात्।। कठोपनिषद्, 2.24

navirato duścharitānnāśānto nāsamāhitaḥ,
nāśāntamanaso vāpi prajñānenainamāpnuyāt.

Kaṭhopaniṣad, 2.24

[Meaning] One who is not indifferent to worldly affairs, free from corruption, free from disturbance, does not know Yoga and is no longer calm and composed in mind cannot realize God by means of knowledge alone or having initiated into Saṁnyāsa.

Therefore,

यच्छेद्वाङ् मनसो प्राज्ञस्तद्यच्छेद् ज्ञान आत्मनि।
ज्ञानमात्मनि महति नियच्छेत्तद्यच्छेच्छान्त आत्मनि।। कठोपनिषद्, 3.13

yachchhedvāṅ manaso prājñastadyachchhed jñāna ātmani,
jñānamātmani mahati niyachchhettadyachchhechhānta ātmani.

Kaṭhopaniṣad, 3.13

[Meaning Let a wise Saṁnyāsī restrain his mind and speech from immoral acts and apply them to the acquisition of knowledge and the realization of his inner Self. Let him use his knowledge for the realization of the Supreme Being, and find rest in Him.

परीक्ष्य लोकान् कर्मचितान् ब्राह्मणो निर्वेदमायान्नास्त्यकृतः कृतेन। तद्विज्ञानार्थं स गुरुमेवाभिगच्छेत् समित्पाणिः श्रोत्रियं ब्रह्मनिष्ठम्।। मुण्डकोपनिषद्, 2.12

parīkṣaya lokān karmachitān brāhmaṇo nirvedamāyānnāstyakṛtaḥ kṛtena, tadvijñānārthaṁ sa gurumevābhigachchhet samitpāṇiḥ śrotriyaṁ brahmaniṣṭham. Muṇḍakopaniṣad, 2.12

[Meaning] Let a Brahman seeking Saṁnyāsī having confirmed that all the worldly enjoyments are attainable by actions, but realization of Supreme Self cannot be attained by actions, should approach with some kind of present in his hand to a preceptor well-versed in the Vedas and process of realization of Brahman to seek guide for self-realization.

But let him desert the company of the following;

अविद्यायामन्तरे वर्तमाना स्वयं धीराः पण्डितम्मन्यमानाः।
जंघन्यमाना परियन्ति मूढा अन्धेनैव नीयमाना यथान्धाः।।

avidyāyāmantare vartamānā svayaṁ dhīrāḥ paṇḍitammanyamānāḥ,
jaṁghanyamānā pariyanti mūḍhā andhenaiva nīyamānā yathāndhāḥ.

अविद्यायां बहुधा वर्तमाना वयं कृतार्था इत्यभिमन्यन्ति बालाः। यत्कर्मिणो न प्रवेदयन्ति रागात्तेनातुराः क्षीणलोकाश्च्यवन्ते।। मुण्डकोपनिषद्, 2.8-9

avidyāyāṁ bahudhā vartamānā vayaṁ kṛtārthā ityabhimanyanti bālāḥ, yatkarmiṇo na pravedayanti rāgāttenāturāḥ kṣīṇalokāśchyavante.

Muṇḍakopaniṣad, 2.8-9

[Meaning] Those ignorance-ridden people who arrogantly consider themselves to be intelligent and wise occupy the species of birds and animals full of ignorance and suffer miseries like the blind following the blind.

Those silly fellows who relish ignorance, believe to have attained the object of their lives through actions, under this fascination, they are not able to realize the truth and help others to do so. Such persons are not born as human beings again and suffer miseries in the lower species of insects, birds, animals and plants in their next lives.

Therefore.

वेदान्तविज्ञानसुनिश्चितार्थाः संन्यासयोगाद्यतयः शुद्धसत्त्वाः ।
ते ब्रह्मलोकेषु परान्तकाले परामृताः परिमुच्यन्ति सर्वे ।। मुण्डकोपनिषद्, 2.6

vedāntavijñānasuniśchitārthāḥ saṁnyāsayogādyatayaḥ śuddhasattvāḥ,

te brahmalokeṣu parāntakāle parāmṛtāḥ parimuchyanti sarve. *Muṇḍakopaniṣad, 2.6*

[Meaning] Those Saṁnyāsī-s whose intellects have become pure due to renunciation, who have properly understood the process of self-realization through Vedānta (last part of Vedas, i.e Upaniṣads). They enjoy immortality in Brahman till the time of expiry of their salvation period and thereafter revert back to life in the mundane world.

न सशरीरस्य सतः प्रियाप्रिययोरपहतिरस्त्यशरीरं वाव सन्तं नप्रियाप्रियेस्पृशतः ।

छान्दोग्य उपनिषद्, 8.12.1

na saśarīrasya sataḥ priyāpriyayorapahatirastyaśarīraṁ vāva santaṁ napriyāpriyespṛśataḥ.

Chhāndogya Upaniṣad, 8.12.1

[Meaning] The embodied soul can never be free from

pleasure or pain, but the same pleasure and pain is not going to impinge on it when it gets disembodied and live in the company of Almighty Brahman.

That is why,

लोकैषणायाश्च वित्तैषणायाश्च पुत्रैषणायाश्चोत्थायाथ भैक्षचर्यं चरन्ति।

शतपथ ब्राह्मण, 14.5.2.1

lokaiṣaṇāyāścha vittaiṣaṇāyāścha putraiṣaṇāyāśchotthāyātha bhaikṣacharyaṁ charanti.

Śatapatha Brāhmaṇa, 14.5.2.1

[Meaning] Saṁnyāsī-s rise above the longings for name and fame, wealth and progeny and live on alms.

They spend every moment of their life to redeem salvation.

प्राजापत्यां निरूप्येष्टिं तस्यां सर्ववेदसं हुत्वा ब्राह्मणः प्रव्रजेत्। यजुर्वेदब्राह्मण

prājāpatyāṁ nirūpyeṣṭiṁ tasyāṁ sarvavedasaṁ hutvā brāhmaṇaḥ pravrajet. Yajurveda Brāhmaṇa

[Meaning] For the realization of God, let a seeker of Brahman take Saṁnyāsa upon performing a yajña and abandoning all external signs like sacred thread, tuft or lock of hair.

प्राजापत्यं निरुप्येष्टिं सर्ववेदसदक्षिणाम् ।
आत्मन्यग्नीन् समारोप्य ब्राह्मणः प्रव्रजेद् गृहात् ॥ मनुस्मृति, 6-38

prājāpatyaṁ nirupyeṣṭiṁ sarvavedasadakṣiṇām,
ātmanyagnīn samāropya brāhmaṇaḥ pravrajed gṛhāt.

Manusmṛti, 6-38

[Meaning] For realization of God, let a seeker of Brahman renounce his house and take Saṁnyāsa upon performing a yajña and abandoning all external signs like sacred thread, tuft or lock of hair. He should impose on himself the practice of five vital forces (prāṇās), i.e. prāṇ, apāna, udāna, samāna, vyāna in place of five fires of Yajña, i.e. Āhavanīya, Gārhapatya, Dakṣiṇāgni, Āvasthya and Sabhya. That is, he should perform prāṇāyāma instead of Yajñas.

यो दत्त्वा सर्वभूतेभ्यः प्रव्रजत्यभयं गृहात् ।
तस्य तेजोमया लोका भवन्ति ब्रह्मवादिनः ॥ मनुस्मृति, 6-39 ॥

yo dattvā sarvabhūtebhyaḥ pravrajatyabhayaṁ gṛhāt,
tasya tejomayā lokā bhavanti brahmavādinaḥ.

Manusmṛti, 6-39

[Meaning] He, who leaves his home for taking Saṁnyāsa after rendering all living beings free from fear, that Brahmavādī (who disseminates the knowledge of God,i.e. Vedas) attains the state of eternal bliss called Mukti.

Question: What is the Dharma (duty) of a Saṁnyāsī?

Answer: Some duties are common to all, e.g. just and impartial treatment, acceptance of truth, and the rejection of falsehood, obedience to the ordinance of God as revealed in the Veda, promotion of public good, but the following duties are specific to Saṁnyāsī-s:

दृष्टिपूतं न्यसेत् पादं वस्त्रपूतं जलं पिबेत् ।
सत्यपूतां वदेद् वाचं मनःपूतं समाचरेत् ॥ मनुस्मृति, 6-46 ॥

dṛṣṭipūtaṁ nyaset pādaṁ vastrapūtaṁ jalaṁ pibet,
satyapūtāṁ vaded vāchaṁ manaḥpūtaṁ samācharet.

Manusmṛti, 6-46

[Meaning] Let a Saṁnyāsī walk carefully, let him take filtered water, let him speak the truth after verifying the facts and let him think before he acts or let him be mindful while taking action.

That is, he should concentrate on his path while walking. He should be ready to accept the truth and reject falsehood.

क्रुद्ध्यन्तं न प्रतिक्रुध्येदाक्रुष्टः कुशलं वदेत् ।
सप्तद्वारावकीर्णां च न वाचमनृतां वदेत् ॥ मनुस्मृति, 6-48 ॥

kruddhyantaṁ na pratikrudhyedākruṣṭaḥ kuśalaṁ vadet,
saptadvārāvakīrṇāṁ cha na vāchamanṛtāṁ vadet.

Manusmṛti, 6-48

[Meaning] He must observe restraint even though he faces fury. He should show compassion even though abused. He should never give wrong information received from seven receptacles, i.e. from one nose, two nostrils, two eyes, two ears.

अध्यात्मरतिरासीनो निरपेक्षो निरामिषः ।
आत्मनैव सहायेन सुखार्थी विचरेदिह ॥ मनुस्मृति, 6-49 ॥

adhyātmaratirāsīno nirapekṣo nirāmiṣaḥ,
ātmanaiva sahāyena sukhārthī vicharediha.

Manusmṛti, 6-49

[Meaning] Having engrossed in spirituality, indifferent to worldly pain and pleasure, pure vegetarian and having sought bliss through self-realization, he should walk on this earth (preaching the gospel of dharma and enlightening the world with knowledge).

कॢप्तकेशनखश्मश्रुः पात्री दण्डी कुसुम्भवान् ।
विचरेन्नियतो नित्यं सर्वभूतान्यपीडयन् ॥ मनु.स्मृति, 6-52 ॥

kḷptakeśanakhaśmaśruḥ pātrī daṇḍī kusumbhavān,
vicharenniyato nityaṁ sarvabhūtānyapīḍayan.

Manusmṛti, 6-52

[Meaning] With his hair, nails, beard and moustache clipped, carrying a suitable water-jar and a staff, wearing ochre-colored garments, let him walk with a tranquil mind, harming none.

इन्द्रियाणां निरोधेन रागद्वेषक्षयेण च ।
अहिंसया च भूतानाममृतत्वाय कल्पते ॥ मनुस्मृति, 6-60 ॥

indriyāṇāṁ nirodhena rāgadveṣakṣayeṇa cha,
ahiṁsayā cha bhūtānāmamṛtatvāya kalpate.

Manusmṛti, 6-60

[Meaning] Let him restrain his senses from evil stimuli, renounce affection and hatred, bear malice to none, and work for immortality (extreme bliss).

दूषितोऽपि चरेद् धर्मं यत्र तत्राश्रमे रतः ।
समः सर्वेषु भूतेषु न लिङ्गं धर्मकारणम् ॥ मनुस्मृति, 6-66 ॥

dūṣito'pi chared dharmaṁ yatra tatrāśrame rataḥ,
samaḥ sarveṣu bhūteṣu na liṅgaṁ dharmakāraṇam.

Manusmṛti, 6-66

[Meaning] Whether condemned or praised, let a Saṁnyāsī irrespective to his affiliation to an Āśrama fulfil his duty toward all beings impartially. The external signs like the staff, the water-jar and the ochre-colored garments do not by any means constitute an effective discharge of his duty.

फलं कतकवृक्षस्य यद्यप्यम्बुप्रसादकम् ।
न नामग्रहणादेव तस्य वारि प्रसीदति ॥ मनुस्मृति, 6-67 ॥

phalaṁ katakavṛkṣasya yadyapyambuprasādakam,
na nāmagrahaṇādeva tasya vāri prasīdati.

Manusmṛti, 6-67

[Meaning] Though the seeds of a clearing-nut tree (Strychnos Potatorum-Botanical name) purify water (when mixed with it in powdered form), yet the mere mention of its name can never do so.

Kataka tree

Botanical name of Kataka tree is Strychnos Potatorum. It is known as Clearing-Nut Tree in English and Nirmali in Hindi. It is a deciduous tree which has a height up to 40 feet (12 meters). The seeds of the tree are commonly used in traditional medicine as well as for purifying water in India and Myanmar.

प्राणायामा ब्राह्मणस्य त्रयोऽपि विधिवत् कृताः ।
व्याहृतिप्रणवैर्युक्ता विज्ञेयं परमं तपः ॥ मनुस्मृति, 6-70 ॥

prāṇāyāmā brāhmaṇasya trayo'pi vidhivat kṛtāḥ,
vyāhṛtipraṇavairyuktā vijñeyaṁ paramaṁ tapaḥ.

Manusmṛti, 6-70

[Meaning] Let a seeker of Brahman, therefore, practice prāṇāyāma accompanied by vyāhṛtis preceded by praṇava sound (syllable Om). At least three prāṇāyāmas done by the seeker will serve the purpose of highest penance.

NB: There are seven vyāhṛtis, viz. Om bhuḥ, Om bhuvaḥ, Om svaḥ (these three can serve a purpose), Om mahaḥ, Om janaḥ, Om tapaḥ, Om satyam.

दह्यन्ते ध्मायमानानां धातूनां हि यथा मलाः ।
तथेन्द्रियाणां दह्यन्ते दोषाः प्राणस्य निग्रहात् ॥ मनुस्मृति, 6-71 ॥

dahyante dhmāyamānānāṁ dhātūnāṁ hi yathā malāḥ,
tathendriyāṇāṁ dahyante doṣāḥ prāṇasya nigrahāt.

Manusmṛti, 6-71

[Meaning] Just as impurities of metals are blown out in a furnace, so does prāṇāyāma treats the body and mind of the impurities.

प्राणायामैर्दहेद् दोषान् धारणाभिश्च किल्बिषम् ।
प्रत्याहारेण संसर्गान् ध्यानेनानीश्वरान् गुणान् ॥ मनुस्मृति, 6-72

prāṇāyāmairdahed doṣān dhāraṇābhiścha kilbiṣam,
pratyāhāreṇa saṁsargān dhyānenānīśvarān guṇān.
Manusmṛti, 6-72

[Meaning] So, impurities of mind and body caused by aggravated vāta should be treated by prāṇāyāma, guilt feeling should be treated by concentration of mind at one point (dhāraṇā), sensual attachments by pratyāhāra (withdrawal of mind from external stimuli), and all qualities that are not Godly and attributable to souls like joy, sorrow, and ignorance should be treated by Dhyāna.

उच्चावचेषु भूतेषु दुर्ज्ञेयामकृतात्मभिः ।
ध्यानयोगेन सम्पश्येद् गतिमस्यान्तरात्मनः ॥ मनुस्मृति, 6-73 ॥

uchchāvacheṣu bhūteṣu durjñeyāmakṛtātmabhiḥ,
dhyānayogena sampaśyed gatimasyāntarātmanaḥ.
Manusmṛti, 6-73

[Meaning] By the practice of Dhyāna yoga (contemplation), let him then observe the presence of Omnipresent God in all small and big objects which are hard to understand by an ignorant and by those who are not yogis.

अहिंसयेन्द्रियासङ्गैर्वैदिकैश्चैव कर्मभिः ।
तपसश्चरणैश्चोग्रैः साधयन्तीह तत्पदम् ॥ मनुस्मृति, 6-75 ॥

ahiṁsayendriyāsaṅgairvaidikaiśchaiva karmabhiḥ,
tapasaścharaṇaiśchaugraiḥ sādhayantīha tatpadam.
Manusmṛti, 6-75

[Meaning] By non-violence, by renunciation of sensory pleasures, by performing duties as prescribed in the Vedas, and by rigorous austerities, a Saṁnyāsī can achieve Mokṣa.

यदा भावेन भवति सर्वभावेषु निःस्पृहः ।
तदा सुखमवाप्नोति प्रेत्य चैह च शाश्वतम् ॥ मनुस्मृति, 6-80 ॥

yadā bhāvena bhavati sarvabhāveṣu niḥspṛhaḥ,
tadā sukhamavāpnoti pretya chaiha cha śāśvatam.

Manusmṛti, 6-80.

[Meaning] When a Saṁnyāsī by his temperament becomes indifferent to desires for all worldly objects, he attains eternal bliss here (as living liberation) and hereafter (liberation after death).

चतुर्भिरपि चैवैतैर्नित्यमाश्रमिभिर्द्विजैः ।
दशलक्षणको धर्मः सेवितव्यः प्रयत्नतः ॥ मनुस्मृति, 6-91 ॥
chaturbhirapi chaivaitairnityamāśramibhirdvijaiḥ,
daśalakṣaṇako dharmaḥ sevitavyaḥ prayatnataḥ.

Manusmṛti, 6-91

[Meaning] Therefore, all educated Brahmacharī-s (knowledge seeker students), Gṛhasthī-s (householders), Vānaprasthī-s (hermits/forest dwellers) and Saṁnyāsī-s (peripatetic monks) should observe ten fold Dharma (ethical and moral code of conduct).

धृतिः क्षमा दमोऽस्तेयं शौचमिन्द्रियनिग्रहः ।
धीर्विद्या सत्यमक्रोधो दशकं धर्मलक्षणम् ॥ मनुस्मृति, 6-92 ॥
dhṛtiḥ kṣamā damo'steyaṁ śauchamindriyanigrahaḥ,
dhīrvidyā satyamakrodho daśakaṁ dharmalakṣaṇam.

Manusmṛti, 6-92

[Meaning]. 1. Patience, 2. forgiveness and forbearance, 3. self-control (to regulate mind towards dharma), 4. non-stealing (never to acquire things without permission, through fraud, betrayal or illegitimate means, 5. purity of body, mind and soul, 6. restraining sense organs from immoral and illegal actions, 7. sharpening of intelligence by avoiding intoxicants, bad company, idleness, lethargy and by use of healthy products, good company, yoga, virtuous acts, and celibacy, 8. acquisition of true knowledge right from earth to God and its proper application for public good, 9.truthfulness (to know a thing in its right perspective, and harmony of thought, word and deed), 10. abstention from anger, all the above form tenfold ethical and moral code of conduct.

अनेन विधिना सर्वांस्त्यक्त्वा सङ्गान् शनैः शनैः ।
सर्वद्वन्द्वविनिर्मुक्तो ब्रह्मण्येवावतिष्ठते ॥ मनुस्मृति, 6-81 ॥

anena vidhinā sarvāṁstyaktvā saṅgān śanaiḥ śanaiḥ,
sarvadvandvavinirmukto brahmaṇyevāvatiṣṭhate.

Manusmṛti, 6-81

[Meaning] Thus a Saṁnyāsī gets established in Brahman by gradually giving up all evils born of attachment to the worldly objects and rising above the joy and sorrow. It is the duty of all Saṁnyāsī-s to enlighten men of all other Āśramas on true nature of all types of their duties, to dissuade them from all kinds of evil conduct, to dispel their doubts, and to persuade them to follow the path of truth and morality.

Question: Does a person from Brāhmaṇa profession (called seeker of Brahman) have the exclusive right to take Saṁnyāsa or people from other professions like Kṣatriya etc. do have the same?

Answer: Brāhmaṇa (seeker of Brahman) alone has this privilege. Brāhmaṇa means a person who is thoroughly learned, who is endowed with moral, ethical and spiritual values, and who believe in public good. Taking Saṁnyāsa without thorough knowledge, moral, ethical and spiritual values, belief in God and renunciation will not help serve the good to the world. So there is a convention that only a person from Brāhmaṇa profession has the right to seek Saṁnyāsa. We may quote Manu (6.97) in this regard:

एष वोऽभिहितो धर्मो ब्राह्मणस्य चतुर्विधः ।

पुण्योऽक्षयफलः प्रेत्य राज्ञां धर्मं निबोधत ॥ मनुस्मृति, 6-97 ॥

ēṣa vo'bhihito dharmo brāhmaṇasya chaturvidhaḥ,
puṇyo'kṣayaphalaḥ pretya rājñāṁ dharmaṁ nibodhata
Manusmṛti, 6-97

[Meaning] Here we have explained that it is the duty of a Brāhmaṇa (seeker of Brahman) to undergo the training of Brahmacharya, Gṛhastha, Vānaprastha and Saṁnyāsa Āśramas. In this life, it yields high moral value and eternal bliss hereafter. Now listen to the duties of Kṣatriyas (ruling profession).

It is clear from the aforementioned that Saṁnyāsa is chiefly recommended for Brāhmaṇas (seeker of Brahman). Kṣatriya, Vaiśa and Śudras can go for other three Āśramas.

Question: What is the necessity of taking Saṁnyāsa?

Answer: As the head is necessary for the body, so is Saṁnyāsa in the Āśrama system. Education, moral and ethical values can never be promoted for want of it. Persons living in other Āśramas can never promote education and moral values being pre-occupied with other duties like pursuing education (Brahmacharya), household work (Gṛhastha) and austerities (Vānaprastha). Besides it is very difficult to maintain impartiality in other Āśramas. A Saṁnyāsī, being free from all worldly bondages, can do more public good when compared to men of other Āśramas. A Saṁnyāsī has more opportunities and scope to promote sciences when compared to others. However, a Saṁnyāsī coming directly from Brahmacharya Āśrama can contribute to the cause of global progress and advancement through true education more than those coming from other Āśramas.

Question: Saṁnyās is contrary to the intention of God, as the God intend to multiply population. Without

Gṛhastha Āśrama, progeny is not possible. Saṁnyāsa is the Chief Āśrama. Should all men take Saṁnyāsa, the human race would become extinct.

Answer: Well, even after marriage some couples don't have children. Many children die soon after their birth. This would also be against the intention of God. If you justify it quoting a statement 'यत्ने कृते यदि न सिध्यति कोत्र दोषः' that is, 'A man is not to be blamed if he succeeds not even after putting efforts.' This is not a justification, rather a fancy of a poet.

Is there any flaw in the above statement. No, not at all. Let me know if a good number of children begotten in Gṛhastha Āśrama fight with each other and get killed, would it not be a big loss to society? A lot of tussles generally follows due to ideological differences. Here comes the role of a Saṁnyāsi. If a Saṁnyāsī is successful in promoting love and friendship among people by preaching Vedic dharma, he can be instrumental in saving the lives of hundreds of thousands of innocent people and thus help contribute to the increase in population equal to thousands of Gṛhastha. Moreover, it is not possible for everybody to take Saṁnyāsa, as the subjugation of passions is not an easy job. Moreover, all those individuals who will be transformed into good persons by Saṁnyāsī-s will be looked upon as their spiritual children.

Question: Saṁnyāsī-s say that they have no duties to perform. They receive food and clothes from others and live in ease. Why should they bother about this world of ignorance? They contend with the idea that they are Brahman. If somebody approaches them, they tell him the same thing that he is also Brahman. He, being Brahman, is not afflicted by pāpa (evil) and puṇya (virtue), because dichotomy of heat and cold is the state of body, hunger and thirst that of the prāṇa, and pleasure and pain that of the mind. The world is changeable, so are all affairs of the world. Therefore it is not the business of wise to get involved in it. Virtue and vice are the functions of the senses and mind, not that of the soul. They teach these and similar other things, whilst you have taught differently on the duties of Saṁnyāsa. Which of these should be held as true and which as false?

Answer: Do you think that they should not do good actions/jobs? Manu has clearly indicated by his statement, 'वैदिकैश्च कर्मभिः' (by doing actions/duties enjoined in Vedas), that Saṁnyāsīs must perform duties enjoined in Vedas. Can they do without a job of eating and covering their body? If they cannot, how can they leave other good jobs/duties due to them? They will certainly be held responsible for not discharging the duties assigned to them. They are indebted to householders for food, clothing and other necessaries of life. If they fail to pay off by doing good to them, they will be known as ungrateful rascals. Thus they will no longer remain assets, rather become a burden to society. If eyes and ears stop their function, then their existence will become meaningless. Likewise, those Saṁnyāsī-s who do not teach the truth, nor pursue and preach Vedic studies, they are a mere burden to the society.

Those who say that why should they bother about the world of ignorance, they support ignorance and inaction in society. The act done by the body, in fact, is prompted by the soul which alone, therefore, suffers or enjoys the fruits thereof.

Those, who take for granted that soul is Brahman, they are languishing in darkness, because the soul is finite, and knows little, whilst Brahman is Infinite and All-knowing. Again Brahman is Eternal, Pure,

Enlightened and never enslaved by His own nature, whilst the soul is sometimes free, at other times not. Brahman can never be subjected to ignorance or confusion, being the Omnipresent and Omniscient, whilst the soul is sometimes ignorant, at other times aware. Brahman, again, does not undergo the cycle of birth and death, whilst the soul reels under the cycle of birth and death. So, their assumption that soul is not different from Brahman is false.

Question: Saṁnyāsī-s are free from all duties. They never touch fire and metals. Is this true or not?

Answer: No. The etymology of the term Saṁnyāsī goes like this:

सम्यङ् नित्यमास्ते यस्मिन् यद्वा सम्यङ् न्यस्यन्ति दुःखानि कर्माणि येन सः संन्यासः। स प्रशस्तो विद्यते यस्य स संन्यासी।

samyaṅ nityamāste yasmin yadvā samyaṅ nyasyanti duḥkhāni karmāṇi yena saḥ saṁnyāsaḥ, sa praśasto vidyate yasya sa saṁnyāsī.

[Meaning] Saṁnyāsa is a condition or stage in which a seeker is in communion with Brahman and obeys His commands, in which all evil actions are renounced. A person who possesses this good nature is called a Saṁnyāsī. In other words, a Saṁnyāsī is a doer of good actions and destroyer of bad actions.

Question: Teaching and preaching are the duties of house-holders. What will, then, Saṁnyāsī, do?

Answer: Let men and women in all Āśramas learn and teach the truth. But a Saṁnyāsī can devote more time and he can be more fair and impartial while doing his duty than that of a Gṛhasthī. It is true that the job of teaching and preaching is assigned to the people from Brāhmaṇa profession where men are supposed to teach men and women to women. However, a Saṁnyāsī can devote more time in travelling when compared to a Gṛhasthi coming from a Brāhmaṇa profession. Besides, it is Saṁnyāsī who reigns supreme when a Brāhmaṇa professional starts deviating from the Vedic path.Therefore, justification of Saṁnyāsa cannot be ruled out.

Question: What about the prevalent convention that a Saṁnyāsī is not required to stay more than one night at one place?

Answer: This is justified to the extent that by staying longer at one place, a Saṁnyāsī cannot do much public good. He will also develop a sentimental attachment to the place and people over there. He may begin to feel love and hatred towards things and persons associated with that place. But if a Saṁnyāsī can do more good by staying at one place, let him do so. We have examples of Saṁnyāsī-s like Pañchaśikha who used to break their journey in the court of king Janaka for even four months. This continued for years. The rule of a short stay in respect of a Saṁnyāsī is, in fact, framed by modern day schools of hypocrite Saṁnyāsī-s. Should a Saṁnyāsī stay longer at one place, our superstitions will be exposed and hypocrisy cannot flourish.

Question: There is a saying:

यतीनां कांचनं दद्यात्ताम्बुलं ब्रह्मचारिणाम्।
चैराणामभयं दद्यात्स नरो नरकं व्रजेत्।।

yatīnāṁ kāṁchanaṁ dadyāttāmbulaṁ brahmachāriṇām,
chairāṇāmabhayaṁ dadyātsa naro narakaṁ vrajet.

[Meaning] Whosoever gives gold to a Saṁnyāsī, betal to students, and freedom to thieves shall attain lower species in the next life.

What is your opinion?

Answer: This slogan is fabricated by those who are opposed to the institutions of Varṇa and Āśrama, who are extremely selfish and orthodox. If Saṁnyāsī-s will receive monetary aid, they will become financially self-reliant and will be able to expose our frauds without any hitch which may not serve our self-interests. If they are dependant on us for the necessaries of their life, they will remain under our control and pressure. When charity, even in respect of ignorant and selfish people, is considered a virtuous act, how can there be any harm when it benefits the learned Saṁnyāsī-s engaged in the activities of the public good?

There is evidence to support our hypothesis. Manu (2-6) says:

विविधानि च रत्नानि विविक्तेषूपपादयेत्।।

vividhāni cha ratnāni viviktesūpapādayet.

[Meaning] One should donate various types of gems to the Saṁnyāsī-s.

Do you think the above-quoted verse meaningless? Because, if the donor of gold to a Saṁnyāsī goes to hell, how can the donations of silver, diamonds and other precious stones send the donor to the heaven?

Questioner: The aforesaid verse is a misreading by Pundit ji. It runs like this: ;fr gLrs /kua n|kr~ that is, 'by giving money in the hands of a Saṁnyāsī, the donor goes to hell.

Answer: This is again a speculation of an ignorant mind. Should a man goes to hell by offering gifts to a Saṁnyāsī in his hands, will he go to heaven if he offers gifts on his feet or offers in a bag. This type of speculative statements cannot be believed. Yes, of course, should a Saṁnyāsī hoards money more than he needs, he may face trouble at the hands of thieves and will be afflicted with the passions. However, a wise Saṁnyāsī would do nothing objectionable, nor would he go astray, because he has already experienced it in his previous Āśramas. If one has taken Saṁnyāsa direct from Brahmacharya Āśrama, he would never allow himself to be trapped by these material attractions because of his strong urge for renunciation.

Question: It is said that if a Saṁnyāsī is invited to a Śrāddha, the spirits of the forefathers of the host leave the venue and pushed to the hell.

Answer: Firstly, the arrival of dead forefathers to attend Śraddha is practically impossible. It is also against Vedas and all canons of logic. In absence of their arrival, who is going to leave the venue? How can the return of manes be possible, when all souls have reborn after death according to their good or bad Sanskāras as per law of God? This is also a false speculation fabricated by glutton and orthodox mendicants. It is true though that wherever a Saṁnyāsī will go, he will put an end to the practice of Śrāddha of dead people which is against the norms of Vedas.

Question: He who takes Saṁnyāsa directly from Brahmacharya Āśrama will find it hard to pull on. It is also very difficult to subdue passions. So, it is better to follow a proper prescribed channel for Saṁnyāsa, that is, through Gṛhastha Āśrama and Vānaprastha.

Answer: Let him not take Saṁnyāsa who fails on above tests, but why should not he who clears all tests? One who has realized the evils of indulgence in sensual pleasures and merits of the preservation of the reproductive element can never go astray. His reproductive element serves as fuel to the fire of thought. Just as a physician and medicines are required by a patient and not by a healthy person, similarly Saṁnyāsa is required by a person who intends to disseminate knowledge, moral and ethical code of conduct and do good to the world at large. Pañchaśikha among men and Gārgī among women are true examples of it.

Therefore, deserving alone are entitled to become Saṁnyāsī-s. If an undeserving person takes Saṁnyāsa, he would ruin himself and others too. As world emperor is called Samrāṭa, so is a Saṁnyāsī Parivrāṭa (peripatetic monk who roams about the whole globe preaching and teaching science and universal values). However, an emperor commands respect in his own country, while a Saṁnyāsī is respected universally. There is a śloka in Chāṇakya Nītiśāstra which reads as under:

विद्वत्त्वं च नृपत्वं च नैव तुल्यं कदाचन्।
स्वदेशे पुज्यते राजा विद्वान् सर्वत्र पूज्यते।।

vidvattvaṁ cha nṛpatvaṁ cha naiva tulyaṁ kadāchan,
svadeśe pujyate rājā vidvān sarvatra pūjyate.

[Meaning] There can be no comparison between a king and a learned man, since the one is respected in his own country, whilst the other is respected everywhere.

Therefore, Brahmacharya Āśrama is required for knowledge, education, and physical strength.

Gṛhastha Āśrama is required to carry out social, national and cultural duties.

Vānaprastha Āśrama is required to give perfection to the process of thinking, contemplation, realization and austerities,

Saṁnyāsa Āśrama is needed for dissemination of Vedic knowledge, the introduction of an ethical and moral code of conduct, preaching the gospel of truth and dispelling doubts and ignorance of the people. However, all those who do not discharge the main duty of

Saṁnyāsa, such as the preaching of truth and moral and ethical code of conduct, they are degraded to the lower species in the next life. Therefore, it behoves Saṁnyāsī-s to devote themselves assiduously to awake the people, who are in doubt, to truth and the teaching of the Vedas as well as the other true Śāstras and to propagate the Vedic values, in order to ensure the progress and advancement of the whole world.

Question: Should mendicants other than Saṁnyāsī-s such as sadhus, vairāgī-s, Gusais and Khākhī-s, etc. be ranked as Saṁnyāsī or not?

Answer: No, they do not possess even a single characteristic of a Saṁnyāsī. They follow anti-Vedic creeds and give preference to the teachings of their preceptors over the Vedas. They sing the praises of their own creed, involve in false practices, further their selfish ends by trapping others into their creeds and cults. Let alone doing any good to the world, they, instead, mislead people and bring about their fall and accomplish their own selfish ends. So, they are not entitled to be included in the Saṁnyāsa Āśrama, rather they are entitled to be associated with Svārtha Āśrama (selfish cult). There is no doubt about it.

Those deserve to be called Saṁnyāsī-s and great persons who themselves tread the path of dharma and make others to tread it, who promote their own happiness as well as that of the whole world here and hereafter.

This is a brief account of Saṁnyāsa Āśrama. In the next chapter, we shall deal with the Science of Governance.

इति श्रीमद् दयानन्दसरस्वतीस्वामिकृते सत्यार्थप्रकाशे सुभाषाविभूषिते वानप्रस्थसंन्यासाश्रमविषये पंचमः समुल्लासः सम्पूर्णः ।।

iti śrīmad dayānandasarasvatīsvāmikṛte satyārthaprakāśe subhāṣāvibhūṣite vānaprasthasaṁnyāsāśramaviṣaye paṁchamaḥ samullāsaḥ sampūrṇaḥ.

Thus ends this fifth chapter on 'Retirement and Renunciation' of Satyarth Prakash by Swami Dayanand Saraswati.

Dayanand has no doubt found the key to the Vedas through his unique system of interpretation. It is for us to now, to use the key and open the portals of Vedic Wisdom

Aurobindo Ghose

CHAPTER 6

अथ राजधर्मान् व्याख्यास्यामः ।

Atha rājadharmān vyākhyāsyāmaḥ.

Now we begin to explain the Science of Governance

We are often given to understand that the System of Governance that is followed in India today was borrowed from the West. It subtly seeks to imply how grateful we must be to the West, read British, for having passed this system to India. The present Chapter of Satyarth Prakash called 'Raja Dharma' shed ample good light on the science of Governance prevalent in India since ancient times and gives one an insight that the system of Governance is not borrowed by India from West, rather the West borrowed it from India.

Research work done by Swami Dayananda was successfully used in a vital political controversy that erupted in the 20th century. When the Brits set about its newly declared goal of setting up responsible Govt in India, an eminent historian Vincent Smith, rushed to prove that the attempt to set up self-governing institutions in India was bound to fail as being alien to it. Sir Shankaran Nair, a member of the Governor-General-in-Council disagreed on the basis of Kashi Prashad Jayaswal's Hindu Polity written to expand Dayananda's hints on the places of the Sabhas in ancient India.

Introduction

राजधर्मान् प्रवक्ष्यामि यथावृत्तो भवेन्नृपः ।
सम्भवश्च यथा तस्य सिद्धिश्च परमा यथा ।। मनु. 7.1

rājadharmān pravakṣayāmi yathāvṛtto bhavennṛpaḥ,
sambhavaścha yathā tasya siddhiścha paramā yathā.
Manu. 7.1

[Meaning] The great Manu says to the Rishis, after discussion on the duties of the four Varṇas (professions) and Aśramas (the four social orders), we shall now describe Rāja Dharma or the duties and qualifications, etc., of rulers, in other words, we shall discuss as to who is fit to be a ruler/administrator, how he is to be selected, and how he can deliver good governance.

ब्राह्मं प्राप्तेन संस्कारं क्षत्रियेण यथाविधि ।
सर्वस्यास्य यथान्यायं कर्त्तव्यं परिरक्षणम् ।। मनु. 7.2

brāhmaṁ prāptena saṁskāraṁ kṣatriyeṇa yathāvidhi,
sarvasyāsya yathānyāyaṁ karttavyaṁ parirakṣaṇam.
Manu. 7.2

[Meaning] Let a Kṣatrīya (a person from ruling profession), who has attained spiritual education/ sanskāras govern the country justly.

The way of good governance is described in Ṛgveda (**3.38.6**) as follow:

त्रीणि राजाना विदथे पुरूणि परि विश्वानि भूषाथः सदांसि ।।

trīṇi rājānā vidathe purūṇi pari viśvāni bhūṣāthaḥ sadāṁsi.

[Meaning] Let the rulers and the ruled form three Assemblies-**1.** Vidyā Ārya Sabhā (Academic Council), **2.** Dharma Ārya Sabhā (Judiciary) and **3.** Rāja Ārya Sabhā (Legislature and executive) for the benefit of the public at large, for the advancement of knowledge, education, culture, values, independence and prosperity.

NB: Here Academic Council is on the top of official hierarchy followed by Judiciary and Legislature.

The *Atharvaveda* (15.2.2; 19.7.6) lays emphasis:

तं सभा च समितिश्च सेना च ।। 15.2.2

taṁ sabhā cha samitiścha senā cha. 15.2.2

[Meaning] Let the three Assemblies, Military Councils, and the Defence forces harmoniously work together to carry on the governance of a country.

A king should address the Assembly thus:

सभ्य सभां मे पाहि ये च सभ्याः सभासदः ।। 19.7.6

sabhya sabhāṁ me pāhi ye cha sabhyāḥ sabhāsadaḥ. 19.7.6

[Meaning] Let the leader of the Assembly abide by the just laws passed by the Assembly, and let other members follow the same.

It means that no single individual should be invested with absolute power. The king, who is the president of the Assembly, and the Assembly itself, should be inter-dependent on each other. Both should be controlled by the people, who in their turn should be governed by the Assembly.

Śatapatha Brāhmaṇa (**13.2.3.7**;**8**) reminds of consequences if this system is not followed in letter and spirit. It says,

राष्ट्रमेव विश्या हन्ति तस्माद्राष्ट्री विशं घातुकः ।। विशमेव राष्ट्रायाद्यां करोति तस्माद्राष्ट्री विशमत्ति न पुष्टं पशुं मन्यत इति ।।

rāṣṭrameva viśyā hanti tasmādrāṣṭrī viśaṁ ghātukaḥ. viśameva rāṣṭrāyādyāṁ karoti tasmādrāṣṭrī viśamatti na puṣṭaṁ paśuṁ manyata iti.

[Meaning] If the king/administrator be independent of the people and enjoy absolute powers, he would impoverish the people, - being despotic and hence arrogant - and oppress them, or, even eat them up, just as a tiger or any other carnivorous animal pounces upon a robust animal and eats it up. A despotic ruler does not let anyone else grow in power, robs the rich, usurps their property by unjust punishment, and meets his selfish end. One man should, therefore, never be given despotic power.

So far as the selection of a president is concerned, the Atharvaveda (6.98.1) advises thus:

इन्द्रो जयाति न परा जयाता अधिराजो राजसु राजयातै ।
चर्कृत्य ईड्यो वन्द्यश्चोपसद्यो नमस्यो भवेह ।।

indro jayāti na parā jayātā adhirājo rājasu rājayātai,
charkṛtya īḍyo vandyaśchopasadyo namasyo bhaveha.

[Meaning] O men! let that man alone among you be made a king -the President of the Assembly - who is a very powerful conqueror of foes, is never beaten by them, has the capacity to become the paramount sovereign, is most enlightened, is worthy of being made a President, who possesses most noble qualities, accomplishments, character and disposition; who is thoroughly worthy of the homage, trust and respect of all.

The *Yajurveda* (9.40) observes:

इमं देवाऽ असपत्नꣳ सुवध्वं महते क्षत्रय महते ज्यैष्ठ्याय महते जानराज्यायेन्द्रस्येन्द्रियाय

imaṁ devā' asapatnaꣳ suvadhvaṁ mahate kṣatraya, mahate jyaiṣṭhyāya mahate jānarājyāyendrasyendriyāya.

[Meaning] O learned men! declare that man with

consensus your king- the Head of the State-who is just, impartial, well-educated, cultured and friend of all. In this way alone you will attain universal sovereignty, be greater than all, manage the affairs of the State, obtain political eminence, acquire wealth, and ride the world of its enemies.

The *Ṛgveda* (**1.39.2**) says:

स्थिरा वः सन्त्वायुधा पराणुदे वीळू उत प्रतिष्कभे ।
युष्माकमस्तु तविषी पनीयसी मा मर्त्यस्य मायिनः ।।

sthirā vaḥ santvāyudhā parāṇude vīḻū uta pratiṣkabhe,
yuṣmākamastu taviṣī panīyasī mā martyasya māyinaḥ.

[Meaning] Rulers! your implements of warfare, (such as, guns, rifles. bows, arrows, etc.) and war materials (such as, gunpowder) be worthy of praise, strong and durable to repel and conquer your enemies. Let your army be a glorious one, so that you may always be victorious. But the aforesaid things shall not be attainable to the contemptible, the despicable, and the unjust.

In other words, it is only as long as men remain honourable, just and virtuous that they are politically great. When they become wicked and unjust, they are absolutely ruined.

Let a nation, therefore, elect the most learned men, as members of the Academic Council, the most devout men, as members of the Judiciary and men of the most praiseworthy character, as members of the Legislative Assembly; and let that great man in it, who possesses most excellent qualities, is highly accomplished, and bears most honourable character, be made the Head or President of the Political Assembly.

Let the three Assemblies harmoniously work together, and make good laws, and let all abide by those laws. Let them all be of one mind in affairs that promote the happiness of all. All men should subordinate themselves to the laws that are calculated to promote general well-being; they should be free in matters relating to individual well-being.

NB: To sum up it can be maintained that the objective of governance is to promote happiness. Equal importance is given to Dharma (Judiciary), legislature and education which with the aid of the military is responsible for governance. It means that Dharma played an important role in society and government responsibility. Education was stressed, that is why, we Indians gave importance to education since it was an important part of our lives from ancient times. Note that the Military is subordinate to the Legislature and is not part of three assemblies. This could be one of the reasons why the Army never ruled India. Adequate safeguards existed to prevent the King from becoming a dictator. Also one of the primary duties of the King was to protect his subjects from enemies. The importance of good laws and enforcement is stressed. That is perhaps one of the biggest failures of Post Independence India. The laws and rules framed by Britishers in the 18th and 19th century were to help them exploit Indian masses and natural resources. Unfortunately, all these rules and laws have been retained by the post -independent Governments in India. That is why people are getting away with worse like murder in India today. Take the stock market, Harshad Mehta, Hiten Dalal, Ketan Parikh and Dawood. The list is endless. Ask yourselves how many governments in medieval and modern India have met these criteria?

Qualifications of the Head of State

Regarding qualifications of the Head of the State, Manu (7. 4, 6, 7) says:

इन्द्राऽनिलयमार्काणामग्नेश्च वरुणस्य च।
चन्द्रवित्तेशयोश्चैव मात्र निर्हृत्य शाश्वतीः।।4

indrā'nilayamārkāṇāmagneścha varuṇasya cha,
chandravitteśayośchaiva mātra nirhṛtya śāśvatīḥ.

तपत्यादित्यवच्चैष चक्षूंषि च मनांसि च।
न चैनं भुवि शक्नोति कश्चिदप्यभिवीक्षितुम्।। 6

tapatyādityavachchaiṣa chakṣūṁṣi cha manāṁsi cha,
na chainaṁ bhuvi śaknoti kaśchidapyabhivīkṣitum.

सोऽग्निर्भवति वायुश्च सोऽर्कः सोमः स धर्मराट्।
स कुबेरः स वरुणः स महेन्द्रः प्रभावतः।। 7

so'gnirbhavati vāyuścha so'rkaḥ somaḥ sa dharmarāṭ,
sa kuberaḥ sa varuṇaḥ sa mahendraḥ prabhāvataḥ

[Meaning] He should be as powerful as electricity, as dear to his people's hearts as their very breath, able to read their minds, and just in his dealings as a judge. He should enlighten people's minds by the spread of knowledge, justice, and righteousness, and dispel ignorance and injustice as the sun dispels darkness and illuminates the world. He should be like one who consumes wickedness like fire, keeps the wicked and the criminal under control like a jailer, gladdens the hearts of the good people like the moon; makes the country rich and prosperous, as a treasurer keeps his treasury full; is powerful and majestic like the sun, keeps the people in fear and awe; and on whom no one in the whole world dares to look with a stern eye. He alone is then fit to be the Head of the State who behaves like fire, air, the sun, the moon, a judge, a treasurer, a jailer while keeping the wicked under control.

The True Ruler/Administrator

Manu (7.17-19; 24-28; 30-31) says:

स राजा पुरुषो दण्डः स नेता शासिता च सः।

चतुर्णामाश्रमाणां च धर्मस्य प्रतिभूः स्मृतः।।

*sa rājā puruṣo daṇḍaḥ sa netā śāsitā cha saḥ,
chaturṇāmāśramāṇāṁ cha dharmasya pratibhūḥ smṛtaḥ.*

दण्डः शास्ति प्रजाः सर्वा दण्ड एवाभिरक्षति।
दण्डः सुप्तेषु जागर्ति दण्डं धर्मं विदुर्बुधाः।।

*daṇḍaḥ śāsti prajāḥ sarvā daṇḍa ēvābhirakṣati,
daṇḍaḥ supteṣu jāgarti daṇḍaṁ dharmaṁ vidurbudhāḥ.*

समीक्ष्य स धृतः सम्यक् सर्वा रञ्जयति प्रजाः।
असमीक्ष्य प्रणीतस्तु विनाशयति सर्वतः।।

*samīkṣaya sa dhṛtaḥ samyak sarvā rañjayati prajāḥ,
asamīkṣaya praṇītastu vināśayati sarvataḥ.*

दुष्येयुः सर्ववर्णाश्च भिद्येरन्सर्वसेतवः।
सर्वलोकप्रकोपश्च भवेद्दण्डस्य विभ्रमात्।।

*duṣyeyuḥ sarvavarṇāścha bhidyeransarvasetavaḥ,
sarvalokaprakopaścha bhaveddaṇḍasya vibhramāt.*

यत्र श्यामो लोहिताक्षो दण्डश्चरति पापहा।
प्रजास्तत्र न मुह्यन्ति नेता चेत्साधु पश्यति।।

*yatra śyāmo lohitākṣo daṇḍaścharati pāpahā,
prajāstatra na muhyanti netā chetsādhu paśyati.*

तस्याहुः सम्प्रणेतारं राजानं सत्यवादिनम्।
समीक्ष्यकारिणं प्राज्ञं धर्मकामार्थकोविदम्।।

*tasyāhuḥ sampraṇetāraṁ rājānaṁ satyavādinam,
samīkṣayakāriṇaṁ prājñaṁ dharmakāmārthakovidam.*

तं राजा प्रणयन्सम्यक् त्रिवर्गेणाभिवर्द्धते।
कामात्मा विषमः क्षुद्रो दण्डेनैव निहन्यते।।

*taṁ rājā praṇayansamyak trivargeṇābhivarddhate,
kāmātmā viṣamaḥ kṣudro daṇḍenaiva nihanyate.*

दण्डो हि सुमहत्तेजो दुर्धरश्चाकृतात्मभिः।
धर्माद्विचलितं हन्ति नृपमेव सबान्धवम्।।

daṇḍo hi sumahattejo durdharaśchākṛtātmabhiḥ,
dharmādvichalitaṁ hanti nṛpameva sabāndhavam.

सोऽसहायेन मूढेन लुब्धेनाकृतबुद्धिना।
न शक्यो न्यायतो नेतुं सक्तेन विषयेषु च।।

so'sahāyena mūḍhena lubdhenākṛtabuddhinā,
na śakyo nyāyato netuṁ saktena viṣayeṣu cha.

शुचिना सत्यसन्धेन यथाशास्त्रनुसारिणा।
प्रणेतुं शक्यते दण्डः सुसहायेन धीमता।।

śuchinā satyasandhena yathāśāstranusāriṇā,
praṇetuṁ śakyate daṇḍaḥ susahāyena dhīmatā.

[Meaning] The authority alone is the real king, the dispenser of justice, the ruler. The authority can ensure surety for the four Varṇas and Aśramas to discharge properly their respective duties.

The authority alone is the true Governor that maintains order among the people. The authority alone is their Protector. The authority keeps awake whilst all the people are fast asleep. The wise, therefore, look upon authority as Dharma or Righteousness.

When rightly exercised the authority makes all men happy but when exercised adversely, i.e., without due regard to the requirement of justice, it ruins the king.

All the four Varṇas (professional classes based on merit and personality) would become corrupt, all Aśramas (orders) would come to an end, there would be nothing but chaos and corruption if the authority was not properly and justly exercised. Where the authority is exercised without favour or fervour, rationally and strictly to suppress injustice and sustain justice, there the people never go astray, and consequently, live in happiness.

He alone is considered a fit person to be invested with authority, who invariably speaks the truth, is thoughtful, highly intellectual and very expert in the accomplishment of dharma (values), artha (means to sustain material and spiritual life) and kama (desire of spiritual, material prosperity).

The authority justly exercised by the king/administrator greatly promotes dharma (values), artha (means to sustain material and spiritual life) and kama (desire of spiritual and material prosperity). But the same authority if invested with a king who is sensual, indolent, crafty, malevolent, mean and low-minded, becomes the means of his ruin.

Great is the power and majesty of authority. It cannot be invested with a man who is uneducated, ignorant and unjust. In that particular case, it surely brings the downfall of the king, state and his subjects who deviates from the path of dharma.

The authority can never be justly exercised by a man who is destitute of knowledge, good learning and culture, has no wise and good men to advise and assist him, and is lost in sensual pleasures.

He alone is fit to exercise authority, who is wise, pure in heart, of truthful character, accompanied by good and learned persons, conducts himself according to the ethics, morality and human values.

Qualifications of Four Chiefs

Manu (**12.100; 110-115**) says:

सैनापत्यं च राज्यं च दण्डनेतृत्वमेव च।
सर्वलोकाधिपत्यं च वेदशास्त्रविदर्हति।।

saināpatyaṁ cha rājyaṁ cha daṇḍanetṛtvameva cha,

sarvalokādhipatyaṁ cha vedaśāstravidarhati.

दशावरा वा परिषद्यं धर्मं परिकल्पयेत्।
त्र्यवरा वापि वृत्तस्था तं धर्मं न विचालयेत्।।

daśāvarā vā pariṣadyaṁ dharmaṁ parikalpayet,
trayavarā vāpi vṛttasthā taṁ dharmaṁ na vichālayet.

त्रैविद्यो हैतुकस्तर्की नैरुक्तो धर्मपाठकः।
त्रयश्चाश्रमिणः पूर्वे परिषत्स्याद्दशावरा।।

traividyo haitukastarkī nairukto dharmapāṭhakaḥ,
trayaśchāśramiṇaḥ pūrve pariṣatsyāddaśāvarā.

ऋग्वेदविद्यजुर्विच्च सामवेदविदेव च।
त्र्यवरा परिषज्ज्ञेया धर्मसंशयनिर्णये।।

ṛgvedavidyajurvichcha sāmavedavideva cha,
trayavarā pariṣajjñeyā dharmasaṁśayanirṇaye.

एकोऽपि वेदविद्धर्मं यं व्यवस्येद् द्विजोत्तमः।
स विज्ञेयः परो धर्मो नाज्ञानामुदितोऽयुतैः।।

ēko'pi vedaviddharmaṁ yaṁ vyavasyed dvijottamaḥ,
sa vijñeyaḥ paro dharmo nājñānāmudito'yutaiḥ.

अव्रतानाममन्त्रणां जातिमात्रेपजीविनाम्।
सहस्रशः समेतानां परिषत्त्वं न विद्यते।।

avratānāmamantraṇāṁ jātimātrepajīvinām,
sahasraśaḥ sametānāṁ pariṣattvaṁ na vidyate.

यं वदन्ति तमोभूता मूर्खा धर्ममतद्विदः।
तत्पापं शतधा भूत्वा तद्वक्तननुगच्छति।।

yaṁ vadanti tamobhūtā mūrkhā dharmamatadvidaḥ,
tatpāpaṁ śatadhā bhūtvā tadvaktananugachchhati.

[Meaning] The four chief offices-Commander-in-Chief of the armed forces, Chief Administrator, Chief Justice, and the Head of State, should be held only by those persons who are well-versed in all the four Vedas and the Śāstras, are conversant with all the sciences and philosophies, devout, and have perfect control over their passions, and hold a noble character.

The above cited four chief offices must have a maximum of 10 persons or minimum of 3 persons in its working committees. No one should try to transgress the rules framed by the committees of above offices.

The above-cited offices must consist of members who are well versed in the four Vedas, Nyāya Śāstra, Nirukta (Etymology) and Dharmaśāstras; they must represent first three Āśramas, viz. Brahmacharya, Gṛhastha and Vānaprastha.

The doubtful cases be referred to a committee consisting of three scholars well versed in Ṛgveda, Yajurveda and Sāmaveda respectively. The decision of this committee will supersede and all are obliged to follow it.

Even the decision of one Saṁnyāsī, who is fully conversant with all the four Vedas and is superior to all the scholars should be considered supreme as compared to the decision taken by myriads of laymen in the society.

Even a meeting of thousands of men cannot be designated an Assembly, if they destitute of such high virtues as self-control or truthful character, be ignorant of the Vedas like illiterate and uneducated men.

Let no man abide by the law laid down by men who are altogether ignorants, and destitute of the knowledge of the Veda. If the laws propounded by ignorant fools are followed one may land into hundreds of problems.

Therefore, let not ignorant fools be ever made members of the three Assemblies - Academic Council, Judiciary and Legislative Assembly. On the other hand let learned and persons of high moral and ethical values only be elected to such high offices.

NB: We all know very well that almost all laws numbering around **35000** were being passed between **1860** and **1935** i.e. over **125** years ago by Britishers to serve the British interest in India. These laws do not address the interest of the Indian people. The need is to revisit and revise the Indian Penal Code (IPC), Code of Civil Procedure (CPC) in the light of Vedas and Dharmaśāstras. Qualifications of Ministers, Legislators, Councillors and Corporators

Manu (7.43-53) says:

त्रैविद्येभ्यस्त्रयीं विद्यां दण्डनीतिं च शाश्वतीम्।

आन्वीक्षिकीं चात्मविद्यां वार्त्तारम्भाँश्च लोकतः।। 43

traividyebhyastrayīṁ vidyāṁ daṇḍanītiṁ cha śāśvatīm, ānvīkṣikīṁ chātmavidyāṁ vārttārambhāṁścha lokataḥ.

[Meaning] Those men alone are fit to occupy such high offices, as of the President, Prime Ministers, Ministers, Legislators, Councillors, and Corporators, who have gained the three kinds of knowledge defined in the Vedas as Karma, UpÈsanÈ and J¤Èna from the experts; who have mastered the science of governance (how to exercise the power and authority) and announcing justice; who have excelled the Divine science of spirituality which consists of the knowledge of the nature, character and attributes of God; who take the opinion of public while pursuing any policy matter involving national and public interest.

इन्द्रियाणां जये योगं समातिष्ठेद्दिवानिशम्।
जितेन्द्रियो हि शक्नोति वशे स्थापयितुं प्रजाः।।44

indriyāṇāṁ jaye yogaṁ samātiṣṭheddivāniśam,
jitendriyo hi śaknoti vaśe sthāpayituṁ prajāḥ.

[Meaning] Let all above-mentioned leaders subdue senses and keep them under control, ever follow the moral and ethical values and avoid what is immoral and unethical. Let them always practice yoga, and meditate on God, for he who cannot control his passions can never keep the people under control.

दश कामसमुत्थानि तथाष्टौ त्रफ़ोधजानि च।
व्यसनानि दुरन्तानि प्रयत्नेन विवर्जयेत्।।45

daśa kāmasamutthāni tathāṣṭau traphodhajāni cha,
vyasanāni durantāni prayatnena vivarjayet.

[Meaning] Let a leader, therefore, most diligently shun (and help others to do the same) eighteen vices which can hardly be abandoned, ten of which are born of lust and eight of anger.

कामजेषु प्रसक्तो हि व्यसनेषु महीपतिः।
वियुज्यतेऽर्थधर्माभ्यां क्रोधजेष्वात्मनैव तु।। 46

kāmajeṣu prasakto hi vyasaneṣu mahīpatiḥ,
viyujyate'rthadharmābhyāṁ krodhajeṣvātmanaiva tu.

[Meaning] A king/administrator addicted to vices born of lust loses his kingdom, wealth and power and even his character. Whilst one who is addicted to vices born of anger may even lose his life.

मृगयाक्षो दिवास्वप्नः परीवादः स्त्रियो मदः।
तौर्य्यत्रिकं वृथाट्या च कामजो दशको गणः।। 47

mṛgayākṣo divāsvapnaḥ parīvādaḥ striyo madaḥ,
tauryyatrikaṁ vṛthāṭyā cha kāmajo daśako gaṇaḥ.

[Meaning] The ten vices due to lust are:

(1) Hunting, (2) gambling, etc. (3) sleeping during day, (4) gossiping or talking of sensual subjects, (5) eve-hunting, (6) use of intoxicants such as alcohol, opium, etc. (7) excessive indulgence in singing, playing and

dancing or hearing and seeing other people do so, (8) and aimless wandering about from place to place.

पैशुन्यं साहसं द्रोह ईर्ष्यासूयार्थदूषणम्।
वाग्दण्डजं च पारुष्यं क्रोधजोऽपि गणोऽष्टकः।।48।।

paiśunyaṁ sāhasaṁ droha īrṣyāsūyārthadūṣaṇam,
vāgdaṇḍajaṁ cha pāruṣyaṁ krodhajo'pi gaṇo'ṣṭakaḥ.

[Meaning] The eight vices due to anger are:

(1) Back-biting, (2) adultery or rape, (3) malice, (4) jealousy or envy, (5) fault finding, (6) abuse of money and means for unsocial activities, (7) use of harsh language, (8) or convicting innocent.

द्वयोरप्येतयोर्मूलं यं सर्वे कवयो विदुः।
तं यत्नेन जयेल्लोभं तज्जावेतावुभौ गणौ।।49।।

dvayorapyetayormūlaṁ yaṁ sarve kavayo viduḥ,
taṁ yatnena jayellobhaṁ tajjāvetāvubhau gaṇau.

[Meaning] Let him persistently shun greed that all wise men hold to be the root cause of both lust and anger. It is greed that gives rise to these both types of passions.

पानमक्षाः स्त्रियश्चैव मृगया च यथाक्रमम्।
एतत्कष्टतमं विद्याच्चतुष्कं कामजे गणे।।50।।

pānamakṣāḥ striyaśchaiva mṛgayā cha yathākramam,
ētatkaṣṭatamaṁ vidyāchchatuṣkaṁ kāmaje gaṇe.

[Meaning] The use of intoxicants, gambling, involvement with women, and hunting-these four are the most pernicious vices that arise from lust.

दण्डस्य पातनं चैव वाक्पारुष्यार्थदूषणे।
क्रोधजेऽपि गणे विद्यात्कष्टमेतत्त्रिकं सदा।।।।51

daṇḍasya pātanaṁ chaiva vākpāruṣyārthadūṣaṇe,
krodhaje'pi gaṇe vidyātkaṣṭametattrikaṁ sadā.

[Meaning] Punishment to innocent, the use of disparaging remarks, the abuse of money and means to promote unsocial activities-these three are the distressing vices born of anger.

सप्तकस्यास्य वर्गस्य सर्वत्रैवानुषिंगणः ।
पूर्वं पूर्वं गुरुतरं विद्याद्व्यसनमात्मवान् । ।52 । ।

saptakasyāsya vargasya sarvatraivānuṣiṁgaṇaḥ,
pūrvaṁ pūrvaṁ gurutaraṁ vidyādvyasanamātmavān.

[Meaning] Out of these seven vices born of lust and anger the preceding ones are worse than the succeeding ones. In other words, the use of disparaging remarks is worse than the abuse of money, convicting the innocent is worse than the use of disparaging remarks. Hunting is worse than punishing the innocent, involvement with women is worse than hunting and the use of intoxicants is worst of all.

व्यसनस्य च मृत्योश्च व्यसनं कष्टमुच्यते ।
व्यसन्यधोऽधो व्रजति स्वर्यात्यव्यसनी मृतः । । 53 । ।

vyasanasya cha mṛtyoścha vyasanaṁ kaṣṭamuchyate,
vyasanyadho'dho vrajati svaryātyavyasanī mṛtaḥ.

[Meaning] It is certain that it is better to die than to be addicted to vices since the longer a wicked man lives, the more immoral and unethical acts he will commit and consequently lower and lower he will sink inviting suffering in proportionate to his omissions and commissions. Whilst he who is free from vices enjoys happiness even after his death.

Therefore, it behoves all men, especially the political leaders/legislators/administrators, to keep aloof from hunting, drinking, and other vices, and instead, to develop a good character and a noble disposition, and to devote themselves to the moral and ethical practices.

Qualifications of Ministers, Officers, Subordinate Staff and Ambassadors to be Appointed

Regarding the qualifications of cabinet ministers, ministers of state, parliamentary secretaries, officers, subordinate staff to be appointed in different departments, and ambassadors, Manu (7-54-57; 60-64) observes thus:

मौलान् शास्त्रविदः शूरांल्लब्धलक्ष्यान् कुलोद्गतान्।
सचिवान् सप्त चाष्टौ वा प्रकुर्वीत परीक्षितान्।।54।।

maulān śāstravidaḥ śūrāṁllabdhalakṣayān kulodgatān,
sachivān sapta chāṣṭau vā prakurvīta parīkṣitān.

[Meaning] Let the Head of a state appoint seven or eight good, and intelligent cabinet ministers endowed with moral and ethical values who are natives of the country, are thoroughly conversant with the Vedas and the Śāstras, are very brave and courageous, whose judgment seldom errs, who come from good family and are well-tried men.

अपि यत् सुकरं कर्म तदप्येकेन दुष्करम्।
विशेषतोऽसहायेन किन्तु राज्यं महोदयम्।।55।।

api yat sukaraṁ karma tadapyekena duṣkaram,
viśeṣato'sahāyena kintu rājyaṁ mahodayam.

[Meaning] Because even an act easy in itself becomes difficult if carried by a man single-handedly. How can then the great work of the governance of a country be carried out by a man single-handedly? It is, therefore, a most dangerous thing to make one man a despotic ruler, or entrust a single man with the sole management of the affairs of the State.

तैः सार्द्धं चिन्तयेन्नित्यं सामान्यं सन्धिविग्रहम्।

स्थानं समुदयं गुप्तिं लब्धप्रशमनानि च।।56।।

taiḥ sārddhaṁ chintayennityaṁ sāmānyaṁ sandhivigraham,
sthānaṁ samudayaṁ gupti labdhapraśamanāni cha.

[Meaning] Let the Head of a State, then, constantly consult with his intelligent and learned cabinet ministers on the affairs of the State, such as (1) peace, (2) war, (3) defence-quietly protecting his own country against a foreign attack and to wait for an opportune time to attack, (4) offence, i.e., attacking an enemy when our position is strong enough to do so, (5) proper management of the internal affairs of the State, the exchequer and the army; (6) restore peace and stability in the newly subjugated countries.

Let him daily reflect on the above mentioned six subjects.

तेषां स्वं स्वमभिप्रायमुपलभ्य पृथक्पृथक्।
समस्तानाञ्च कार्य्येषु विदध्याद्धितमात्मनः।।57।।

teṣāṁ svaṁ svamabhiprāyamupalabhya pṛthakpṛthak,
samastānāñcha kāryyeṣu vidadhyāddhitamātmanaḥ.

[Meaning] Having ascertained the individual opinion of each of his cabinet ministers and other members of the assembly, let him abide by the decision of the majority and do what is best in his self-interest and interest of others.

अन्यानपि प्रकुर्वीत शुचीन् प्रज्ञानवस्थितान्।
सम्यगर्थसमाहर्तन् अमात्यान् सुपरीक्षितान्।।60।।

anyānapi prakurvīta śuchīn prajñānavasthitān,
samyagarthasamāhartan amātyān suparīkṣitān.

[Meaning] Let him likewise appoint other ministers of state or parliamentary secretaries who are men of great integrity, highly intellectual, of resolute minds, of great organizing power and of vast experience.

निवर्त्तेतास्य यावद्भिरितिकर्तव्यता नृभिः।
तावतोऽतन्द्रितान् दक्षान् प्रकुर्वीत विचक्षणान्।।61।।

nivarttetāsya yāvadbhiritikartavyatā nṛbhiḥ,
tāvato'tandritān dakṣān prakurvīta vichakṣaṇān.

[Meaning] Let him appoint good, energetic, strong, and intelligent officers, as per requirement.

तेषामर्थे नियुञ्जीत शूरान् दक्षान् कुलोद्गतान्।
शुचीन् आकरकर्मान्ते भीरून् अन्तर्निवेशने।।62।।

teṣāmarthe niyuñjīta śūrān dakṣān kulodgatān,
śuchīn ākarakarmānte bhīrūn antarniveśane.

[Meaning] Let strong men of great integrity and of noble lineage fill positions of subordinate staff in various ministries involving great responsibility and risk, whilst let timid and faint-hearted men be appointed as home Minister and other officials under him for the administration of internal (home) affairs.

दूतं चैव प्रकुर्वीत सर्वशास्त्रविशारदम्।
इंगिताकारचेष्टज्ञं शुचि दक्षं कुलोद्गतम्।।63।।

dūtaṁ chaiva prakurvīta sarvaśāstraviśāradam,
iṁgitākāracheṣṭajñaṁ śuchi dakṣaṁ kulodgatam.

[Meaning] Let him also appoint foreign minister and ambassadors who come from a good family, are well versed in all the Śāstras, perfectly honest, able to read the minds of others and to predict future developments by observing the state of affairs of a country.

अनुरक्तः शुचिर्दक्षः स्मृतिमान् देशकालवित्।
वपुष्मान्वीतभीर्वाग्मी दूतो राज्ञः प्रशस्यते।।64।।

anuraktaḥ śuchirdakṣaḥ smṛtimān deśakālavit,
vapuṣmānvītabhīrvāgmī dūto rājñaḥ praśasyate.

[Meaning] He alone is a fit person to be appointed a

foreign minister and ambassador who excels in political affairs, is of irreproachable character, pure at heart, highly intelligent and endowed with an excellent memory, who can adapt himself to the manners and customs of different countries and different times, is good looking, fearless and a master of elocution.

Duties of Ministers and other officials

Manu (7.65; 66; 68; 70; 74-78) describes the duties and responsibilities of various ministers and officers. Accordingly,

अमात्ये दण्ड आयत्तो दण्डे वैनयिकी क्रिया।
नृपतौ कोशराष्ट्रे च दूते सन्धिविपर्ययौ।।65।।

amātye daṇḍa āyatto daṇḍe vainayikī kriyā,
nṛpatau kośarāṣṭre cha dūte sandhiviparyayau.

[Meaning] The power to enforce the law should be vested in a Law Minister who would see that the justice is administered properly, Finance Ministry should be under the control of the Head of State, deptt. of peace and war with other countries under that of the Foreign Minister and Ambassadors, and everything under the control of the Assembly, i.e. the Head of state and all ministers are responsible to State Assembly.

दूत एव हि सन्धत्ते भिनत्त्येव च संहतान्।
दूतस्तत्कुरुते कर्म भिद्यन्ते येन वा न वा।।66।।

dūta ēva hi sandhatte bhinattyeva cha saṁhatān,
dūtastatkurute karma bhidyante yena vā na vā.

[Meaning] It is the Foreign Minister alone who can make peace between enemies, or war between friends. He should so strive as to divide enemies united against his country.

बुद्ध्वा च सर्वं तत्त्वेन परराजचिकीर्षितम्।
तथा प्रयत्नमातिष्ठेद्यथात्मानं न पीडयेत्।।68।।

buddhvā cha sarvaṁ tattvena pararājachikīrṣitam,
tathā prayatnamātiṣṭhedyathātmānaṁ na pīḍayet.

[Meaning] Thus having learnt the designs of his enemy let the Head of a state, as well as the members of his council, ministers and others, endeavor in a way that the state interests are not compromised.

धनुर्दुर्गं महीदुर्गमब्दुर्गं वार्क्षमेव वा।
नृदुर्गं गिरिदुर्गं वा समाश्रित्य वसेत्पुरम्।।70।।

dhanurdurgaṁ mahīdurgamabdurgaṁ vārkṣameva vā,
nṛdurgaṁ giridurgaṁ vā samāśritya vasetpuram.

[Meaning] The Head of state should reside in a walled city which cannot be targeted by enemy's arms, difficult to be approached by land or sea and is located on a hilly terrain under the thick cover of trees guarded by armed forces.

एकः शतं योधयति प्राकारस्थो धनुर्धरः।
शतं दशसहस्राणि तस्माद् दुर्गं विधीयते।।74।।

ēkaḥ śataṁ yodhayati prākārastho dhanurdharaḥ,
śataṁ daśasahasrāṇi tasmād durgaṁ vidhīyate.

[Meaning] Because one brave, well-armed soldier placed behind a wall is a match for a hundred and a hundred for thousands. It is therefore, extremely necessary to build walled cities.

तत्स्यादायुधसम्पन्नं धनधान्येन वाहनैः।
ब्राह्मणैः शिल्पिभिर्यन्त्रैर्यवसेनोदकेन च।।75।।

tatsyādāyudhasampannaṁ dhanadhānyena vāhanaiḥ,
brāhmaṇaiḥ śilpibhiryantrairyavasenodakena cha.

[Meaning] Let the city be well equipped with ordnance depots, godowns of different kinds of grain and other foodstuffs, transportation facilities, learned scholars and teachers, technocrats, various kinds of machines, fodder and provisions of adequate water supply, etc.

तस्य मध्ये सुपर्याप्तं कारयेद् गृहमात्मनः ।
गुप्तं सर्वर्त्तुकं शुभ्रं जलवृक्षसमन्वितम् ।।76।।

tasya madhye suparyāptaṁ kārayed gṛhamātmanaḥ,
guptaṁ sarvarttukaṁ śubhraṁ jalavṛkṣasamanvitam.

[Meaning] In the centre of the city let the Head of state erect for himself a white house, well-protected, suited to all weathers, provided with parks and gardens around it, and well-supplied with water. It should have space enough to cater to the needs of all the state functions

तदध्यास्योद्वहेद्भार्यां सवर्णां लक्षणान्विताम् ।
कुले महति सम्भूतां हृद्यां रूपगुणान्विताम् ।।77।।

tadadhyāsyodvahedbhāryāṁ savarṇāṁ lakṣaṇānvitām,
kule mahati sambhūtāṁ hṛdyāṁ rūpaguṇānvitām.

[Meaning] Having settled the affairs of the State, let him choose a life partner resembling his own temperament, nature and person, born of a high family, endowed with charming personality, beauty and other excellent qualities. (Let him walk down the aisle with only one wife and should not have relationship with a woman other than his married wife).

पुरोहितं प्रकुर्वीत वृणुयादेव चिर्त्वजम् ।
तेऽस्य गृह्याणि कर्माणि कुर्य्युर्वैतानिकानि च ।।78।।

purohitaṁ prakurvīta vṛṇuyādeva chirtvajam,
te'sya gṛhyāṇi karmāṇi kuryyurvaitānikāni cha.

[Meaning] Since the Head of a state remains busy day and night in the affairs of the State, so it is advisable for him to engage a Purohita (priest for household rites) and a Ṛtvik (Minister of Vedic allegorical rites) to perform for him the Gṛhya Karmas (household ceremonies or Sanskaras) suitable for different occasions of household life and the Śrauta Yajñas/Vaitānika karmas (Vedic allegorical rituals) suitable for various seasons and explain various aspects of creation.

Tax Collection

On the issue of tax collection Manu (7-80-83; 86; 91-97) says:

सांवत्सरिकमाप्तैश्च राष्ट्रादाहारयेद् बलिम् ।
स्याच्चाम्नायपरो लोके वर्त्तेत पितृवन्नृषु । ।80 । ।

sāṁvatsarikamāptaiścha rāṣṭrādāhārayed balim,
syāchchāmnāyaparo loke vartteta pitṛvannṛṣu.

[Meaning] Let the king collect annual tax through respected, trustworthy and accomplished men possessed of excellent character. Let the Head of a state, his ministers, assembly members and other officials, follow the eternal principles taught by the Vedas, and let them behave towards people like parents.

अध्यक्षान्विविधान्कुर्यात् तत्र तत्र विपश्चितः ।
तेऽस्य सर्वाण्यवेक्षेरन्नृणां कार्याणि कुर्वताम् ॥ 81 ॥

adhyakṣānvividhānkuryāt tatra tatra vipaśchitaḥ,
te'sya sarvāṇyavekṣerannṛṇāṁ kāryāṇi kurvatām.

[Meaning] Let all the state departments be headed by accomplished and learned officers. They should supervise the works done by all the officials working under them. Let them honour those who discharge their duties satisfactorily, whilst punish those who fail to do so.

Respect for Education and Teacher

आवृत्तानां गुरुकुलाद्विप्राणां पूजको भवेत् ।
नृपाणामक्षयो ह्येष निधिर्ब्राह्मो विधीयते ॥ 82 ॥

āvṛttānāṁ gurukulādviprāṇāṁ pūjako bhavet,
nṛpāṇāmakṣayo hyeṣa nidhibrāhmo vidhīyate.

[Meaning] In order to disseminate the quality education and knowledge of the Veda, which is called a true the undepleted revenue of the state, let the Head of state and his Assembly show due respect to graduating students as well as their teachers. This helps the growth of education and the progress of a country.

War Ethics

समोत्तमाधमै राजा त्वाहूतः पालयन् प्रजाः ।
न निवर्तेत संग्रामात् क्षात्रं धर्ममनुस्मरन् ॥ 83 ॥

samottamādhamai rājā tvāhūtaḥ pālayan prajāḥ,
na nivarteta saṁgrāmāt kṣātraṁ dharmamanusmaran.

[Meaning] If a king, devoted to the welfare of his people, is challenged by an enemy of equal, greater, or less standing, let him mindful of the duty of a Kṣatriya never withdraw from going to war. (Let him fight skillfully so as to ensure his victory).

आहवेषु मिथोऽन्योन्यं जिघांसन्तो महीक्षितः ।
युध्यमानाः परं शक्त्या स्वर्गं यान्त्यपरांगमुखाः ॥ 86 ॥

āhaveṣu mitho'nyonyaṁ jighāṁsanto mahīkṣitaḥ,
yudhyamānāḥ paraṁ śaktyā svargaṁ yāntyaparāṁgamukhāḥ.

[Meaning] Those kings who, with the object of defeating their enemies, fight fearlessly in a best possible manner and never take flight from battlefiled rejoice in life.

However, it is sometimes advisable to go into hiding in order to ensure victory over his enemy. Let him not perish foolishly like that of a tiger who succumbs to a gunshot under high tempers.

न च हन्यात्स्थलारूढं न क्लीबं न कृतांजलिम् ।
न मुक्तकेशं नासीनं न तवास्मीति वादिनम् ॥ 91 ॥

na cha hanyātsthalārūḍhaṁ na klībaṁ na kṛtāṁjalim,
na muktakeśaṁ nāsīnaṁ na tavāsmīti vādinam.

[Meaning] In the field of battle, never strike innocent people, nor one who is a eunuch, one who has surrendered, nor one whose hair is scattered over his eyes, nor one who is sitting at ease, nor one who pleads for mercy.

न सुप्तं न विसन्नाहं न नग्नं न निरायुधम् ।
नायुध्यमानं पश्यन्तं न परेण समागतम् ॥ 92 ॥

na suptaṁ na visannāhaṁ na nagnaṁ na nirāyudham,
nāyudhyamānaṁ paśyantaṁ na pareṇa samāgatam.

[Meaning] Never strike one who is asleep, nor one who is unconscious or in a fit, nor one who is disarmed, nor one who is naked, nor one who is a mere spectator, nor one who is only a camp-follower.

नायुधव्यसनं प्राप्तं नार्त्तं नातिपरिक्षतम् ।
न भीतं न परावृत्तं सतां धर्ममनुस्मरन् ॥ 93 ॥

nāyudhavyasanaṁ prāptaṁ nārttaṁ nātiparikṣatam,
na bhītaṁ na parāvṛttaṁ satāṁ dharmamanusmaran.

[Meaning] Nor one who is smarting under the pain of wounds, nor one who is in a miserable condition, nor one who is seriously wounded, nor one who is terrified, nor one who is running away (from the battle field).

They may be arrested and made war prisoners. They may be provided with food, drink and other necessaries of life. The wounded should be medically attended to. They should never be teased or made to suffer in any way. They should be made to work that suits them. The king should especially see that no one strikes a woman, a child, an old man, a wounded man and one who is diseased or afflicted with sorrow. Let him protect and bring up their children as if they were his own, and let their women be also well looked after. He should look upon them as he would upon his own daughter or sisters. Nor should he never look upon them with the eye of lust. After the country has stabilized, let him deport all of them, from whom he does not fear a fresh war or revolt, to their own countries or homes; but let him keep in prison all others who, he fears, may cause a disturbance.

Note: Thus we find that war ethics was prevalent in India since the times of yore. That is why the Indians comply with these rules of war ethics till today. Let us take the example of last war of Kargil. Every time Indians came across dead Pakistanis, they buried them if they were alive they were taken the prisoner and released later. The Pakis either killed our soldiers or cut their organs and sent them back. The same is the case with Bangladesh when they killed 16 BSF jawans. Muslim invaders raped our women and razed our temples. How many times have we heard Hindu rulers raping women or razing a place of worship as a sign of conquest? The award winning movie Gladiator shows how gruesome the Greeks of 2000 years ago were, they had no scruples, killed innocent people mercilessly. On the other hand, lets go 5000 years back in 'India of the Mahabharat period'. We find that war used to be stopped at sunset, a person who was injured or without arms was never attacked, in short, there were certain rules that governed war ethics. The question that we need to ask ourselves is that must we become ruthless, have the killer instinct and kill our enemies without mercy like them or observe restraint allowing our jawans to die in the process.

यस्तु भीतः परावृत्तः संग्रामे हन्यते परैः ।
भर्त्तुर्यद् दुष्कृतं किंचित्तत्सर्वं प्रतिपद्यते ॥ 94 ॥

yastu bhītaḥ parāvṛttaḥ saṁgrāme hanyate paraiḥ,

bhartturyad duṣkṛtaṁ kiṁchittatsarvaṁ pratipadyate.

यच्चास्य सुकृतं किंचिदमुत्रार्थमुपार्जितम् ।
भर्त्ता तत्सर्वमादत्ते परावृत्तहतस्य तु ॥ 95 ॥

yachchāsya sukṛtaṁ kiṁchidamutrārthamupārjitam,
bharttā tatsarvamādatte parāvṛttahatasya tu.

[Meaning] The soldier, who cowardly turns his back on a field of battle and is slain (by the enemy), is thus rightly punished for his disloyalty to his master who shall take unto himself all the honour due to the deceased on account of his past good conduct which begets happiness here and hereafter. The soldier, who is killed whilst running away from the field of battle, shall never obtain happiness. All his good work is nullified by this act of cowardice. He alone wins laurels who fights faithfully.

रथाश्वं हस्तिनं छत्रं धनं धान्यं पशून्स्त्रियः ।
सर्वद्रव्याणि कुप्यं च यो यज्जयति तस्य तत् ॥ 96 ॥

rathāśvaṁ hastinaṁ chhatraṁ dhanaṁ dhānyaṁ paśūnstriyaḥ,
sarvadravyāṇi kupyaṁ cha yo yajjayati tasya tat.

[Meaning] Here it may be reminded that the vehicles, horses, elephants, tents, grains, wealth, cattle, godowns and various other articles won in war goes to the winner as his lawful property.

राज्ञश्च दद्युरुद्धारमित्येषा वैदिकी श्रुतिः ।
राज्ञा च सर्वयोधेभ्यो दातव्यमपृथग्जितम् ॥ 97 ॥

rājñaścha dadyuruddhāramityeṣā vaidikī śrutiḥ,
rājñā cha sarvayodhebhyo dātavyamapṛthagjitam.

[Meaning] The winners should share the sixteenth part of their booty with the state, and so should the latter share the sixteenth part of the collective booty with the whole army. Let martyr's wife and children have his share. The wife and children of martyrs' should be well looked after by the state. When the children are grown up, the state should offer them suitable jobs. Let no one, who is desirous of augmenting the prosperity of his State and of gaining fame, victory, and happiness, transgress this law.

Liabilities of the Head of a State and his Assembly

Manu (7.99; 101; 104; 106-107; 110-117; 120-124) describes the responsibilities of the Head of State and his Assembly.

अलब्धं चैव लिप्सेत लब्धं रक्षेत्प्रयत्नतः ।
रक्षितं वर्द्धयेच्चैव वृद्धं पात्रेषु निःक्षिपेत् ॥ 99 ॥

alabdhaṁ chaiva lipseta labdhaṁ rakṣetprayatnataḥ, rakṣitaṁ varddhayechchaiva vṛddhaṁ pātreṣu niḥkṣipet.

[Meaning] The Head of State and his Assembly should concentrate on development in their states. They should strive to achieve the targets in various areas of development and financial growth, whatever is achieved should be maintained and the surplus funds be invested in the priority sectors like development of education, science and technology, dissemination of spiritual, ethical and moral values, educational aid to the poor and needy students, remuneration to scholars and spiritual masters including funding to disabled and orphans.

अलब्धमिच्छेद्दण्डेन लब्धं रक्षेदवेक्षया ।
रक्षित वर्द्धयेद् वृद्ध्या वृद्धं दानेन निःक्षिपेत् ॥ 101 ॥

alabdhamichchheddaṇḍena labdhaṁ rakṣedavekṣayā, rakṣita varddhayed vṛddhyā vṛddhaṁ dānena niḥkṣipet.

[Meaning] Having acquainted with the above mentioned fourfold objectives, the Head of state should strive to achieve it actively without fail. The law and order in state is the mainstay for achieving targets. Constant supervision helps in maintenance of achieved targets and the profitable investments help in surplus growth. The surplus can be allocated to the priority areas.

अमाययैव वर्तेत न कथंचन मायया।
बुध्येतारिप्रयुक्तां च मायां नित्यं स्वसंवृतः ॥ 104 ॥

amāyayaiva vatemrta na kathaṁchana māyayā,
budhyetāriprayuktāṁ cha māyāṁ nityaṁ svasaṁvṛtaḥ.

[Meaning] Let him be honest in his dealings and never be dishonest. He should be intelligent enough to be aware of the evil designs of his opponents for the safety and security of himself and the state.

नास्य छिद्रं परो विद्याच्छिद्रं विद्यात्परस्य तु।
गूहेत्कूर्म इवांगानि रक्षेद्विवरमात्मनः ॥ 105 ॥

nāsya chhidraṁ paro vidyāchchhidraṁ vidyātparasya tu,
gūhetkūrma ivāṁgāni rakṣedvivaramātmanaḥ.

[Meaning] He should manage in a way that his opponents are not able to break into his loophole or weakness, but he should be able to secure the weak points of his opponents. He should be able to conceal his weak points like a tortoise hides his limbs.

वकवच्चिन्तयेदर्थान् सिंहवच्च पराक्रमेत्।
वृकवच्चावलुम्पेत शशवच्च विनिष्पतेत् ॥ 106 ॥

vakavachchintayedarthān siṁhavachcha parākramet,
vṛkavachchāvalumpeta śaśavachcha viniṣpatet.

[Meaning] Let him attentively capture an opportunity to strengthen the economy like a heron to capture a fish.

Having strengthened economy, let him put forth his strength like a lion to vanquish the enemy; like a leopard let him lay an ambush for the enemies of the state; let him escape from a powerful enemy like a hare and then overtake him by stratagem.

एवं विजयमानस्य येऽस्य स्युः परिपन्थिनः ॥
तानानयेद्वशं सर्वान् सामादिभिरूपक्रमैः ॥ 107 ॥

ēvaṁ vijayamānasya ye'sya syuḥ paripanthinaḥ,
tānānayedvaśaṁ sarvān sāmādibhirūpakramaiḥ.

[Meaning] Let such a victorious sovereign reduce all dacoits, robbers and the like to submission by conciliating them, by giving them presents or by turning them against each other. If he fails to restrain them by those means let him do so by inflicting heavy punishment on them.

यथोद्धरति निर्दाता कक्षं धान्यं च रक्षति ।
तथा रक्षेन्नृपो राष्ट्रं हन्याच्च परिपन्थिनः ॥ 110 ॥

yathoddharati nirdātā kakṣaṁ dhānyaṁ cha rakṣati,
tathā rakṣennṛpo rāṣṭraṁ hanyāchcha paripanthinaḥ.

[Meaning] As a farmer separates the husk from the corn without injuring the latter, so should a king exterminate dacoits and burglars, and thus protect his state and people.

मोहाद्राजा स्वराष्ट्रं यः कर्षयत्यनवेक्षया ।
सोऽचिराद्भ्रश्यते राज्याज्जीविताच्च सबान्धवः ॥ 111 ॥

mohādrājā svarāṣṭraṁ yaḥ karṣayatyanavekṣayā,
so'chirādbhṛśyate rājyājjīvitāchcha sabāndhavaḥ.

[Meaning] The king, who through neglect of duty and lack of understanding oppresses his people, soon loses his kingdom and perishes with his persons before his time.

शरीरकर्षणात्प्राणाः क्षीयन्ते प्राणिनां यथा।
तथा राज्ञामपि प्राणाः क्षीयन्ते राष्ट्रकर्षणात्॥ 112 ॥

śarīrakarṣaṇātprāṇāḥ kṣīyante prāṇināṁ yathā,
tathā rājñāmapi prāṇāḥ kṣīyante rāṣṭrakarṣaṇāt.

[Meaning] Just as living beings lose their lives through the failure of their bodily strength, so do Head of states lose their power by oppressing the people.

राष्ट्रस्य संग्रहे नित्यं विधानमिदमाचरेत्।
सुसंगृहीतराष्ट्रो हि पार्थिवः सुखमेधते॥ 113 ॥

rāṣṭrasya saṁgrahe nityaṁ vidhānamidamācharet,
susaṁgṛhītarāṣṭro hi pārthivaḥ sukhamedhate.

[Meaning] Therefore, Head of state and the assembly so strive as to gain success in governance. The well protected and prosperous nation bring perpetual happiness to the Head of the State.

द्वयोस्त्रयाणां पंचानां मध्ये गुल्ममधिष्ठितम्।
तथा ग्रामशतानां च कुर्य्याद्राष्ट्रस्य संग्रहम् ॥ 114 ॥

dvayostrayāṇāṁ paṁchānāṁ madhye gulmamadhiṣṭhitam,
tathā grāmaśatānāṁ cha kuryyādrāṣṭrasya saṁgraham.

[Meaning] Let him, therefore, have an administrative office over two, three, five and a hundred villages, wherein he should appoint the required number of officials to carry on government business.

ग्रामस्याधिपतिं कुर्य्याद्दशग्रामपतिं तथा।
विंशतीशं शतेशं च सहस्त्रपतिमेव च॥ 115 ॥

grāmasyādhipatiṁ kuryyāddaśagrāmapatiṁ tathā,
viṁśatīśaṁ śateśaṁ cha sahastrapatimeva cha.

[Meaning] Let him appoint an official at the head of one village, the second one over ten such villages, a third one over twenty, a fourth one over one hundred villages, and a fifth one over a thousand such villages.

ग्रामदोषान्समुत्पन्नान् ग्रामिकः शनकैः स्वयम्।
शंसेद् ग्रामदशेशाय दशेशो विंशतीशिनम्। ॥ 116 ॥

grāmadoṣānsamutpannān grāmikaḥ śanakaiḥ svayam,
śaṁsed grāmadaśeśāya daśeśo viṁśatīśinam.

[Meaning] Let the administrator of one village daily report to the administrator of ten villages of all crimes committed within his jurisdiction and the administrator of ten villages submit his report to the administrator of twenty villages.

विंशतीशस्तु तत्सर्वं शतेशाय निवेदयेत्।
शंसेद् ग्रामशतेशस्तु सहस्रपतये स्वयम्॥ 117 ॥

viṁśatīśastu tatsarvaṁ śateśāya nivedayet,
śaṁsed grāmaśateśastu sahasrapataye svayam.

[Meaning] Let the administrator of twenty report all such matters to the administrator of hundred every day and the administrator of hundred, to the administrator of one thousand, in other words, five administrator of twenty, to an administrator of one hundred, ten administrators of a hundred, to an administrator of ten thousand, and the administrator of ten thousand to the state assembly which governs the affairs of entire state and all state assemblies, to the national assembly representing the whole nation and national assemblies to a world council.

तेषां ग्राम्याणि कार्याणि पृथक्कार्याणि चैव हि।
राज्ञोऽन्यः सचिवः स्निग्धस्तानि पश्येदतन्द्रितः ॥ 120 ॥

teṣāṁ grāmyāṇi kāryāṇi pṛthakkāryāṇi chaiva hi,
rājño'nyaḥ sachivaḥ snigdhastāni paśyedatandritaḥ.

[Meaning] Over every ten thousand villages let him appoint two governors (presiding officials), one of whom should preside over the Assembly, whilst the other should tour all over the state and diligently inspect the work and conduct of all the magistrates and other Govt. officials.

नगरे नगरे चैकं कुर्यात्सर्वार्थचिन्तकम् ।
उच्चैः स्थानं घोररूपं नक्षत्राणामिव ग्रहम् ॥ 121 ॥

nagare nagare chaikaṁ kuryātsarvārthachintakam,
uchchaiḥ sthānaṁ ghorarūpaṁ nakṣatrāṇāmiva graham.

[Meaning] For the purpose of holding the meetings of town/city councils let him erect a Town Hall in every big town or a city. It should be lofty, capacious, and beautiful like the moon among other constellations, wherein the learned and experienced members of the town/city council deliberate over the affairs of their town/city, and enact such laws as will promote the welfare of the people and advance the cause of education and enlightenment.

स ताननुपरिक्रामेत्सर्वानेव सदा स्वयम् ।
तेषां वृत्तं परिणयेत्सम्यग्राष्ट्रेषु तच्चरैः ॥ 122 ॥

sa tānanuparikrāmetsarvāneva sadā svayam,
teṣāṁ vṛttaṁ pariṇayetsamyagrāṣṭreṣu tachcharaiḥ.

[Meaning] Let the inspecting governor have detectives under him who should come from various classes of society and through them let him secretly know perfectly the conduct -good or bad- of the Government servants as well as that of the people. Let him punish those who do not faithfully discharge their duties, and honour those whose conduct is praiseworthy.

राज्ञो हि रक्षाधिकृताः परस्वादायिनः शठाः ।
भृत्या भवन्ति प्रायेण तेभ्यो रक्षेदिमाः प्रजाः ॥ 123 ॥

rājño hi rakṣādhikṛtāḥ parasvādāyinaḥ śaṭhāḥ,
bhṛtyā bhavanti prāyeṇa tebhyo rakṣedimāḥ prajāḥ.

[Meaning] Let the Head of the State appoint such men guardians of his people as are virtuous, well-experienced, learned and of good lineage; under such learned officials let him also place men who are very wicked as burglars and robbers, i.e., who live by seizing what belongs to others. It will help to keep those men from the pursuit of their wicked ways, as well as, to protect the public properly.

ये कार्यिकेभ्योऽर्थमेव गृह्णीयुः पापचेतसः ।
तेषां सर्वस्वमादाय राजा कुर्यात्प्रवासनम् ॥124 ॥

ye kāryikebhyo'rthameva gṛhṛṇīyuḥ pāpachetasaḥ,
teṣāṁ sarvasvamādāya rājā kuryātpravāsanam.

[Meaning] Let the Head of the State punish properly the Judges and those officials who are conferred with magisterial powers who accept a bribe either from the plaintiff or the defendant in a case and, therefore, announce the unjust decision. The Head of the State should confiscate their property and banish them to a place from where they are not allowed to return.

Were those man to go unpunished, it would encourage other officials to commit similar wicked crimes, whilst the infliction of punishment would serve to check them. But let those officials be paid a handsome amount of salaries for their services to be given monthly or annually so that they may keep them in comfort and even make them rich. Let an old official in consideration of his services be granted a pension equal to half of his pay. This pension must last only so long as he lives, not after. But let his children be properly honoured or given Government appointments according to their qualifications. Let his wife and children be given an allowance by the State enough for their subsistence which should be stopped if they turn wicked. Let the king constantly follow this policy.

Taxation

Rules of taxation system are ordained by Manu as under:

यथा फलेन युज्येत राजा कर्ता च कर्मणाम् ।
तथाऽवेक्ष्य नृपो राष्ट्रे कल्पयेत् सततं करान् ॥ मनु० 7.128 ॥

yathā phalena yujyeta rājā kartā cha karmaṇām,
tathā'vekṣaya nṛpo rāṣṭre kalpayet satataṁ karān.
Manu, 7.128

[Meaning] Let the king in conjunction with the Assembly, after a lot of consideration, so levy taxes in his dominions as to ensure the happiness of both the rulers and the ruled.

यथाऽल्पाल्पमदन्त्याद्यं वार्योकोवत्सषट्पदाः ।
तथाऽल्पाल्पो ग्रहीतव्यो राष्ट्राद् राज्ञाब्दिकः करः ॥ मनु० 7.129

yathā'lpālpamadantyādyaṁ vāryokovatsaṣaṭpadāḥ,
tathā'lpālpo grahītavyo rāṣṭrād rājñābdikaḥ karaḥ.
Manu, 7.129

[Meaning] Let the king draw an annual revenue from his people little by little just as the leech, the suckling calf and the bee take their food little by little.

नोच्छिन्द्यादात्मनो मूलं परेषां चातितृष्णया ।
उच्छिन्दन् ह्यात्मनो मूलमात्मानं तांश्च पीडयेत् ॥ मनु० 7.139

nochchhindyādātmano mūlaṁ pareṣāṁ chātitṛṣṇayā,
uchchhindan hyātmano mūlamātmānaṁ tāṁścha pīḍayet. *Manu, 7.139*

[Meaning] Let him not, through extreme covetousness, destroy the very roots of his own and others' happiness, since he, who cuts off the roots of happiness and temporal prosperity, brings nothing but misery on himself as well as on others.

तीक्ष्णश्चैव मृदुश्च स्यात् कार्यं वीक्ष्य महीपतिः ।
तीक्ष्णश्चैव मृदुश्चैव राज भवति सम्मतः ॥ मनु० 7.140 ॥

tīkṣaṇaśchaiva mṛduścha syāt kāryaṁ vīkṣaya mahīpatiḥ,
tīkṣaṇaśchaiva mṛduśchaiva rāja bhavati sammataḥ ॥

Manu, 7.140

[Meaning] The king who can be both gentle and stern as occasion demands is highly honoured. He should be gentle to the good and stern towards the wicked.

एवं सर्वं विधायैदमितिकर्तव्यमात्मनः ।
युक्तश्चैवाप्रमत्तश्च परिरक्षेदिमाः प्रजाः ॥ मनु० 7.142 ॥

evaṁ sarvaṁ vidhāyaidamitikartavyamātmanaḥ,
yuktaśchaivāpramattaścha parirakṣedimāḥ prajāḥ.

Manu, 7.142.

[Meaning] Having thus arranged the affairs of the State let him devote himself to the protection and welfare of his people with diligent attention.

विक्रोशन्त्यो यस्य राष्ट्राद् ह्रियन्ते दस्युभिः प्रजाः ।
सम्पश्यतः सभृत्यस्य मृतः स न तु जीवति ॥ मनु० 7.143 ॥

vikrośantyo yasya rāṣṭrād hriyante dasyubhiḥ prajāḥ,
sampaśyataḥ sabhṛtyasya mṛtaḥ sa na tu jīvati.

Manu, 7.143

[Meaning] Know that King as well as his ministers to be dead, not alive, the lives and property of whose subjects are looted by ruffians whilst they lament and cry aloud for help.

क्षत्रियस्य परो धर्मः प्रजानामेव पालनम् ।
निर्दिष्टफलभोक्ता हि राजा धर्मेण युज्यते ॥ मनु० 7.144 ॥

kṣatriyasya paro dharmaḥ prajānāmeva pālanam,
nirdiṣṭaphalabhoktā hi rājā dharmeṇa yujyate.

Manu, 7.144

[Meaning] Promotion of the happiness of their subjects, therefore, is the highest duty of kings. The king who discharges this duty faithfully, levies taxes and governs the country with the help of the assembly enjoys happiness, but he who does otherwise is afflicted with misery and suffering.

King's Routine

उत्थाय पश्चिमे यामे कृतशौचः समाहितः ।
हुताग्निर्ब्राह्मणांश्चार्च्य प्रविशेत् स शुभां सभाम् ॥ मनु० 7-145

utthāya paśchime yāme kṛtaśauchaḥ samāhitaḥ,
hutāgnirbrāhmaṇāṁśchārchya praviśet sa śubhāṁ sabhām. Manu, 7-145

[Meaning] Let the king rise in the last watch of the night, have a wash, meditate on God with his whole attention, perform Homa, pay his respects to the devoutly learned men, take his meal and enter the audience chamber.

तत्र स्थितः प्रजाः सर्वाः प्रतिनन्द्य विसर्जयेत् ।
विसृज्य च प्रजाः सर्वा मन्त्रयेत् सह मन्त्रिभिः ॥ मनु० 7-146 ॥

tatra sthitaḥ prajāḥ sarvāḥ pratinandya visarjayet,
visṛjya cha prajāḥ sarvā mantrayet saha mantribhiḥ.
Manu, 7-146.

[Meaning] Let him standing there show respect to the people present. Having dismissed them, let him take stock of state affairs in consultation with his Council of Ministers.

गिरिपृष्ठं समारुह्य प्रासादं वा रहोगतः ।
अरण्ये निःशलाके वा मन्त्रयेदविभावितः ॥ मनु० 7-147 ॥

giripṛṣṭhaṁ samāruhya prāsādaṁ vā rahogataḥ,
araṇye niḥśalāke vā mantrayedavibhāvitaḥ.
Manu, 7-147

[Meaning] Thereafter let him go out for a walk or a ride, seek the top of a mountain wilderness, where there is not even the tiniest tree (to hide a person), or a sequestered house and discuss (state affairs) with them in all sincerity.

यस्य मन्त्रं न जानन्ति समागम्य पृथग्जनाः ।
स कृत्स्नां पृथिवीं भुङ्क्ते कोशहीनोऽपि पार्थिवः ॥ मनु॰ 7-148 ॥

yasya mantraṁ na jānanti samāgamya pṛthagjanāḥ,
sa kṛtsnāṁ pṛthivīṁ bhuṅkte kośahīno'pi pārthivaḥ.
Manu, 7-148

[Meaning] That king whose secrets cannot be unravelled by people combinedly, in other words, whose plans are deep, pure, centred on the public good, and confidential shall rule the whole earth, even though poor.

Let him never do even a single thing without the approval of the members of his council.

Six Kinds of Tactics

आसनं चैव यानं च सन्धिं विग्रहमेव च ।
कार्यं वीक्ष्य प्रयुञ्जीत द्वैधं संश्रयमेव च ॥ मनु॰ 7-161 ॥

āsanaṁ chaiva yānaṁ cha sandhiṁ vigrahameva cha,
kāryaṁ vīkṣaya prayuñjīta dvaidhaṁ saṁśrayameva cha. Manu, 7-161

[Meaning] The king and another person in authority should keep it in mind that it is their duty to adopt after due deliberation one of the following six measures as occasion demands:

1. Inaction or Remaining quiet
2. Attack/March
3. Treaty with the enemy.

4. War against wicked enemies

5. Division of forces

6. Seeking alliance with a powerful king

सन्धिं तु द्विविधं विद्याद् राजा विग्रहमेव च ।
उभे यानासने चैव द्विविधः संश्रयः स्मृतः ॥ मनु० 7-162 ॥

sandhiṁ tu dvividhaṁ vidyād rājā vigrahameva cha,
ubhe yānāsane chaiva dvividhaḥ saṁśrayaḥ smṛtaḥ.

Manu, 7-162

[Meaning] Let the king thoroughly acquaint himself with the twofold nature of each of these tactics.

समानयानकर्मा च विपरीतस्तथैव च ।
तदा त्वायतिसंयुक्तः सन्धिर्ज्ञेयो द्विलक्षणः ॥ मनु० 7-163 ॥

samānayānakarmā cha viparītastathaiva cha,
tadā tvāyatisaṁyuktaḥ sandhirjñeyo dvilakṣaṇaḥ.

Manu, 7-163

[Meaning] The two kinds of peace are - (1), treaty with enemy, and (2) alliance with another for his opposition. But let the king always go on doing whatever is necessary for the present or will be required for the future.

स्वयङ्कृतश्च कार्यार्थमकाले काल एव वा ।
मित्रस्य चैवापकृते द्विविधो विग्रहः स्मृतः ॥ मनु० 7-164 ॥

svayaṅkṛtaścha kāryārthamakāle kāla ēva vā,
mitrasya chaivāpakṛte dvividho vigrahaḥ smṛtaḥ.

Manu, 7-164

[Meaning] War is of two kinds: (1) when it is waged on account of personal reasons, and (2) when it is waged timely or untimely on account of an injury to a friendly power or an ally.

एकाकिनश्चात्ययिके कार्ये प्राप्ते यदृच्छया ।
संहतस्य च मित्रेण द्विविधं यानमुच्यते ॥ मनु० 7-165 ॥

ēkākinaśchātyayike kārye prāpte yadṛchchhayā,
saṁhatasya cha mitreṇa dvividhaṁ yānamuchyate.
Manu, 7-165

[Meaning] The two kinds of attack are called expeditions against the enemy under the unforeseen circumstances with or without allies.

क्षीणस्य चैव क्रमशो दैवात् पूर्वकृतेन वा ।
मित्रस्य चानुरोधेन द्विविधं स्मृतमासनम् ॥ मनु० 7-166 ॥

kṣīṇasya chaiva kramaśo daivāt pūrvakṛtena vā,
mitrasya chānurodhena dvividhaṁ smṛtamāsanam.
Manu, 7-166

[Meaning] Remaining quiet or inaction is of two kinds-firstly, when it is done when the king's own power is weakened through some cause, and secondly when he remains quiet on the advice of his ally.

बलस्य स्वामिनश्चैव स्थितिः कार्यार्थसिद्धये ।
द्विविधं कीर्त्यते द्वैधं षाड्गुण्यगुणवेदिभिः ॥ मनु० 7-167 ॥

balasya svāminaśchaiva sthitiḥ kāryārthasiddhaye,
dvividhaṁ kīrtyate dvaidhaṁ ṣāḍguṇyaguṇavedibhiḥ.
Manu, 7-167

[Meaning] The division of the force means to divide one's rank and file into two sections in order to gain victory.

अर्थसम्पादनार्थं च पीड्यमानस्य शत्रुभिः ।
साधुषु व्यपदेशश्च द्विविधः संश्रयः स्मृतः ॥ मनु० 7-168 ॥

arthasampādanārthaṁ cha pīḍyamānasya śatrubhiḥ,
sādhuṣu vyapadeśaścha dvividhaḥ saṁśrayaḥ smṛtaḥ.
Manu, 7-168

[Meaning] Twofold Protection or alliance means seeking protection of or alliance with a powerful ruler or a great man in self-defence when threatened by an enemy or when on the offensive.

यदाऽवगच्छेदायत्यामाधिक्यं ध्रुवमात्मनः ।
तदात्वे चाल्पिकां पीडां तदा सन्धिं समाश्रयेत् ॥ मनु० 7-169 ॥

yadā'vagachchhedāyatyāmādhikyaṁ dhruvamātmanaḥ,
tadātve chālpikāṁ pīḍāṁ tadā sandhiṁ samāśrayet.

Manu, 7-169

[Meaning] When a king ascertains that by going to war at present time he will suffer, whilst by waiting and going to war at some future time he will certainly gain in power and vanquish his enemy, let him, then make peace with him and patiently wait for that favourable opportunity.

यदा प्रहृष्टा मन्येत सर्वास्तु प्रकृतीर्भृशम् ।
अत्युच्छ्रितं तथात्मानं तदा कुर्वीत विग्रहम् ॥ मनु० 7-170 ॥

yadā prahṛṣṭā manyeta sarvāstu prakṛtīrbhṛśam,
atyuchchhritaṁ tathātmānaṁ tadā kurvīta vigraham.

Manu, 7-170

[Meaning] When he finds his people and the army considerable happy, prosperous and full of spirits and himself the same, let him then declare war against his foe.

यदा मन्येत भावेन हृष्टं पुष्टं बलं स्वकम् ।
परस्य विपरीतं च तदा यायाद् रिपुं प्रति ॥ मनु० 7-171 ॥

yadā manyeta bhāvena hṛṣṭaṁ puṣṭaṁ balaṁ svakam,
parasya viparītaṁ cha tadā yāyād ripuṁ prati.

Manu, 7-171

[Meaning] When he finds his forces contented, jubilant and ready for action, and those of his enemy the reverse, let him then attack or march against his foe.

यदा तु स्यात् परिक्षीणो वाहनेन बलेन च ।
तदासीत प्रयत्नेन शनकैः सान्त्वयन्नरीन् ॥ मनु० 7-172 ॥

yadā tu syāt parikṣīṇo vāhanena balena cha,
tadāsīta prayatnena śanakaiḥ sāntvayannarīn.

Manu, 7-172

[Meaning] When he finds his army lacking in strength and transport, he should carefully and gradually pacify enemy and stay at home.

मन्येतारिं यदा राजा सर्वथा बलवत्तरम् ।
तदा द्विधा बलं कृत्वा साधयेत् कार्यमात्मनः ॥ मनु० 7-173 ॥

manyetāriṁ yadā rājā sarvathā balavattaram,
tadā dvidhā balaṁ kṛtvā sādhayet kāryamātmanaḥ.

Manu, 7-173.

[Meaning] When he finds his foe much stronger than himself, let him accomplish his object by doubling or dividing his force.

यदा परबलानां तु गमनीयतमो भवेत् ।
तदा तु संश्रयेत् क्षिप्रं धार्मिकं बलिनं नृपम् ॥ मनु० 7-174 ॥

yadā parabalānāṁ tu gamanīyatamo bhavet,
tadā tu saṁśrayet kṣipraṁ dhārmikaṁ balinaṁ nṛpam. *Manu, 7-174*

[Meaning] When it becomes clear to him that his enemies will soon march against him, let him then seek speedily the protection of or an alliance with a just and powerful king.

निग्रहं प्रकृतीनां च कुर्याद् योऽरिबलस्य च ।
उपसेवेत तं नित्यं सर्वयत्नैर्गुरुं यथा ॥ मनु० 7-175 ॥

nigrahaṁ prakṛtīnāṁ cha kuryād yo'ribalasya cha,
upaseveta taṁ nityaṁ sarvayatnairguruṁ yathā.

Manu, 7-175

[Meaning] Let a king treat him who would help him in restoring peace and order among his people or in keeping his army under control or his enemy in check, as he would treat his Guru.

यदि तत्रापि सम्पश्येद् दोषं संश्रयकारितम् ।
सुयुद्धमेव तत्रापि निर्विशङ्कः समाचरेत् ॥ मनु० 7-176 ॥

yadi tatrāpi sampaśyed doṣaṁ saṁśrayakāritam,
suyuddhameva tatrāpi nirviśaṅkaḥ samācharet.

Manu, 7-176

[Meaning] But if he finds his protector or ally full of evil designs, let him then fight him too fearlessly.

Let him never be hostile to a king who is just and virtuous. On the other hand, let him always be on friendly terms with him. All the aforesaid tactics are to be applied in order to vanquish a wicked man in power.

सर्वोपायैस्तथा कुर्यान्नीतिज्ञः पृथिवीपतिः ।
यथाऽस्याभ्यधिका न स्युर्मित्रोदासीनशत्रवः ॥ मनु० 7-177 ॥

sarvopāyaistathā kuryānnītijñaḥ pṛthivīpatiḥ,
yathā'syābhyadhikā na syurmitrodāsīnaśatravaḥ.

Manu, 7-177

[Meaning] Let a king who is a true statesman, apply such tactics as neither his allies, neutral powers nor his foes may grow in power or gain any great advantage over him.

आयतिं सर्वकार्याणां तदात्वं च विचारयेत् ।
अतीतानां च सर्वेषां गुणदोषौ च तत्त्वतः ॥ मनु० 7-178 ॥

āyatiṁ sarvakāryāṇāṁ tadātvaṁ cha vichārayet,
atītānāṁ cha sarveṣāṁ guṇadoṣau cha tattvataḥ.

Manu, 7-178

[Meaning] Let him thoroughly deliberate over the advantages and disadvantages of his past actions, his present and future duties.

आयत्यां गुणदोषज्ञस्तदात्वे क्षिप्रनिश्चयः ।
अतीते कार्यशेषज्ञः शत्रुभिर्नाभिभूयते ॥ मनु० 7-179 ॥

āyatyāṁ guṇadoṣajñastadātve kṣipraniśchayaḥ,
atīte kāryaśeṣajñaḥ śatrubhirnābhibhūyate.

Manu, 7-179

[Meaning] Then let him strive to ward off bad results and promote good results. That king shall never be vanquished by his enemies who can foresee the good and evil results likely to follow from the measures that he would take in the future, who acts according to his convictions in the present without delay and knows his failures in the past.

यथैनं नाभिसन्दध्युर्मित्रोदासीनशत्रवः ।
तथा सर्वं संविदध्यादेष सामासिको नयः ॥ मनु० 7-180 ॥

yathainaṁ nābhisandadhyurmitrodāsīnaśatravaḥ,
tathā sarvaṁ saṁvidadhyādeṣa sāmāsiko nayaḥ.

Manu, 7-180

[Meaning] Let a statesman, especially a king, viz., the President of the Assembly, so endeavour that the power of his allies, natural powers and foes may be kept within limits and not otherwise. Never should he be negligent of this. This alone is, in brief, true statesmanship.

Invasion

कृत्वा विधानं मूले तु यात्रिकं च यथाविधि ।
उपगृह्यास्पदं चैव चारान् सम्यग् विधाय च ॥ मनु० 7-184 ॥

kṛtvā vidhānaṁ mūle tu yātrikaṁ cha yathāvidhi,
upagṛhyāspadaṁ chaiva chārān samyag vidhāya cha.

Manu, 7-184

[Meaning] Before a king begins his march against his enemy, let him secure the safety of his dominions, provide himself with all that is necessary for the expedition, take the necessary number of troops, carriages and other conveyances, weapons, fire-arms, etc. and dispatch his spies in all quarters.

संशोध्य त्रिविधं मार्गं षड्विधं च बलं स्वकम् ।
साम्परायिककल्पेन यायादरिपुरं प्रति ॥ मनु० 7-185 ॥

saṁśodhya trividhaṁ mārgaṁ ṣaḍvidhaṁ cha balaṁ svakam,
sāmparāyikakalpena yāyādaripuraṁ prati. Manu, 7-185

[Meaning] Having been confirmed that all the three zones - land, water and air - are clear and well secured, let him travel on land by means of vehicles, on foot, on horseback, or on elephants, on water by ships, and through air by airplanes and the like. He should be well equipped with infantry, cavalry, elephants, war vehicles, weapons of war, provisions and other necessary things, and proceed gradually towards the chief city of the enemy giving some excuse for his March.

शत्रुसेविनि मित्रे च गूढे युक्ततरो भवेत् ।
गतप्रत्यागते चैव स हि कष्टतरो रिपुः ॥ मनु० 7-186 ॥

śatrusevini mitre cha gūḍhe yuktataro bhavet,
gatapratyāgate chaiva sa hi kaṣṭataro ripuḥ.
Manu, 7-186

[Meaning] In his conversation let him be very careful, and keep a strict vigil on the movements of a man who is in collusion with the enemy and passes him vital information, whilst make a show of friendship; because he who keeps his enmity secret and makes a show of friendship must be looked upon as the most dangerous foe.

दण्डव्यूहेन तन् मार्गं यायात् तु शकटेन वा ।
वराहमकराभ्यां वा सूच्या वा गरुडेन वा ॥ मनु० 7-187 ॥

daṇḍavyūhena tan mārgaṁ yāyāt tu śakaṭena vā,
varāhamakarābhyāṁ vā sūchyā vā garuḍena vā.
Manu, 7-187

[Meaning] Let the king see that all officers learn the

science and art of war, as well as he himself and other people. It is only those warriors who are well trained in the art of war that can fight well on the field of battle. Let them be well drilled in the following battle arrays:

1. Daṇḍa vyuha (marching troops in file)

2. Śakaṭa vyuha (marching troops in column.

3. Varāha vyuha (marching troops in square).

4. Makara vyuha (marching troops in the formation of an alligator)

5. Sūci vyuha (marching troops in wedge-like formation)

6. Garuḍa vyuha (advancing in skirmishing order)

यतश्च भयमाशङ्केत् ततो विस्तारयेद् बलम् ।
पद्मेन चैव व्यूहेन निविशेत सदा स्वयम् ॥ मनु० 7-188 ॥

yataścha bhayamāśaṅket tato vistārayed balam,
padmena chaiva vyūhena niviśeta sadā svayam.

Manu, 7-188

[Meaning] Let him extend his troops to the flank from which he apprehends danger. Let him stay in the centre arraying his troops around him like the petals of a lotus flower.

सेनापतिबलाध्यक्षौ सर्वदिक्षु निवेशयेत् ।
यतश्च भयमाशङ्केत् प्राचीं तां कल्पयेद् दिशम् ॥ मनु० 7-189

senāpatibalādhyakṣau sarvadikṣu niveśayet,
yataścha bhayamāśaṅket prāchīṁ tāṁ kalpayed diśam.

Manu, 7-189

[Meaning] Let him place his Generals and Commanding Officers with their brave troops in all the eight directions. Let him turn the front of the whole army towards the direction of the potential threat. He must also have his flanks and rear well guarded, otherwise, the enemy may attack him on these positions.

गुल्मांश्च स्थापयेदाप्तान् कृतसञ्ज्ञान् समन्ततः ।
स्थाने युद्धे च कुशलानभीरूनविकारिणः ॥ मनु० 7-190 ॥

gulmāṁścha sthāpayedāptān kṛtasañjñān samantataḥ,
sthāne yuddhe cha kuśalānabhīrūnavikāriṇaḥ.

Manu, 7-190

[Meaning] On all sides let him place those soldiers who are well-trained in the art of war, firm in their places like the pillars of a roof, virtuous, clever in charging and sustaining a charge, fearless and faithful.

संहतान् योधयेदल्पान् कामं विस्तारयेद् बहून् ।
सूच्या वज्रेण चैवैतान् व्यूहेन व्यूह्य योधयेत् ॥ मनु० 7-191 ॥

saṁhatān yodhayedalpān kāmaṁ vistārayed bahūn,
sūchyā vajreṇa chaivaitān vyūhena vyūhya yodhayet.

Manu, 7-191.

[Meaning] When he has to fight a numerically strong army, let him then arrange his troops in close formation or quickly deploy as occasion demands. When he has to fight his way into a city, a fort or the ranks of his enemy, let him arrange his troops in the form of sūci (needle), such as marching them in the form of echelon or in the form of a (vajra) double-edged sword that cuts both ways; let them fight as well as advance.

Before artillery or musketry fire let him order his troops to crawl like snakes till they get near the guns, shoot or capture the gunners and turn those very guns on the enemy or shoot him with his rifles. Or let him make old soldiers run on horses before the guns, keep good soldiers in the middle and thus attack the enemy. Let him shoot the enemy, scatter his forces or capture them by a vigorous assault.

स्यन्दनाश्वैः समे युध्येदनूपेनोद्विपैस्तथा ।
वृक्षगुल्मावृते चापैरसिचर्मायुधैः स्थले ॥ मनु० 7-192 ॥

syandanāśvaiḥ same yudhyedanūpenodvipaistathā,
vṛkṣagulmāvṛte chāpairasicharmāyudhaiḥ sthale.

Manu, 7-192

[Meaning] On level ground let him fight on foot, on horseback, or in vehicles manufactured specially for fighting a war, on the sea on warships or fighter boats, in shallow waters on elephants, among trees and bushes with arrows. And in sandy places with swords and shields.

प्रहर्षयेद् बलं व्यूह्य तांश्च सम्यक् परीक्षयेत् ।
चेष्टाश्चैव विजानीयादरीन् योधयतामपि ॥ मनु० 7-194 ॥

praharṣayed balaṁ vyūhya tāṁścha samyak parīkṣayet,
cheṣṭāśchaiva vijānīyādarīn yodhayatāmapi.

Manu, 7-194

[Meaning] When his troops are engaged in fighting, let him cheer and encourage them. Let him closely monitor the behaviour of his troops see whether they discharge their duty faithfully or not and also keep a close vigil on the movements of enemy's army.

At the close of a battle let him gladden the hearts of those who have distinguished themselves, by making nice speeches, providing them with everything they need, looking after their comfort, and helping them in every other way. Let him never engage in a fight without forming his troops into the necessary array of battle.

उपरुध्यारिमासीत राष्ट्रं चास्योपपीडयेत् ।
दूषयेच्चास्य सततं यवसान्नोदकैन्धनम् ॥ मनु० 7-195 ॥

uparudhyārimāsīta rāṣṭraṁ chāsyopapīḍayet,
dūṣayechchāsya satataṁ yavasānnodakaindhanam.

Manu, 7-195

[Meaning] Let him, if occasion arises, surround the enemy and detain him, harass his country, and cut off his supply of grass, water, food and fuel.

भिन्द्याच्चैव तडागानि प्राकारपरिखास्तथा ।
समवस्कन्दयेच्चैनं रात्रौ वित्रासयेत् तथा ॥ मनु० 7-196 ॥

bhindyāchchaiva taḍāgāni prākāraparikhāstathā,
samavaskandayechchainaṁ rātrau vitrāsayet tathā.

Manu, 7-196

[Meaning] Let him destroy the reservoirs, city walls, and trenches of his enemy, alarm him by night and adopt other measures to vanquish him.

प्रमाणानि च कुर्वीत तेषां धर्मान् यथोदितान् ।
रत्नैश्च पूजयेदेनं प्रधानपुरुषैः सह ॥ मनु० 7-203 ॥

pramāṇāni cha kurvīta teṣāṁ dharmān yathoditān,
ratnaiścha pūjayedenaṁ pradhānapuruṣaiḥ saha.

Manu, 7-203

[Meaning] Having conquered his foe, let him, if necessary, depose him from the throne and appoint another righteous man from the same dynasty as the king), let him have a treaty signed by him to the effect that he would carry out his orders, in other words that he would adopt a just system of Governance, serve his people and protect them.

Let him give him the aforesaid advice and leave such men with him as would prevent any further disturbance. Let him honour his vanquished foe with the gifts of gems and other valuable presents. (Let him not behave so meanly as to deprive him even of his subsistence. Even if he were to keep him as his prisoner, let him show him such respect as may free him from the sorrow consequent on his defeat and make his life happy.

आदानमप्रियकरं दानं च प्रियकारकम् ।

अभीप्सितानामर्थानां काले युक्तम् ॥ मनु०7-204 ॥

ādānamapriyakaraṁ dānaṁ cha priyakārakam,
abhīpsitānāmarthānāṁ kāle yuktam. Manu, 7-204

[Meaning] Because the seizure of others' property in this world gives rise to hatred, whilst the bestowal of gifts on others is the cause of love. Let him especially do the right for him at the right moment, it is a laudable thing to fulfil the desire of the vanquished foe.

Let him never taunt him, nor laugh at him, nor poke fun at him, not even remind him of his defeat. Instead, let him always show him respect by addressing him as his own brother.

The qualifications of a friend

हिरण्यभूमिसंप्राप्त्या पार्थिवो न तथैधते ।
यथा मित्रं ध्रुवं लब्ध्वा कृशमप्यायतिक्षमम् ॥ मनु० 7-208 ॥

hiraṇyabhūmisaṁprāptyā pārthivo na tathaidhate,
yathā mitraṁ dhruvaṁ labdhvā kṛśamapyāyatikṣamam
Manu, 7-208

[Meaning] A king does not gain in power so much by the acquisition of gold and territory as by securing a friend who is firm, loving and far-seeing. Such a friend is valuable no matter whether he is powerful enough to help him in the attainment of his wishes or is even weak.

धर्मज्ञं च कृतज्ञं च तुष्टप्रकृतिमेव च ।
अनुरक्तं स्थिरारम्भं लघुमित्रं प्रशस्यते ॥ मनु० 7-209 ॥

dharmajñaṁ cha kṛtajñaṁ cha tuṣṭaprakṛtimeva cha,
anuraktaṁ sthirārambhaṁ laghumitraṁ praśasyate.
Manu, 7-209

[Meaning] It is laudable for a king to secure a friend-feeble though he be who knows what is right, remembers gratefully any kindness shown to him, is cheerful in temper, affectionate and persevering.

प्राज्ञं कुलीनं शूरं च दक्षं दातारमेव च ।
कृतज्ञं धृतिमन्तं च कष्टमाहुररिं बुधाः ॥ मनु० 7-210 ॥

prājñaṁ kulīnaṁ śūraṁ cha dakṣaṁ dātārameva cha,
kṛtajñaṁ dhṛtimantaṁ cha kaṣṭamāhurariṁ budhāḥ.

Manu, 7-210

[Meaning] Let him bear in mind that it is not proper to make a foe of a man who is eminently wise, comes from an excellent family, and is brave, courageous, clever, liberal-minded, grateful, firm, and patient. Whosoever makes such a man his foe is sure to suffer.

आर्यता पुरुषज्ञानं शौर्यं करुणवेदिता ।
स्थौललक्ष्यं च सततमुदासीनगुणोदयः ॥ मनु० 7-211 ॥

āryatā puruṣajñānaṁ śauryaṁ karuṇaveditā,
sthaulalakṣayaṁ cha satatamudāsīnaguṇaudayaḥ.

Manu, 7-211

[Meaning] He is called neutral (i.e., neither an avowed friend nor a declared foe) who is possessed of good qualities, knowledge of mankind, valour, the kindness of heart, and who never discloses the secret of his heart.

एवं सर्वमिदं राजा सह सम्मन्त्र्य मन्त्रिभिः ।
व्यायम्याप्लुत्य मध्याह्ने भोक्तुमन्तःपुरं विशेत् ॥ मनु० 7-216

ēvaṁ sarvamidaṁ rājā saha sammantraya mantribhiḥ,
vyāyamyāplutya madhyāhne bhoktumantaḥpuraṁ viśet. Manu, 7-216

[Meaning] Let a king get up early in the morning, perform his daily duties, worship God, perform Homa himself or have it done by his chaplain, consult with his ministers, (inspect and review his troops, cheer their spirits, inspect stables of horses and elephants, cowsheds, etc. stores of arms and ammunition, hospitals and the Treasury, in short, inspect everything with his own eyes and point out shortcoming). Let him then do physical exercise and, thereafter, in the middle of the day enter his private apartments to dine with his family. (His food should be well tested and be such as will promote health, strength, energy and intellect. It should consist of various kinds of eatables, drink, and sweets, juicy and fragrant dishes as well as condiments, sauce, etc., that may keep him free from disease. Let him thus promote the welfare of his people).

Rate of Taxes

पंचाशद्भाग आदेयो राज्ञा पशुहिरण्ययोः ।
धान्यानामष्टमो भागः षष्ठो द्वादश एव च ॥ मनु0 7.130 ॥

paṁchāśadbhāga ādeyo rājñā paśuhiraṇyayoḥ,
dhānyānāmaṣṭamo bhāgaḥ ṣaṣṭho dvādaśa ēva cha.

Manu, 7.130

[Meaning] Let the king take from traders and artisans one-fiftieth part of their profits in silver and gold, and one-sixth, one-eighth, or one-twelfth of agricultural produce. (If he takes it in cash instead of in kind, then too let him take it in such a way that the farmers and others would not suffer from poverty or for want of necessaries of life such as food, drink and so on. Because when the people are rich, healthy and have an abundance of necessaries of life, the king flourishes. Let him, therefore, make his subjects happy as he would make his own children, and let the people regard the king, his ministers and other officials as their natural protectors, since it is a fact that the farmers and other wealth producers are the real sources of the state economy. The king is their guardian. If there were no subjects whom would he rule? Or on the other hand, if there were no king whose subjects will they be called? Let both the rulers and the ruled be independent of each other in the performance of their respective duties, but let them subordinate themselves to each other in all those matters that require mutual harmony and co-operation. Let not the rulers go against the voice of the people, nor let the people and ministers do anything against the wish of the ruler. The political duties of kings have thus been briefly described.

Let those who want to study this subjects in detail consult the four Vedas, the Manu Smṛti, the Śukra-nīti, the Mahābhārata and other books. The method of administering justice may be studied from the eighth and ninth chapters of Manu, but they are also described below:

The administration of justice

प्रत्यहं देशदृष्टैश्च शास्त्रदृष्टैश्च हेतुभिः ।
अष्टादशसु मार्गेषु निबद्धानि पृथक् पृथक् ॥ मनु॰ 8-3 ॥

pratyahaṁ deśadṛṣṭaiścha śāstradṛṣṭaiścha hetubhiḥ,
aṣṭādaśasu mārgeṣu nibaddhāni pṛthak pṛthak.

Manu, 8-3.

[Meaning] - Let the King, the Court and the Judge daily decide justly law suits which are classified under eighteen heads, according to the laws of the land and the teachings of the Dharm Śāstra. If it be found necessary to undertake fresh legislation in respect of matters which are not governed by any law in the Law books of Ṛṣis-let such laws be framed as will promote the welfare of the rulers and the ruled.

तेषामाद्यं ऋणादानं निक्षेपोऽस्वामिविक्रयः ।
सम्भूय च समुत्थानं दत्तस्यानपकर्म च ॥ मनु॰ 8-4 ॥

teṣāmādyaṁ ṛṇādānaṁ nikṣepo'svāmivikrayaḥ,

sambhūya cha samutthānaṁ dattasyānapakarma cha.
Manu, 8-4

वेतनस्यैव चादानं संविदश्च व्यतिक्रमः ।
क्रयविक्रयानुशयो विवादः स्वामिपालयोः ॥ मनु० 8-5 ॥

vetanasyaiva chādānaṁ saṁvidaścha vyatikramaḥ,
krayavikrayānuśayo vivādaḥ svāmipālayoḥ. Manu, 8-5

सीमाविवादधर्मश्च पारुष्ये दण्डवाचिके ।
स्तेयं च साहसं चैव स्त्रीसङ्ग्रहणमेव च ॥ मनु० 8-6 ॥

sīmāvivādadharmaścha pāruṣye daṇḍavāchike,
steyaṁ cha sāhasaṁ chaiva strīsaṅgrahaṇameva cha.
Manu, 8-6

स्त्रीपुन्धर्मो विभागश्च द्यूतमाह्वय एव च ।
पदान्यष्टादशैतानि व्यवहारस्थिताविह ॥ मनु० 8-7 ॥

strīpundharmo vibhāgaścha dyūtamāhvaya ēva cha,
padānyaṣṭādaśaitāni vyavahārasthitāviha. Manu, 8-7

[Meaning] These are the following eighteen causes of disputes:

(1) Debt

(2) Deposit-the dispute arises when a man deposits an article with another and is refused its return on demand

(3) Sale by one person of a thing is owned by another.

(4) Association of some persons against a particular individual for a criminal purpose

(5) Refusal to return a loan

(6) Non-payment or inadequate payment of one's wages

(7) Backing out of the agreement or contract

(8) Disputes with regard to sale or purchase

(9) Disputes between the owner of an animal and the man who looks after it

(10) Boundary disputes

(11) Assault

(12) Slander

(13) Larceny, burglary, and dacoity

(14) Violence

(15) Adultery

(16) Disregard of conjugal duties.

(17) Disputes about inheritance

(18) Gambling-with animate as well as inanimate things

एषु स्थानेषु भूयिष्ठं विवादं चरतां नृणाम् ।
धर्मं शाश्वतमाश्रित्य कुर्यात् कार्यविनिर्णयम् ॥ मनु० 8-8 ॥

ēṣu sthāneṣu bhūyiṣṭhaṁ vivādaṁ charatāṁ nṛṇām,
dharmaṁ śāśvatamāśritya kuryāt kāryavinirṇayam.

Manu, 8-8

[Meaning] Let the judge observe the eternal law of justice and decide all these cases of disputes among men justly, that is, without partiality.

धर्मो विद्धस्त्वधर्मेण सभां यत्रोपतिष्ठते ।
शल्यं चास्य न कृन्तन्ति विद्धास्तत्र सभासदः ॥ मनु० 8-12 ॥

dharmo viddhastvadharmeṇa sabhāṁ yatropatiṣṭhate,
śalyaṁ chāsya na kṛntanti viddhāstatra sabhāsadaḥ.

Manu, 8-12

[Meaning] Where Justice is defeated by injustice in courts of law, all the judges who constitute the bench to decide it also deserve to be looked upon as defeated

सभां वा न प्रवेष्टव्यं वक्तव्यं वा समञ्जसम् ।

अब्रुवन् विब्रुवन् वाऽपि नरो भवति किल्बिषी ॥ मनु० 8-13 ॥

sabhāṁ vā na praveṣṭavyaṁ vaktavyaṁ vā samañjasam,
abruvan vibruvan vā'pi naro bhavati kilbiṣī. Manu,8-13

[Meaning] Either a just and virtuous man should not enter an Assembly (or a Court of justice), or, when he does enter it, should invariably speak the truth. He who looks on injustice perpetrated before his own eyes and still remains mute spectator is the greatest sinner.

यत्र धर्मो ह्यधर्मेण सत्यं यत्रानृतेन च ।
हन्यते प्रेक्षमाणानां हतास्तत्र सभासदः ॥ मनु० 8-14 ॥

yatra dharmo hyadharmeṇa satyaṁ yatrānṛtena cha,
hanyate prekṣamāṇānāṁ hatāstatra sabhāsadaḥ.
Manu, 8-14

[Meaning] Where dharma (justice) is killed by adharma (injustice) and truth by falsehood, while judges or members of assembly look on as a mute spectator, there they are also deemed as killed.

धर्म एव हतो हन्ति धर्मो रक्षति रक्षितः ।
तस्माद् धर्मो न हन्तव्यो मा नो धर्मो हतोऽवधीत् ॥मनु० 8-15 ॥

dharma ēva hato hanti dharmo rakṣati rakṣitaḥ,
tasmād dharmo na hantavyo mā no dharmo hato'vadhīt. Manu, 8-15

[Meaning] Dharma (moral and ethical values and justice) kills if it is killed, protects if it is protected. So, dharma should not be killed, least killed dharma kill us.

वृषो हि भगवान् धर्मस्तस्य यः कुरुते ह्यलम् ।
वृषलं तं विदुर्देवास्तस्माद् धर्मं न लोपयेत् ॥ मनु० 8-16 ॥

vṛṣo hi bhagavān dharmastasya yaḥ kurute hyalam,
vṛṣalaṁ taṁ vidurdevāstasmād dharmaṁ na lopayet.
Manu, 8-16

[Meaning] Dharma (moral values and justice) showers happiness and prosperity in the nation. It's killer or violator is called by scholars as Vṛṣala (Śudra). Therefore, dharma should not be killed or violated.

एक एव सुहृद् धर्मो निधनेऽप्यनुयाति यः ।
शरीरेण समं नाशं सर्वमन्यद् हि गच्छति ॥ मनु० 8-17 ॥

eka ēva suhṛd dharmo nidhane'pyanuyāti yaḥ,
śarīreṇa samaṁ nāśaṁ sarvamanyad hi gachchhati.

Manu, 8-17

[Meaning] Dharma (Sanskāras) alone, in this world, is the true friend that accompanies a man even after death; all other companions become extinct with the extinction of the body. Dharma never forsakes a man.

Note: As per Indian philosophical tradition, sanskāras act as the seed of next life. Good sanskaras lead an individual to the species of human beings and bad sanskāras destined him to take birth in lower species of animals, birds, insects and plants. That is why Manu also says that Dharma (Sanskāras) alone accompany body after death and nothing else.

पादोऽधर्मस्य कर्तारं पादः साक्षिणं ऋच्छति ।
पादः सभासदः सर्वान् पादो राजानमृच्छति ॥ मनु० 8-18 ॥

pādo'dharmasya kartāraṁ pādaḥ sākṣiṇaṁ ṛchchhati,
pādaḥ sabhāsadaḥ sarvān pādo rājānamṛchchhati.

Manu, 8-18

[Meaning] When injustice is done with favour or fervour to one party, the injustice is divided into four equal parts. The first quarter of injustice is shared by the party in the cause, the second quarter is shared by the witnesses, third by the judges (or members of the assembly), and fourth by the President of the Assembly or Chief Justice.

राजा भवत्यनेनास्तु मुच्यन्ते च सभासदः ।
एनो गच्छति कर्तारं निन्दाऽर्हो यत्र निन्द्यते ॥ मनु० 8-19 ॥

rājā bhavatyanenāstu muchyante cha sabhāsadaḥ,
ēno gachchhati kartāraṁ nindā'rho yatra nindyate.

Manu, 8-19

[Meaning] Where condemnable is condemned, praiseworthy is praised, punishable is punished, and honourable is honoured, in that court (or assembly) the Presiding Judge and other Judges (or the President and the members of the Assembly) cannot be held guilty, but the real culprit is held guilty.

Witnesses and their qualifications

आप्ताः सर्वेषु वर्णेषु कार्याः कार्येषु साक्षिणः ।
सर्वधर्मविदोऽलुब्धा विपरीतांस्तु वर्जयेत् ॥ मनु० 8-63 ॥

āptāḥ sarveṣu varṇeṣu kāryāḥ kāryeṣu sākṣiṇaḥ,
sarvadharmavido'lubdhā viparītāṁstu varjayet.

Manu, 8-63

[Meaning] Among all Varṇas (professional classes) those persons alone are eligible as witnesses who are men of character, good learning, straightforward, who know their duty properly and are truthful and free from covetousness. Never should men of opposite character be considered eligible to depose the witness.

स्त्रीणां साक्ष्यं स्त्रियः कुर्युर्द्विजानां सदृशा द्विजाः ।
शूद्राश्च सन्तः शूद्राणां अन्त्यानामन्त्ययोनयः ॥ मनु० 8-68 ॥

strīṇāṁ sākṣayaṁ striyaḥ kuryurdvijānāṁ sadṛśā dvijāḥ,
śūdrāścha santaḥ śūdrāṇāṁ antyānāmantyayonayaḥ.

Manu, 8-68

[Meaning] Let women be witnesses for women, the intellectuals for intellectuals, service providers for service providers, and aliens for aliens (aliens were incorporated into Indian society as the last fifth Varṇa).

साहसेषु च सर्वेषु स्तेयसङ्ग्रहणेषु च ।
वाग्दण्डयोश्च पारुष्ये न परीक्षेत साक्षिणः ॥ मनु० 8-72 ॥

sāhaseṣu cha sarveṣu steyasaṅgrahaṇeṣu cha,
vāgdaṇḍayośća pāruṣye na parīkṣeta sākṣiṇaḥ.

Manu, 8-72

[Meaning] Let a judge never deem it extremely necessary to examine too strictly the witnesses in cases of violence, theft, adultery, the use of abusive language and assault, all these things being done in the private, witnesses are not easily available in such cases.

बहुत्वं परिगृह्णीयात् साक्षिद्वैधे नराधिपः ।
समेषु तु गुणोत्कृष्टान् गुणिद्वैधे द्विजोत्तमान् ॥मनु० 8-73 ॥

bahutvaṁ parigṛhṇīyāt sākṣidvaidhe narādhipaḥ,
sameṣu tu guṇotkṛṣṭān guṇidvaidhe dvijottamān.

Manu, 8-73

[Meaning] If there be contradictory evidence let him accept as true the evidence of the majority; if the conflicting parties are equal in number, that of those distinguished by good qualities; on a difference between equally distinguished witnesses, that of the best among intellectuals, viz., sages, seers and Yatis (Saṁnyāsī-s)- the teachers of altruistic welfare of humanity.

समक्षदर्शनात् साक्ष्यं श्रवणाच्चैव सिध्यति ।
तत्र सत्यं ब्रुवन् साक्षी धर्मार्थाभ्यां न हीयते ॥ मनु० 8-74 ॥

samakṣadarśanāt sākṣayaṁ śravaṇāchchaiva sidhyati,
tatra satyaṁ bruvan sākṣī dharmārthābhyāṁ na hīyate.

Manu, 8-74

[Meaning] Two kinds of evidence are admissible, (1) what has been seen and (2) what has been heard by the witnesses. A witness who speaks the truth in a court of law is never deprived of dharma (morality, spirituality and knowledge) and artha (material needs and prosperity).

साक्षी दृष्टश्रुतादन्यद् विब्रुवन्नार्यसंसदि ।
अवाङ्नरकमभ्येति प्रेत्य स्वर्गाच्च हीयते ॥ मनु० 8-75 ॥

sākṣī dṛṣṭaśrutādanyad vibruvannāryasaṁsadi,
avāṅnarakamabhyeti pretya svargāchcha hīyate.

Manu, 8-75

[Meaning] A witness, who says anything in a court of law or in an assembly of good men, different from what he had seen or heard falls from divinity (if ever attained by him) and after death attains lower species where he shall not able to make use of his/her tongue.

स्वभावेनैव यद् ब्रूयुस्तद् ग्राह्यं व्यावहारिकम् ।
अतो यदन्यद् विब्रूयुर्धर्मार्थं तदपार्थकम् ॥ मनु० 8-78 ॥

svabhāvenaiva yad brūyustad grāhyaṁ vyāvahārikam,
ato yadanyad vibrūyurdharmārthaṁ tadapārthakam.

Manu, 8-78

[Meaning] Let only that which a witness declares naturally be received as evidence, but what he says on being tutored by others be considered useless for the purposes of evidence by a judge.

सभान्तः साक्षिणः प्राप्तानर्थिप्रत्यर्थिसंनिधौ ।
प्राड् विवाकोऽनुयुञ्जीत विधिनाऽनेन सान्त्वयन् ॥ मनु० 8-79

sabhāntaḥ sākṣiṇaḥ prāptānarthipratyarthisaṁnidhau,
prāḍ vivāko'nuyuñjīta vidhinā'nena sāntvayan.

Manu, 8-79

[Meaning] The witnesses being assembled in the court, let the judge or the counsels in the presence of the plaintiffs and defendants address them in the following manner.

यद् द्वयोरनयोर्वेत्थ कार्येऽस्मिंश्चेष्टितं मिथः ।
तद् ब्रूत सर्वं सत्येन युष्माकं ह्यत्र साक्षिता ॥ मनु० 8-80 ॥

yad dvayoranayorvettha kārye'smiṁścheṣṭitaṁ mithaḥ,
tad brūta sarvaṁ satyena yuṣmākaṁ hyatra sākṣitā.

Manu, 8-80

[Meaning] O witnesses! whatever you know with regard to the matter before us in relation to both parties declare truthfully, for your evidence is needed in this case.

सत्यं साक्ष्ये ब्रुवन् साक्षी लोकान् आप्नोत्यपुष्कलान् ।
इह चानुत्तमां कीर्तिं वागेषा ब्रह्मपूजिता ॥ मनु० 8-81 ॥

satyaṁ sākṣaye bruvan sākṣī lokān āpnotyapuṣkalān,
iha chānuttamāṁ kīrtiṁ vāgeṣā brahmapūjitā.

Manu, 8-81

[Meaning] A witness who speaks the truth shall attain happy and prosperous life hereafter; he will attain glory here and hereafter because the speech has been declared in the Vedas as the cause of honour and disgrace. He who invariably speaks the truth is worthy of honour, while he who falsifies his speech is disgraced.

सत्येन पूयते साक्षी धर्मः सत्येन वर्धते ।
तस्मात् सत्यं हि वक्तव्यं सर्ववर्णेषु साक्षिभिः ॥ मनु० 8-83 ॥

satyena pūyate sākṣī dharmaḥ satyena vardhate,
tasmāt satyaṁ hi vaktavyaṁ sarvavarṇeṣu sākṣibhiḥ.

Manu, 8-83

[Meaning] By truthfulness, a witness is exalted and truthfulness promotes Justice. It behoves witnesses from all Varṇas (professional classes), therefore, to speak the truth and nothing but the truth.

आत्मैव ह्यात्मनः साक्षी गतिरात्मा तथाऽत्मनः ।
माऽवमंस्थाः स्वमात्मानं नृणां साक्षिणमुत्तमम् ॥ मनु० 8-84

ātmaiva hyātmanaḥ sākṣī gatirātmā tathā'tmanaḥ,
mā'vamaṁsthāḥ svamātmānaṁ nṛṇāṁ sākṣiṇamuttamam. Manu, 8-84

[Meaning] Verily, the soul itself is its own witness; the soul itself is its own motive power. O man! you as the chief witness on behalf of others destroy not the purity of your own soul; in other words, you know better what is in your own mind what is true and what is false.

यस्य विद्वान् हि वदतः क्षेत्रज्ञो नाभिशङ्कते ।
तस्मान्न देवाः श्रेयांसं लोकेऽन्यं पुरुषं विदुः ॥ मनु० 8-86 ॥

yasya vidvān hi vadataḥ kṣetrajño nābhiśaṅkate,
tasmānna devāḥ śreyāṁsaṁ loke'nyaṁ puruṣaṁ viduḥ. Manu, 8-86

[Meaning] The wise considers no man greater than one whose discerning soul feels no misgivings when speaks.

एकोऽहमस्मीत्यात्मानं यस्त्वं कल्याण मन्यसे ।
नित्यं स्थितस्ते हृद्येष पुण्यपापैक्षिता मुनिः ॥ मनु० 8-91 ॥

ēko'hamasmītyātmānaṁ yastvaṁ kalyāṇa manyase,
nityaṁ sthitaste hṛdyeṣa puṇyapāpaikṣitā muniḥ.
Manu, 8-91

[Meaning] O man! if you are happy to think that you are the sole witness of the case, you are mistaken, as the real witness of your good or bad deeds resides in your heart.

लोभान्मोहाद् भयात्मैत्रात् कामात् क्रोधात् तथैव च ।
अज्ञानाद् बालभावात्च साक्ष्यं वितथमुच्यते ॥ मनु० 8-118 ॥

lobhānmohād bhayātmaitrāt kāmāt krodhāt tathaiva cha,
ajñānād bālabhāvātcha sākṣayaṁ vitathamuchyate.
Manu, 8-118

[Meaning] Witness deposed due to covetousness, confusion, terror, friendship, lust, hunger, anger, ignorance and childishness must be declared false.

एषामन्यतमे स्थाने यः साक्ष्यमनृतं वदेत् ।
तस्य दण्डविशेषांस्तु प्रवक्ष्याम्यनुपूर्वशः ॥ मनु० 8-119 ॥

eṣāmanyatame sthāne yaḥ sākṣayamanṛtaṁ vadet,
tasya daṇḍaviśeṣāṁstu pravakṣayāmyanupūrvaśaḥ.

Manu, 8-119

[Meaning] Should a witness give false evidence from either of the above-cited motives, there should be a provision of specific punishment to them which is prescribed below:

लोभात् सहस्रं दण्ड्यस्तु मोहात् पूर्वं तु साहसम् ।
भयाद् द्वौ मध्यमौ दण्डौ मैत्रात् पूर्वं चतुर्गुणम् ॥ मनु० 8-120

lobhāt sahasraṁ daṇḍyastu mohāt pūrvaṁ tu sāhasam,
bhayād dvau madhyamau daṇḍau maitrāt pūrvaṁ chaturguṇam. Manu, 8-120

कामाद् दशगुणं पूर्वं क्रोधात् तु त्रिगुणं परम् ।
अज्ञानाद् द्वे शते पूर्णे बालिश्यात्शतमेव तु ॥ मनु० 8-121 ॥

kāmād daśaguṇaṁ pūrvaṁ krodhāt tu triguṇaṁ param,
ajñānād dve śate pūrṇe bāliśyātśatameva tu.

Manu, 8-121

[Meaning] If a witness commits perjury due to greed he shall be imposed a fine of one thousand bills in local currency; if due to confusion initial fine (five times less) of 200; if due to terror double of initial known as moderate, i.e. 400; if due to friendship four times of initial, i.e. 800; if due to lust 10 times of initial, i.e. 2000; if due to anger three times of moderate, i.e. 1200; if due to ignorance 200; and if due to childishness 100 only.

उपस्थमुदरं जिह्वा हस्तौ पादौ च पञ्चमम् ।
चक्षुर्नासा च कर्णौ च धनं देहस्तथैव च ॥ मनु० 8-125 ॥

upasthamudaraṁ jihvā hastau pādau cha pañchamam, chakṣurnāsā cha karṇau cha dhanaṁ dehastathaiva cha. *Manu, 8-125*

अनुबन्धं परिज्ञाय देशकालौ च तत्त्वतः ।
सारापराधो चालोक्य दण्डं दण्ड्येषु पातयेत् ॥ मनु० 8-126 ॥

anubandhaṁ parijñāya deśakālau cha tattvataḥ,
sārāparādho chālokya daṇḍaṁ daṇḍyeṣu pātayet.
Manu, 8-126

[Meaning] Punishment may be inflicted through following means: (attachment of) property, the (castration of) genital organs, stomach, tongue, hands, feet, eyes; ears, nose, and body.

Thedegrees of various punishments to be given shall be decided having fully ascertained the motive behind offence, time and place of offence, and having considered the worth of offender to bear the punishment, nature and magnitude of the offence.

अधर्मदण्डनं लोके यशोघ्नं कीर्तिनाशनम् ।
अस्वर्ग्यं च परत्रापि तस्मात् तत् परिवर्जयेत् ॥ मनु० 8-127 ॥

adharmadaṇḍanaṁ loke yaśoghnaṁ kīrtināśanam,
asvargyaṁ cha paratrāpi tasmāt tat parivarjayet.
Manu, 8-127

[Meaning] The infliction of unjust punishment tarnishes reputation and honour in this world. It causes great misery and intense suffering even in next life after death. Let a judge, therefore, avoid infliction of unjust punishment.

अदण्ड्यान् दण्डयन् राजा दण्ड्यांश्चैवाप्यदण्डयन् ।
अयशो महदाप्नोति नरकं चैव गच्छति ॥ मनु० 8-128 ॥

adaṇḍyān daṇḍayan rājā daṇḍyāṁśchaivāpyadaṇḍayan,
ayaśo mahadāpnoti narakaṁ chaiva gachchhati.

Manu, 8-128

[Meaning] A judge who convicts innocent, and acquits the guilty, brings infamy on himself in this life and after death, he sinks into the lower species (animals, birds, Insects etc). Let the guilty, therefore, be invariably punished, and the innocent be never punished.

वाग्दण्डं प्रथमं कुर्याद् धिग्दण्डं तदनन्तरम् ।
तृतीयं धनदण्डं तु वधदण्डमतः परम् ॥ मनु० 8-129 ॥

vāgdaṇḍaṁ prathamaṁ kuryād dhigdaṇḍaṁ tadanantaram,
tṛtīyaṁ dhanadaṇḍaṁ tu vadhadaṇḍamataḥ param.

Manu, 8-129

[Meaning] For the first offence let the offender be warned, for the second be reprimanded with the phrase like 'shame be upon you', for the third be fined, and for the fourth be given corporal punishment, such as flogging and caning, or imprisonment or death penalty.

येन येन यथाङ्गेन स्तेनो नृषु विचेष्टते ।
तत् तदेव हरेत् तस्य प्रत्यादेशाय पार्थिवः ॥ मनु० 8-334 ॥

yena yena yathāṅgena steno nṛṣu vicheṣṭate,
tat tadeva haret tasya pratyādeśāya pārthivaḥ.

Manu, 8-334

[Meaning] With whatever limb an offender commits an offence, even of that limb shall the judge/king deprive him in order to set an example for others and prevent the repetition of the same crime.

पिताऽचार्यः सुहृत्माता भार्या पुत्रः पुरोहितः ।
नादण्ड्यो नाम राज्ञोऽस्ति यः स्वधर्मे न तिष्ठति ॥ मनु० 8-335

pitā'chāryaḥ suhṛtmātā bhāryā putraḥ purohitaḥ,
nādaṇḍyo nāma rājño'sti yaḥ svadharme na tiṣṭhati.

Manu, 8-335

[Meaning] Whosoever-be he is a father; tutor, friend, wife, son, or family priest - deviates from the path of duty be punished. In other words, when a judge sits on the seat of justice, let him be just and show partiality to none while passing judgement.

कार्षापणं भवेद् दण्ड्यो यत्रान्यः प्राकृतो जनः ।
तत्र राजा भवेद् दण्ड्यः सहस्रमिति धारणा ॥ मनु० 8-336 ॥

kārṣāpaṇaṁ bhaved daṇḍyo yatrānyaḥ prākṛto janaḥ,
tatra rājā bhaved daṇḍyaḥ sahasramiti dhāraṇā.

Manu, 8-336

[Meaning] Where an ordinary man is fined one rupee, a member of the judiciary, executive or legislature shall be fined a thousand, i.e., the punishment inflicted on a member of the executive, judiciary and legislature should be a thousand times heavier than that on an ordinary man.

The range of punishment may vary from heavy to moderate to light according to the official hierarchy and protocol of officials in Government administration. The punishment should be set such that even the lowest official in Government administration, should be punished not less than eight times as heavily as an ordinary man would be, for if the government officials or servants be not punished more severely than ordinary people, they would tyrannize them. As a Lion requires a severer punishment than a goat to be well broken, similarly do the rulers (from the highest officials to the lowest worker of the State), require heavier punishment than ordinary people.

अष्टापाद्यं तु शूद्रस्य स्तेये भवति किल्बिषम् ।
षोडशैव तु वैश्यस्य द्वात्रिंशत् क्षत्रियस्य च ॥ मनु० 8.337 ॥

aṣṭāpādyaṁ tu śūdrasya steye bhavati kilbiṣam,

ṣoḍaśaiva tu vaiśyasya dvātriṁśat kṣatriyasya cha.

Manu, 8.337

ब्राह्मणस्य चतुःषष्टिः पूर्णं वाऽपि शतं भवेत् ।
द्विगुणा वा चतुःषष्टिस्तद्दोषगुणविद् हि सः ॥ मनु० 8.338 ॥

brāhmaṇasya chatuḥṣaṣṭiḥ pūrṇaṁ vā'pi śataṁ bhavet,
dviguṇā vā chatuḥṣaṣṭistaddoṣaguṇavidd hi saḥ.

Manu, 8.338

[Meaning] The punishment should be proportional to the knowledge, position and reputation of a person. For example, if an offence (monetary or relating to property) is committed by a person coming from an uneducated and labour class, he should be fined eight times the amount of damage caused by him. If the offender comes from the class of producers, merchants or traders, he is liable to be fined sixteen times the amount of damage. If the offender happens to be from Judiciary, executive, defence, or legislature class, he is liable to be fined thirty-two times the damage. If the offence comes from intellectual class, he is liable to be fined sixty-four or a hundred, or even one hundred and twenty-eight times the damage caused by him.

ऐन्द्रं स्थानमभिप्रेप्सुर्यशश्चाक्षयमव्ययम् ।
नोपेक्षेत क्षणमपि राजा साहसिकं नरम् ॥ मनु० 8.344 ॥

aindraṁ sthānamabhiprepsuryaśaśchākṣayamavyayam,
nopekṣeta kṣaṇamapi rājā sāhasikaṁ naram.

Manu, 8.344

[Meaning] Let not the ruler and any other person in authority, who desires unending prosperity and glory, delay even for a single moment the punishment of a man who has committed terrorism and other atrocious violence.

वाग्दुष्टात् तस्कराच्चैव दण्डेनैव च हिंसतः ।

साहसस्य नरः कर्ता विज्ञेयः पापकृत्तमः ॥ मनु० 8.345 ॥

vāgduṣṭāt taskarāchchaiva daṇḍenaiva cha hiṁsataḥ,
sāhasasya naraḥ kartā vijñeyaḥ pāpakṛttamaḥ.

Manu, 8.345

[Meaning] A man who commits violence is more wicked and a more grievous offender than a slander, a thief, and even one who assaults another without provocation.

साहसे वर्तमानं तु यो मर्षयति पार्थिवः ।
स विनाशं व्रजत्याशु विद्वेषं चाधिगच्छति ॥ मनु० 8.346 ॥

sāhase vartamānaṁ tu yo marṣayati pārthivaḥ,
sa vināśaṁ vrajatyāśu vidveṣaṁ chādhigachchhati.

Manu, 8.346

[Meaning] A ruler, who tolerates and forgives a man that perpetrates crimes and atrocities, incurs the public wrath and soon perishes.

न मित्रकारणाद् राजा विपुलाद् वा धनागमात् ।
समुत्सृजेत् साहसिकान् सर्वभूतभयावहान् ॥ मनु० 8.347 ॥

na mitrakāraṇād rājā vipulād vā dhanāgamāt,
samutsṛjet sāhasikān sarvabhūtabhayāvahān.

Manu, 8.347.

[Meaning] Neither due to friendship nor even at the offer of immense wealth should a ruler let a criminal, who commits violent acts, go unpunished.

Let ruler inflict just punishment, such as life imprisonment or death on terrorists and ultras.

गुरुं वा बालवृद्धौ वा ब्राह्मणं वा बहुश्रुतम् ।
आततायिनमायान्तं हन्यादेवाविचारयन् ॥ मनु० 8-350 ॥

guruṁ vā bālavṛddhau vā brāhmaṇaṁ vā bahuśrutam,
ātatāyinamāyāntaṁ hanyādevāvichārayan.

Manu, 8-350

[Meaning] Let him put a man, who is convicted of terror activities to death without a moment's hesitation, be he is a preceptor, a child, or an elderly person, a visionary person, or a great scholar.

नाततायिवधे दोषो हन्तुर्भवति कश्चन ।
प्रकाशं वाऽप्रकाशं वा मन्युस्तं मन्युमृच्छति ॥ मनु० 8.351 ॥

nātatāyivadhe doṣo hanturbhavati kaśchana,
prakāśaṁ vā'prakāśaṁ vā manyustaṁ manyumṛchchhati. Manu, 8.351

[Meaning] There is nothing wrong in passing a death sentence on a terrorist, whether he commits crime publicly or privately. It is like anger opposing anger.

यस्य स्तेनः पुरे नास्ति नान्यस्त्रीगो न दुष्टवाक् ।
न साहसिकदण्डघ्नो स राजा शक्रलोकभाक् ॥ मनु० 8.386 ॥

yasya stenaḥ pure nāsti nānyastrīgo na duṣṭavāk,
na sāhasikadaṇḍaghno sa rājā śakralokabhāk.
Manu, 8.386

[Meaning] Most excellent is the ruler in whose realm there is neither a thief nor an adulterer, nor a slanderer, nor a perpetrator of atrocious violence, nor heinous crime, nor a violator of the law.

भर्तारं लङ्घयेद् या तु स्त्री ज्ञातिगुणदर्पिता ।
तां श्वभिः खादयेद् राजा संस्थाने बहुसंस्थिते ॥ मनु० 8-371 ॥

bhartāraṁ laṅghayed yā tu strī jñātiguṇadarpitā,
tāṁ śvabhiḥ khādayed rājā saṁsthāne bahusaṁsthite.
Manu, 8-371

[Meaning] Should a wife desert her husband out of her family pride and misconduct herself with other persons, let the ruler punish her to be devoured by dogs publicly.

पुमांसं दाहयेत् पापं शयने तप्त आयसे ।

अभ्यादध्युश्च काष्ठानि तत्र दह्येत पापकृत् ॥ मनु० 8-372 ॥

pumāṁsaṁ dāhayet pāpaṁ śayane tapta āyase,
abhyādadhyuścha kāṣṭhāni tatra dahyeta pāpakṛt.
Manu, 8-372

[Meaning] Similarly should a husband forsake his wife and misconduct himself with other women, let the ruler punish him to be burnt alive publicly on a red hot iron-bed.

Questions and Answers on Governance

Question: - Who shall punish the ruler or his/her spouse, the judges or their spouses, if any one of them commits such wicked crimes as adultery?

Answer: The assembly (or the court of justice). They should be punished even more severely than other people.

Question: Why will a ruler or king and other VVIPS accept punishment from assembly or the court of justice?

Answer: A ruler is but a man endowed with virtue and favoured by fortune. If he goes unpunished, why would others obey the law? Besides, if the people and other persons in authority and the assembly would deem it fit to punish the ruler, how can he lonely refuse to undergo punishment? Should an offender, be he a king or other VVIP, enjoy immunity from punishment, he would simply indulge into unlawful activities and unleash havoc taking law for a ride. Remember the teaching of the Vedic text that says, 'Verily the justice[182] alone rules.'

---

[182] Today we have the rule of law, but in Vedic period there was the rule of justice. Today judge announces the decision as per law, but one may get justice or may not. Sometimes an innocent person is convicted and sometimes

Yes, the justice is the true Dharma. Whosoever takes the justice for a ride, he would be the most wicked and meanest of persons.

Question: How can it be right to award such harsh punishments, since man has no power to revive a limb or the dead to life?

Answer: Whosoever calls it harsh punishment is ignorant of the true principles of good governance. The award of harsh punishment on one man sends a message aloud to hoards of others to prevent them from committing similar crimes. It also helps them to be steadfast in righteousness. Truly speaking, this so-called harsh punishment awarded on one criminal will be as small as the size of a *Rai* seed (a kind of mustard plant) when distributed among all members of society, whilst the so-called light punishment, by its failure to check crime, increase crime million fold, as the crime rate is inversely proportional to the sentence. That is, harsher the punishment, lower the crime rate, lighter the punishment, higher the crime rate. Take for an example, a community of one thousand persons. If every one of them be punished, say, one rupee each, the total punishment will be one thousand rupees, whilst if one man in this community of one thousand persons be punished, say, one hundred rupees and should that punishment succeed in preventing the repetition of similar crimes, the total punishment will not be more than a hundred rupees, which is ten times less than one thousand rupees. Thus the seemingly light punishment, in the long run, turns out to be the severe and heavier

---

the real culprit is acquited. Should there be a rule of justice an offender can never go scot free. So the need is for the rule of justice and not that of law.

one.

दीर्घाध्वनि यथादेशं यथाकालं तरो भवेत् ।
नदीतीरेषु तद् विद्यात् समुद्रे नास्ति लक्षणम् ॥ मनु० ॥ 406-8

dīrghādhvani yathādeśaṁ yathākālaṁ taro bhavet,
nadītīreṣu tad vidyāt samudre nāsti lakṣaṇam.

Manu, 8-406.

[Meaning] Let the king impose a toll on all the ships and boats passing up and down sea-canals (or bays) and rivers-big and small-proportionate to the length of the country that they traverse; at sea, no settled duty can be imposed, hence let him do what best suits the occasion.

Let him in such cases make laws that may prove beneficial both to the state and the proprietors of ships. It also sets aside the notion that sea navigation was not prevalent in ancient times.

Let him always protect his subjects, who go to different foreign lands by means of these ships, wherever they are. Let them never suffer in any way.

अहन्यहन्यवेक्षेत कर्मान्तान् वाहनानि च ।
आयव्ययौ च नियतावाकरान् कोशमेव च ॥ मनु० ॥ 419-8

ahanyahanyavekṣeta karmāntān vāhanāni cha,
āyavyayau cha niyatāvākarān kośameva cha.

Manu, 8-419

[Meaning] Let a ruler routinely assess the results of various measures (adopted for the public good). Order inspection of elephants, horses and other conveyances, take stock of income and expenditure of state, natural resources and treasury.

एवं सर्वानिमान् राजा व्यवहारान् समापयन् ।
व्यपोह्य किल्बिषं सर्वं प्राप्नोति परमां गतिम् ॥ मनु० ॥ 420-8

ēvaṁ sarvānimān rājā vyavahārān samāpayan,

vyapohya kilbiṣaṁ sarvaṁ prāpnoti paramāṁ gatim.

Manu, 8-420

[Meaning] A ruler who discharges all these duties most faithfully is freed from all blames of bad governance, and attains the highest state of bliss hereafter.

Question: Is the system of Governance provided in Sanskrit texts perfect or imperfect?

Answer: Perfect, because all other systems of Governance on globe prevailed in past or shall prevail, have been derived from Sanskrit texts. The laws that have not been declared expressly have been provided for by the Sanskrit texts.

प्रत्यहं लोकदृष्टैश्च शास्त्रदृष्टैश्च हेतुभिः ॥ मनु 0

pratyahaṁ lokadṛṣṭaiścha śāstradṣṭaiścha hetubhiḥ.

Manusmṛti

[Meaning] Let the Parliament composed of scholars, frame such laws as conform to the Śāstras and are just and beneficial to the rulers and the ruled.

Let the king, as well as his advisers, bear in mind that early marriage must not be allowed, nor the marriage of grown-ups without their consent. Let a ruler encourage the practice of Brahmacharya; let him put an end to the practice of prostitution and the custom of polygamy, etc. so that both body and soul may be transformed. For if only soul (mental power and knowledge) be transformed, a man of great physical power may vanquish hundreds of intellectuals/scholars. On the other hand, if physical power alone is developed, the objectives of good Governance can never be achieved. The Proper balance of both is must, nor the discords, division, mutual disputes, quarrels and feuds will ultimately ruin the nation. There is nothing more prejudicial to the growth of physical and mental powers than prostitution and excessive sexual indulgence.

Kṣatriya professionals, should, in particular, be technically and physically powerful, if they become corrupt, the system of governance in the country will collapse. The dictum "As is the ruler, so shall be the ruled' should never be lost sight of. It, therefore, behoves the rulers and other VVIPS never to misconduct themselves. Instead, let them always set good examples to others in the matter of just and righteous living.

Thus the duties of rulers are briefly described here. Those, who want to study them in detail can refer to the Vedas, the seventh, eighth and ninth chapters of Manu, the Śukranīti, Vidurnīti, Rājadharma, and Āpaddharma chapters of Śāntiparva of the Mahābhārata. They should perfectly master the science and art of governance, and rule one country or empire or the whole earth. Let us all understand the below-given statement of the Yajurveda:

वयं प्रजापतेः प्रजा अभूम। (यजुर्वेद)

vayaṁ prajāpateḥ prajā abhūma. Yajurveda

[Meaning] We are the subjects of the God-the Creator.

He is true king and we all are His humble subjects. May we in this world, through His mercy, be privileged to occupy kingly and other high offices and may He make us the means of advancing His Eternal Justice. Now, we shall deal with the subject of God and Veda in the ensuing chapter.

इति श्रीमद्दयानन्दसरस्वतीस्वामिकृते सत्यार्थप्रकाशे सुभाषाविभूषिते राजधर्मविषये षष्ठः समुल्लासः सम्पूर्णः॥

iti śrīmaddayānandasarasvatīsvāmikṛte satyārthaprakāśe subhāṣāvibhūṣite rājadharmaviṣaye ṣaṣṭhaḥ samullāsaḥ sampūrṇaḥ.

Thus ends this sixth chapter on 'Governance' of Satyarth Prakash by Swami Dayanand Saraswati.

Rare Pictures of Swami Dayananda

Seated on Padmasan with cloth wrapped around his chest

Rishi Dayananda made a stop over at Meerut on his way to Hradwar at Kumbh Mela in 1867 (Vikrama Samvat 1924). During his stay at Meerut, this sketch was made. From this sketch, the age of Rishi Dayananda appears to be between 35-40. There is a glow on his face. This sketch was discovered by Yudhisthir Mimamsaka from Meerut while he was searching the Letters of Rishi Dayananda. Its photocopy was published in Arya Gazette, a Urdu paper published from Lahore in Samvat 1983. It was a special issue dedicated to Swami Dayananda.

Seated on the chair wearing a saffron robe and holding a stick with silver handle in his hands

In this picture, Rishi Dayananda has covered his body completely with clothes and holding a stick with a silver handle. This picture was taken in Dehradun either in the month of Kartika or Margashirsh in Nov. 1880 (Saṁvat 1937). From the Biography of Swami Dayananda written by Devendra Babu, it is clear that in Dehradun, Swamiji's photo was taken.

Swami Ji in the pose of Samadhi

This photo was sketched in Meerut in 1879 (Saṁvat 1936). Its copy was printed in the Autobiography of Swami Shraddhananda. It appears that this photo was mentioned by Swami Dayananda in a letter to Shyamji Krishna Verma on January 17, 1879.

Seated on the ground with turban over head and holding an open book before him

In this photo Rishi Dayananda is seen seated on the ground with turban whose tail part is visible outside on the neck. In the front an open book is placed and a stick with a silver knob is lying close by. Swami ji looking weak, as he was suffering from dysentery then. This photo was taken in 1879 (Saṁvat 1936). Its small copy was given to Pt. Bhagvadatta by Mahatama Hansraj. He made a big photo out of it and installed the same in the Lal Chand Library of Dayananda College Lahore.

Seated on a Chair dressed in saffron robes with turban tied over his head

This sketch was made by Babu Harishchandra Cintamani during the time of second visit of Swami Dayananda to Bombay in 1875 (Saṁvat 1932). Mention of this sketch is available at page 4 of '*Swami Dayananda Jiwan Charit*' by Sh. Devendra Babu. Here it may be pointed out that Harishchandra Chintamani was the manager of Vedabhashya of Swami Dayananda. Since he did some mismanagement with the funds collected for the Vedabhashya, he was fired by Swamiji from this responsibility. Thus he turned rebellion. In this photo Swami Ji has given his side pose.

Front look : Seated on a Chair

This photo was taken in Bombay in 1875 (Saṁvat 1931). In this photo saffron clad Rishi Dayanada is seated on the chair. He has a turban tied over his head also holding a stick. This photo was discovered by Swami Satyananda from Bombay. Since the photo was in dilapidated condition, so feet of Rishi Dayananda are not visible. On the basis of this photo a block was prepared and was printed in the first edition of '*Śrimad Dayananda Prakash*'. This book was available in Lal Chand library of Lahore. From there it was brought at the residence of Pt. Bhagavaddata C Block No. 9, Model Town, Lahore. During the partition it got destroyed along with other literature.

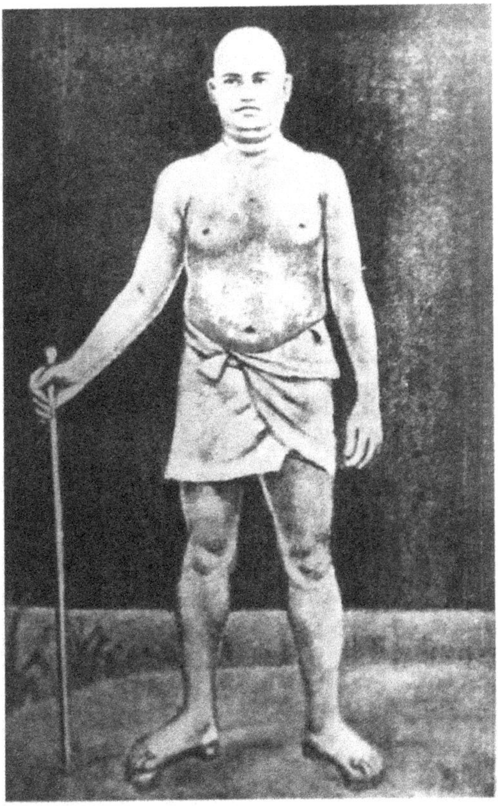

Dayananda as a recluse holding a stick in his hands

This sketch of Rishi Dayananda was taken in Vikrama Saṁvat 1924 i.e. c 1867 in Hardwar during the *Kumbh Mela* at a place where Pākhaṇḍa Khaṇḍana (extermination of hypocrisy) flag was installed. This is known by the old persons contemporary to Rishi Dayananda. On the basis of this sketch, a big sketch was prepared by an art studio in Poona. This sketch was seen by Yudhisthir Mimansak on 25th December 1926 in the custody of an old gentleman named as Jhunni Lal in Farrukhabad. Similar type of photo was published by Ram Vilas Sarda in '*Arya Dharmendra Jivan*'. The same photo has been published in the '*History of Arya Samaj Lucknow*'. Similar type of photo taken from the original plate was seen by Yudjisthir Mimansak in the custody of Babu Jivan lal S/o Babu Anandi Lal ji master (secretary of Arya Samaj Meerut in 1880). Babu Jivan Lal informed Mimansak ji that this photo was the original photo.

Seated on the chair with Brahmachari Ramananda

In this picture, Rishi Dayananda is seated on the chair. He is wearing Kharau (wooden shoe). Alongside is standing Brahmchari Ramananda. This photo was taken in Shahpura in the beginning of Saṁvat 1940. Its dispatch to Ramanand has been mentioned by Swami Dayananda himself in one of his letters addressed to him.

www.ingramcontent.com/pod-product-compliance
Lightning Source LLC
Chambersburg PA
CBHW022057090426
42743CB00008B/636
* 9 7 8 8 1 8 7 7 1 0 6 4 6 *